SHARING LIFE

Sharing Life

Stories of L'Arche Founders

CAROLYN WHITNEY-BROWN

AFTERWORD BY JEAN VANIER

Paulist Press
New York / Mahwah, NJ

Title page and chapter opener image adapted from artwork by Santos from Choluteca, Honduras.

The Scripture quotations contained herein are from the New Revised Standard Version: Catholic Edition, Copyright © 1989 and 1993, by the Division of Christian Education of the National Council of the Churches of Christ in the United States of America. Used by permission. All rights reserved.

Cover art: Detail of Dayspring chapel doors at L'Arche Daybreak, painted by Carolyn Whitney-Brown using art by L'Arche community members in Canada and Honduras. Photograph by Warren Pot.
Cover design by Carolyn Whitney-Brown
Book design by Lynn Else

Library of Congress Cataloging-in-Publication Data is available upon request.

ISBN 978-0-8091-5431-9 (paperback)
ISBN 978-1-58768-826-3 (e-book)

Published by Paulist Press
997 Macarthur Boulevard
Mahwah, New Jersey 07430
www.paulistpress.com

Printed and bound in the
United States of America

CONTENTS

CONTENTS

PREFACE

The room is a sea of bright banners, colorful clothing, and chatter in twenty languages including sign language. It is June 2017 and more than five hundred L'Arche members from five continents have gathered in Belfast, Ireland. A quarter have intellectual disabilities. They are Christian, Hindu, Muslim, Jewish, Buddhist, and some unaffiliated with any faith tradition. They represent 154 communities in 38 countries, or they would, except that visa difficulties prevented representatives attending from Burkina Faso, Ivory Coast, Zimbabwe, or Uganda. The communities in Haiti are recovering from last year's hurricane but have managed to come. Delegates have arrived from Syria and the West Bank. The sheer joy in the room is contagious.

L'Arche Canada founder Steve Newroth believes that the most healing thing anyone can hear is for someone to say, "I want to share my life with you." In 1964, Jean Vanier and several people with intellectual disabilities decided to live together. From that simple beginning, L'Arche has grown into an international movement and Jean Vanier became known as a peacemaker, philosopher, and spiritual guide for millions of people. He won many honors, including the 2015 Templeton Prize. Until his death on May 7, 2019, at the age of ninety, Jean continued to live in the original L'Arche community.

SHARING LIFE

"L'Arche has passed from an idealization of our history to a more mature understanding," announced the international leaders to the 2017 federation. This book is part of that effort, beginning with the evolution of Jean Vanier's founding story of L'Arche in France, then the stories of the founders of L'Arche in Canada, India, United States, United Kingdom, Ivory Coast, Haiti, and Honduras.

We all share our lives—in our families, gathering places, neighborhoods, world. These L'Arche founders' stories offer not only inspiring narratives of sharing life together, but also the familiar challenges and struggles inherent in this work of building a world where the contribution of each person is welcomed. We hope that each story offers you renewed inspiration in creating more diverse, welcoming, and celebratory communities.

ACKNOWLEDGMENTS

Carolyn Whitney-Brown: My thanks to Jean Vanier and all the founders who entrusted me with their remarkable stories. Thanks also to Jean-Christophe Pascal who initiated the project, to Eileen Glass who provided wise counsel and insight along the way, and to the Centre for Studies in Religion and Society at the University of Victoria, British Columbia, for inviting me to present an earlier version of the introduction as part of their 2016 lecture series. I am also grateful to Thérèse Vanier's friends Teresa de Bertodano and Ann Shearer for reading and improving Thérèse's chapter. Martha Bala, Katharine Hall, and Janet Whitney-Brown all worked with founders to articulate their stories. Thanks most of all to Geoff Whitney-Brown whose generous editing, revisions, and suggestions made this book shorter and better.

Steve Newroth: Had the core members who came to Daybreak not flourished and responded to our life together with such resounding enthusiasm, there would be nothing to write. They were truly such loyal, communicative, and buoyant personalities that it was a pleasure to share their company. To Ann, my wife—partner and codirector of Daybreak—for the years and skill she gave to the building of Daybreak, for which she was rarely recognized, I extend my love and heartfelt thanks. Deep gratitude also to one of my dearest friends and mentors, Jean Vanier, for his guidance and leadership. Finally, thanks to all the assistants, volunteers, and board members who joined us in breaking new ground by combining scriptural values with the delivery of services for people with intellectual disabilities.

Gabrielle Einsle: I leave my part in the foundation of L'Arche in India to God's mercy and honor—and the good will and patience of those who started it with me, as well as those who carry it on today. Thank you, Srinivas, Shyamsunder, Aramuda, Peter, Kashi, Madhu, Dr. Reddy, Nandan, Saroja, Ronald, John, Martha, Dorothy, Tom, Hazel, Chris, Léo....Not to forget Gerald Arbuckle (anthropologist) at whose request at the International Federation at Assisi in 2005 I began to write our story. He accompanied the process, "Identity and Mission of L'Arche." I thank all who carry this process on.

Fr. George Strohmeyer: I delight in celebrating "founding" companions: Sr. Barbara Ann Karsznia, OSB, cofounder of L'Arche in Erie; Fr. Stephen Somerville of Toronto, who introduced both Barbara and me to Jean Vanier; Jean, who preached the gospel with unheard-of authority; Steve and Ann Newroth and Sr. Sue Mosteller of L'Arche Daybreak and Fr. Jim O'Donnell of Cleveland, all of whom welcomed Barbara and me with unconditional support; Donna, Shirley, Bill, and John, who stepped out onto the unmarked path as cofounders, and by crossing the threshold of the opened door, prepared the way for all hoping to find the gift of meaning, purpose, and relationship while entering the give-and-take of the absolutely ordinary events of daily life with growing, selfless attention.

Dawn Follett/Barraqué: I thank Jean Vanier for his discernment, accompaniment, and supportive friendship. Thanks to all those in Bouaké who trusted "without seeing" and whose support was essential: Dom Denis Martin and the Benedictine community; Angèle, Marie, Monique, members of Clair Logis; Mr. Sebastien Djibo, Dr. Baba Coulibaly, and other first board members; and our neighbors "le Vieux" and Maman and their children who welcomed generations of community members and remain faithful in their friendship today. Sincere thanks to people working with L'Arche International over the years finding financial and human support. Last, my thanks to all I have not named but who were active in the founding years of the community and all those who have carried the community since.

Robert Larouche: To Jean-Robert, Jolibois, Yveline, and Jacqueline, who were pillars in the foundation of the community of L'Arche in Haiti and with whom these words became real: "I chose you. And I appointed you to go and bear fruit, fruit that will last" (John 15:16).

Nadine Tokar: I feel so grateful to all those who contributed to make this crazy adventure a reality, still living today. My warm gratitude to Jean Vanier who dared to trust us and supported us faithfully. A tender thanks to my very first companions with whom bonds remain living despite distance and years: Marcia, Lita, Régine, Micky, Jorge, Noly, Vilma Luz, Yvan, Sandra, Maria Conchita, Olga, René, and so many others. My profound gratitude to those who preceded us to heaven, but who remain so present in my heart and essential to our community history: thanks to you Rafaelito, Dona Maria, Claudia, Jorge, Esperancita, Brenda, Oscar. My thanksgiving to all who continue this journey, faithfully, every day. And then finally, how to give thanks to God, "the source of all"!

Introduction

"THERE WAS A LIGHTNESS IN US"

The Story of L'Arche Trosly with Jean Vanier, 1964

CAROLYN WHITNEY-BROWN

With regards to Jean Vanier, it's true that it's he who opened Trosly, but I would like to say that when one opens a home, one is not alone. If Jean had not known Raphaël Simi, Philippe Seux, Jacques Dudouit and me, he could not have started L'Arche!

> Jean-Pierre Crépieux (nicknamed "Pierrot"),
> the fourth core member of L'Arche[1]

Jean Vanier took me out of a center where I had been placed by social workers. It had really been desolate there.... When I came to L'Arche, there was no electricity, none. We used candles for lighting. It was fun! There were no toilets or showers, but I felt like I was exploding with joy.

Philippe Seux, founding core member of L'Arche[2]

In 1964, before the existence of group homes or community living for people with intellectual disabilities, Canadian philosophy professor Jean Vanier began sharing a house in a French village with men from a nearby institution and called it L'Arche. It was a radical and unprecedented move. Within twelve years, more than forty new L'Arche communities had opened in eleven countries. Philippe Seux, one of the first members of L'Arche, describes "exploding with joy" as they began the first L'Arche community together.

"That was the spirit of it," Jean Vanier explains, recalling how during dinner in the first months of L'Arche, when a government inspector was their guest, they passed him a fake mustard jar with a cloth snake on a spring inside. "We would play jokes, and everyone was laughing. There was that spirit of fun, of craziness, which for me is the spiritual life." He describes a key dynamic discovered in the early years of L'Arche as it expanded rapidly, "The important thing is how to participate in having fun together. The first thing is doing acts of justice, taking people who have been treated cruelly out of those situations. Then the second thing is that the assistants are changed. And the third thing is that we come together, and we don't know who is changing who and it doesn't matter, but we have fun. This is part of the complexity."[3]

Of course, no one has fun all the time. Suggesting that the founders were lighthearted does not mean they were superficial. L'Arche specializes in suffering, even anguish. Jean and all the founders in this book and their companions lived through times of struggle. What kept them going? Not only a sense of duty or commitment to social justice, but something deeper. As I looked for a unifying characteristic of the founders and the people they welcomed, I kept discovering a kind of interior buoyancy, an ability to rise again and again. It was a quality of the heart that lifted them through the most dark and heavy times. They may have been lighthearted, but in terms of sheer courage and commitment to community with people with intellectual disabilities, they were not lightweights.

This book has its roots in the Identity and Mission process that was led by L'Arche International in the early 2000s, which acknowledged the importance of founding stories throughout the federation: "We tend to idealize the time of the foundation and as a result, we are not able to appropriate important values and formative experiences of the story and integrate them into our personal journey. This also limits the potential power of the founding story to challenge and to transform us." In response, L'Arche International asked me to begin gathering stories of early founders. I invited the founding directors of the first L'Arche community in each country to share their experiences, especially things that they might not have shared publicly at celebratory anniversary celebrations or in fund-raising brochures. Assuming L'Arche International was right that romanticized stories limit L'Arche's understanding of itself, then exploring tensions and stresses of the time, personal, institutional, and cultural, could be liberating. The purpose was not to suggest that pain is more significant than joy, but to listen to these founding stories in light of a fundamental L'Arche philosophy. L'Arche often uses the term "core members" to refer to the community members with intellectual disabilities, because they are at the core of the community. In a similar way, the rejected, seemingly incoherent or broken stories of L'Arche history may hold something essential.

I was prepared for stories of pain, of disillusionment, even of anger, and I certainly did hear those. But what I hadn't expected was the energy that ran underneath all those stories, even the most painful ones. The pain only hurt so much because the relationships and commitment were deep, and there was always a sense of light when the founders described those relationships. As nineteenth-century English poet William Blake put it, "Joy & Woe are woven fine / A Clothing for the soul divine / Under every grief & pine / Runs a joy with silken twine."

Nadine Tokar, founder of L'Arche in Honduras, was cautious about whether one can look to a founding story for clarity about why a community evolved as it did in the following decades. "Maybe," she said. "I don't know."

> But we had fun. It was beautiful. The time of the foundation of a community is a very special time because it is really a time when you can touch the grace of God. Really you touch it—it is incredible. It gives you energy because you know you are not alone. You are on the right path. After that time, it's not to touch the grace but to trust it—it's different. I am happy with what we lived. One of my good friends from those early days reminds me that we were crazy together: what people today may not know is that even though at times it was hard, we really had a lot of fun.

I asked Robert Larouche, founder of L'Arche in Haiti, whether he would call the early founders lighthearted. He responded, "There was a lightness in us. We were all living that lightness in these beginnings. I can't wait to read all the other stories to touch that reality again. It is still there in many ways, I am sure, in all of us."

Robert and Nadine say three important things.[4] The founders were living in a unique time, with an interior disposition of confidence. Robert looks forward to reading these stories because they will allow him to touch again that experience in their lives. And he is sure that the light or lightness of those times lives on in each of them still, more than four decades later. In a 2017 book of autobiographical reflections, Jean Vanier wrote that while he was certainly older than in 1964, he still found in L'Arche the freedom to be silly, the laughter, and times of silence together in prayer "just like the first day" of L'Arche.[5]

L'Arche is or has been in nearly forty countries around the world. This book presents the stories of the founders of just eight countries. Why the founding directors? The founding directors' story is key. They know the story from multiple perspectives because they held authority at various levels: in the community with core members and assistants; with boards, governments, social services, and volunteers; with L'Arche on regional and zone levels; and internationally—they held the vision and led the choices around who to welcome and where to live.

The precedent for looking to the founding director to tell the story is, of course, Jean Vanier himself. Over more than half a century, he told the founding story of L'Arche more times than anyone can count. Every retelling of the Trosly story bases itself on Jean Vanier's narrative. Therefore, Jean and I decided I would not ask him to rehearse it again for this book. Instead, I begin by exploring how Jean's founding story of L'Arche in Trosly evolved over more than half a century, and how Jean himself has been interpreted as a symbol with nearly mythical status.

JEAN VANIER AND L'ARCHE TROSLY

This is a story about a story, tracing a few strands in the making and remaking of the L'Arche creation myth. Jean Vanier's founding story of Trosly is pivotal because it is the first story: the first founder, the first community, the first national story, the first international story. Because of that, people have looked to it for authority, permission, and precedence. This first story also holds a particular grip on peoples' imaginations because a personal relationship with Jean was behind most of the new communities founded over the next three decades. What is remarkable is how the original founding story evolved over the past fifty years, continuing to deepen and become more complex.

Jean Vanier was born in 1928 into a Canadian diplomatic family. He joined the British navy in 1941 when he was thirteen, then continued in the Canadian navy. By his early twenties, Jean had visited communities such as the Catholic Worker house in New York and decided to leave his military career to follow Jesus in a new way. He spent six years as part of a student community near Paris called L'Eau Vive, then eight years seeking his vocation. After completing his PhD on Aristotle's ethics of happiness, Jean briefly taught at University of Toronto. Then, in August 1964, Jean moved to France and began L'Arche.

In January 1965, five months after L'Arche began, Canada's national television network (CBC) broadcasted an interview with Jean across the country. In it, Jean described his vision of homes for people with disabilities (called "mentally deficient" in the language of the time) as a place "where they can feel they are loved, where we live all together without this kind of distinction between the director and those who are directed, where they all feel that we are a family together, brothers and sisters if you like, in a very happy family atmosphere where we eat together, where we live together."[6] Right from the start, the founding story of L'Arche had two strands: first, the values and vision that Jean expressed in the CBC interview, and second, the narrative details of what happened. In a 1967 interview with Peter Flemington for the Canadian church TV network, Jean offered this narrative:

> I discovered the plight of the mentally handicapped. They are often put into hospitals or asylums, and in general they haven't got a place where their personality

can flower out and they can be happy. I felt that I was called to do something in this particular situation, and I was able to buy a house in this village. It was rather dilapidated and falling to bits and there was no electricity—there was water. And so in August 1964 I began there. I took two boys from an asylum, Raphaël and Philippe, and we started out together. This is how it began, in a very simple way, and a very poor way. Many people felt that we were crazy because of the extreme poverty and felt that it was bad to do this with boys in this sort of poverty, without electricity and so on, but we found in this first small L'Arche house that the boys have seen it grow, have painted it themselves, have chosen the colors. Gradually the toilets are being built—there are no longer outhouses. This has made them feel that it is really their house and it's their home.[7]

THREE IN AN ARK

The one-sentence version of the story, told for roughly the first twelve years, goes like this: In 1964, working with his mentor Père Thomas Philippe, Jean welcomed Raphaël Simi and Philippe Seux to live with him in an old house in a little French village, and knew that his decision was irrevocable. In his first public "Letter to Friends," written soon after the beginning, Jean wrote, "On the fourth of August our little community settled in Trosly-Breuil, and on the fifth of August (the feast day of Our Lady of the Snows) our first two 'boys' arrived, driven by Mme Martin from an institution. Dr. Preaut, Père Thomas, some friends, and I were there to welcome them. We want to love one another as Christ taught us: gently, humbly and mercifully. Love is the distinctive feature of the message of the

Gospels."[8] Readers could visualize Jean Vanier and his two new friends, three men in their new home. Jean named immediately that "the generosity of many friends" has made it possible to begin L'Arche, emphasizing that "L'Arche is not the work of just a small group of people." The very fact that Jean was writing circular letters attests to the wider community that was supporting the new L'Arche project.

LAUGHTER, SUFFERING, AND A GOSPEL-CENTERED THEOLOGY OF THE BODY

Jean immediately put his unique stamp on the project. He had a lively sense of fun, and Raphaël and Philippe nurtured that. They enjoyed getting to know each other. Raphaël and Philippe opened for Jean aspects of the heart that he had previously overlooked. When Jean spoke to CBC in January 1965, he noted that his new friends "are not deficient cordially, in their hearts, and they are not deficient spiritually either." He beamed as he described their ability to awaken something new in him, something deeper than social success or achievement. He recognized, with respect and perhaps even a touch of envy, their capacity to love.

He was also keenly aware of their suffering. In a 1992 lecture at Harvard University, Jean recalled, "In 1964 I took from an asylum two men, Raphaël and Philip, and we began to live together. I did not know I was founding the first of many L'Arche communities. I simply felt called to live with these two men who had suffered rejection and a lot of inner pain and perhaps with a few others like them. When I had begun living with them, I soon discovered the immense pain in their hearts."[9]

As L'Arche took shape, Père Thomas provided theological insight, especially into the importance of touch, of taking the body seriously as a means of grace, creating a unique spirituality that drew many people. In the first issue of the new magazine *Letters of L'Arche,* Père Thomas asked how Jesus's church of the poor can remain open to God, noting that mystics can spend years struggling only to find that what they sought was very simple and accessible: "It is as if God must bind up our imaginative and reasoning capacities which have become useless, in order to give Himself to us, in his person, through a substantial 'touch'...the mystic finally discovers the profound truth of these words spoken so simply by Our Lord: 'Unless you become like little children, you will never enter the Kingdom of Heaven.'" Père Thomas implies that this spirituality is available to everyone because it is not dependent on intellectual "reasoning capacities" but requires only openness to God.[10] To live well with Philippe and Raphaël, Jean had to set aside his abstract ideas and reasoning and give himself to the moment. As he said to CBC in January 1965, Jean found himself learning to play, to laugh. Living with Raphaël and Philippe was liberating his inner child. Right from the start, L'Arche was about living in a "happy family atmosphere," having fun, physically being together, playing, laughing, and genuinely enjoying each other.

Jean came to realize and say, "L'Arche is founded upon the body."[11] For example, in 1991 he explained that "there is communication of the heart through our bodies" and "a whole new mode of communicating through the way we touch, and look and laugh, the way we listen, the way we are present to others." He found in living with people with disabilities that "they are more sensitive to body language than to verbal language, though both are necessary."[12] In 2007, he again affirmed, "The first element in our relationships at L'Arche centers on the body—eating meals together, dressing, bathing, touching—just physically caring for people, being attentive to the body, attentive to medical care, revealing to them in a concrete way that they are loved. It's about compassion, about recognizing what is common among us—the body."[13]

A RAPIDLY EVOLVING STORY

The story of the founding of L'Arche has evolved. The earliest version of the story, such as that depicted on CBC in 1965, focused on Jean and his personal decision to welcome Raphaël and Philippe. The version that has emerged since is not essentially different, but further elements make it more complex, more interdependent, less heroic, more messy, and certainly more human.

The community itself expanded rapidly. Friends came to help, and the little household was able to welcome more people. Jean recalls, "Every evening there would be prayer. It would be just the rosary, we would say ten Hail Marys, you know, something like that. We would sing something. It didn't last too long. But people entered into that, and there were people who loved singing. There was Pierrot [Jean-Pierre Crépieux] who came in December 1964—he was a great guy and he loved singing, sometimes folk songs of Paris. There was singing and praying, and times of silence. I would say it was right from the beginning. The spiritual life was just really around the table, almost the same as today. For me the spiritual life is more the quality of the love. Spiritual life is not just about prayers, it's about the quality of attention. It's the growing deep respect of people. We had fun! Every meal was fun."

Early in 1965, the local institution where Père Thomas was chaplain suddenly needed a new director and Jean, at Père Thomas's urging, agreed to take it on. When the residents from the Val Fleuri entered the life of the community, L'Arche became more than a tiny, eccentric, one-house experiment. The Val Flueri was a small institution, understaffed and often violent, with an entirely different relationship to government services and expectations. Jean sums it up as "the huge weight of the Val. Taking on the Val was not fun, oh no—it was horrible." Developing any kind of prayer life seemed impossible, and the community at the Val did not begin to pray together for five years. But in July 1965, the entire community went on pilgrimage to Lourdes. "Living together was difficult, but going on a trip was super," Jean recalls.[14]

Through the first decade, the founding story was often told as a call-and-response reminiscing at community events. Jean would lead the telling, calling on members of the community to chime in, prompting individuals: "Do you remember that first night?" or "Do you remember when…?" Thus the story of the founding of the first L'Arche community evolved as interactive oral history, conversations among those who had remained in the community. Jean was linking people in the room to their own place in the L'Arche story, creating a history for people with little family history of their own. In a sense, there was little interest at that time in L'Arche history for its own sake or for future generations. The purpose of the founding story was to build belonging. In that context, it makes sense that many people's contribution to L'Arche would be forgotten from the narrative since the development of the story focused on those who continued the story together.

FOUR IN THE ARK: DANY

Sometime in the 1980s, Jean described the first night in the new house with himself and not just two but three men. The third was named Dany. No one present had ever before heard of Dany, though Jean was sure it had never been a secret. In the 1989 anniversary edition of *Letters of L'Arche*, Jean wrote that on August 5, 1964, Madame Martin, the director of the

St. Jean-les-deux-Jumeaux institution, had selected not two but three men to come to this new home. The first day and night were exhausting and chaotic. Dany had hallucinations and ran into the street. Dany could not hear and Jean relied on words. Dany had psychological issues that were beyond Jean's experience: "Dany was a deeply emotionally disturbed man who could not hear and could not speak. He was living so much in his own world of pain and dreams that he was not able to stay with us for more than one day." Realizing that Dany needed a more structured situation, Jean called Madame Martin from the nearest pay phone in the village, and she came to return with Dany to the institution.[15]

The new addition of Dany to the founding story showed L'Arche immediately began with an unsuccessful attempt to welcome someone with needs too complex for the first L'Arche house. As Kathryn Spink phrased it in her 1990 book, *Jean Vanier and L'Arche: A Communion of Love*, "So it was that from the very first night of the founding of L'Arche Jean Vanier was to experience the need to make choices and to know suffering; his own suffering and sense of failure and the suffering of the men who had come to live with him."[16] For many people in L'Arche, hearing about Dany for the first time decades after that first night, there was something reassuring in finding that the founding story included failure and limitations.

Perhaps it is amazing that Raphaël and Philippe did not beg to go home after that first bewildering night. Of course, they probably knew Dany at the institution, and were at least somewhat accustomed to life in an overcrowded, loud, confusing building. The new home that seemed so unbearable to Jean might have seemed relatively calm to Raphaël and Philippe, with far fewer residents. They might have found the noise and chaos of that first night more familiar than Jean did. Fortunately, Raphaël and Philippe boldly carried on with the new L'Arche experiment. Maybe they saw that Jean needed them, too.

OTHER SUPPORT AROUND JEAN INTEGRATED INTO THE STORY

Any version of L'Arche's founding story that focuses solely on Jean Vanier as independent is misleading. As he acknowledged in his first letter, he had enormous support right from the first day. This support around Jean was never secret, but Jean recorded more specific details in the 1980s. For example, in *The Challenge of L'Arche*, Jean wrote, "I had no previous knowledge of handicapped people. In so many ways I was ignorant. I had a great deal to learn about handicapped people and life in community…but we were learning to live together, to care for each other, to listen, and to have fun. Some people in the village cared for us because we were poor."[17] Jean also credited the hidden spiritual support of contemplative orders, who supported L'Arche in prayer.

Some of Jean's personal friends came by to visit and volunteer briefly. For example, soon after L'Arche began, Raymond Jolliffe (later Lord Hylton) came for a week in the middle of August 1964 and dug up the garden. He had become a family friend while serving Jean's father when Georges Vanier held the diplomatic post of Secretary to the High Commission of Canada in London. A 2015 anniversary online book titled *The Beginnings of L'Arche: Recollections of the First Years in Trosly, 1964–1968* collects interviews, memoirs, and letters from the time that give readers a vivid sense of meals, holidays, decisions, and most of all, the enormous cast of friends, family, social workers, vowed religious, doctors, psychiatrists, government bureaucrats, philanthropists, and neighbors who supported Jean and helped create L'Arche.[18] In later versions of the founding story, mention of professional advice and friendships with government officials has often been missing, leaving newcomers to L'Arche with a sense that Jean and his untrained friends bumbled along with the grace of God and good hearts. It is important to hold in mind their efforts to develop competence, along with openness to ideas and insights from all disciplines. Jean's second circular letter, dated June 1965, emphasizes, "L'Arche, while taking its inspiration directly from the Gospels, wants to make full use of psychiatry and medicine, and to work in collaboration with local authorities."[19] For Jean, struggling to understand thirty-two men at the Val, diagnoses and professional expertise were lifesavers.

Jean's public letters reveal how much he travelled, starting within months of founding L'Arche. Because Jean's life as a speaker and teacher took him away from the new community often, support was needed for the L'Arche community as well as for Jean personally. He told of a meeting at Christmas 1965 with the twenty assistants from the Val and the original L'Arche house in the calm of a neighboring abbey. After a time of sharing in smaller groups, Jean was stunned, even shocked, to hear all the frustration of the community. His travels had left him out of touch with its daily life. They created a community council and drafted a constitution to help clarify responsibilities and how the community would fulfill its mission for the growth of both core members and assistants.[20]

More people came to help, many of whom went on to found other L'Arche communities. In his 2007 collection of letters, *Our Life Together*, Jean reflected, "As I was travelling around the world living the excitement of the birth of new communities, others were living the day-to-day life of community with all its pain and conflicts, with all its celebrations and the joys.... I could not have done all this travelling if others were not there living so faithfully and beautifully what I was preaching."[21] This wide circle offering generous and often sacrificial commitment was a great gift because Jean's gifts were unusual and needed a strong network of support to flourish. The huge cast of people who came to support the community allowed Jean to travel, to teach, and to proclaim the mission of L'Arche. In other words, they made it possible for their friend Jean Vanier to become the internationally recognized Jean Vanier.

In 1968, Jean led his first retreat, and a movement of affordable, accessible retreats called Faith and Sharing began, which continues to the present.

> It was because of the enthusiasm engendered at my St. Michael's lectures that I was asked to give that famous retreat at Mary Lake, which started something completely new. In the history of L'Arche, Mary Lake is very important because of the discovery that L'Arche was based in evangelical values and so people were excited. It was a response, a clear response to Vatican II, while there were a lot of unclear responses of anger against authority. We were new and it was exciting, and it was grounded in reality. It was living with the poor. It made sense to people.

People at the retreat found their spiritual lives transformed by Jean's encouragement to pray by simply abiding in Jesus. Jean credited Père Thomas: "I learned from him to pray is not just to say prayers but to be prayerful, to remain quietly in the presence of God, to simply be in communion with Jesus."[22]

This retreat led directly to the founding of L'Arche in Canada, as Our Lady's Missionaries' superior Sr. Rosemary offered the property that became L'Arche Daybreak in 1969.

WHAT IS A FOUNDER?

Through the 1980s, Jean tried to distance himself from the word *founder*, feeling that it implied a plan and ownership, when he felt he had simply followed his intuition and let L'Arche grow organically as God directed it. Kathryn Spink noted in 1990 that Jean "disclaimed that title. Growth in community meant the progression from 'my work' to 'our work' to 'God's work.' More specifically, the role of founder belonged as much to Père Thomas…and to the handicapped people." In her revised version of the book, Spink confirmed, "In 2004 Jean Vanier stood by that insistence."[23]

For a time, Jean referred to both himself and Père Thomas as founders, as in his 1999 "Letter to my Brothers and Sisters in L'Arche and in Faith and Light": "As founder of L'Arche with Père Thomas, and of Faith and Light with Marie-Hélène Mathieu, I like to say over and over again what a treasure we have received."[24] Yet after Père Thomas's death in 1993, Jean had begun to reveal more about how the founding of L'Arche brought painful stresses between the two, whose vision for the community diverged almost immediately. Key points of disagreement beginning in 1965 included whether L'Arche should expand beyond Trosly, spread to other countries, remain exclusively Roman Catholic or be open to becoming ecumenical and interfaith, and whether communities could welcome female core members. Perhaps it is obvious that they would disagree: Père Thomas was born and raised in a large family in rural France and lived most of his life in France, while Jean was born in Switzerland to a diplomatic family and travelled widely with his family and in his naval career. Sometime in L'Arche's fourth decade, partially as a fruit of the L'Arche International Identity and Mission process, the founding story of L'Arche began to acknowledge more of this complicated relationship between Jean and Père Thomas.[25] This was seen as a helpful expansion of the story: L'Arche was founded, not just in the simple unity of the two—one lay, one ordained—but also in their commitment to each other despite deep ideological differences. Jean says he came to Père Thomas as a very young man to be born, to discover his identity, and Père Thomas became his spiritual father, but almost immediately after beginning L'Arche, disagreements between the two forced Jean to take responsibility for the community and grow beyond his father, as sons do.

Like the new inclusion of Dany in the story, this revelation of tension and conflict was welcomed. Jean has suggested that the tension between the two men saved L'Arche because it prevented L'Arche from being too dependent on one person's inspiration. Throughout the 2000s, the evolving story of the founding of Trosly suggested that the continued faithfulness in disagreement of Jean and Père Thomas could offer a model for community. In 2008, theologian Christian Salenson identified the tension between Père Thomas and Jean around questions of community direction, ecclesial relations, and interfaith choices as two anchors that hold an arch. Using the "L'Arche" image of a rainbow and an arch, he noted that an arch is held in place by tension. He urged L'Arche members to stay with the tension because tension and paradox are intrinsic to the central identity of L'Arche. "This tension between the gifts of Père Thomas and the gifts of Jean is creative. This tension is a cornerstone in the foundation of L'Arche."[26]

RAPHAËL SIMI AND PHILIPPE SEUX AS FOUNDERS

By 2010, Jean was willing to identify himself as the primary founder of L'Arche. Père Thomas was an inspiration, Jean explained, but not a founder. More recently, Raphaël Simi and Philippe Seux have been recognized as cofounders of L'Arche with their own stories and history. In 2014, the L'Arche International website included short biographies of these two men who said yes to an extraordinary and unprecedented invitation from an unknown Canadian stranger. Previous versions of the founding story had stated only that Raphaël and Philippe had come from an overcrowded and often violent institution. The new biographical information is interesting. Although Raphaël was thirty-six years old and Philippe only twenty-two, both men had lived with their mothers until being orphaned less than two years previously. Thus both were more accustomed to life in a family household than in an institution.[27] As quoted earlier, Philippe Seux vividly describes his experience of beginning L'Arche:

> Jean Vanier took me out of a center where I had been placed by social workers. It had really been desolate there. There was no village nearby, there was no way of communicating with the outside world, and we were always inside surrounded by four walls. When he took me out of there, I felt so relieved: "phew!" When I came to L'Arche, there was no electricity, none. We used candles for lighting. It was fun! There were no toilets or showers, but I felt like I was exploding with joy.[28]

FIVE IN THAT ARK? JEAN-LOUIS COÏC

Kathryn Spink's 1990 history described the first day of the new community as a day of welcome. Madame Martin brought with her the three men and a celebratory meal, which was shared by a few other friends, including Père Thomas, Dr. and Madame Preaut, and others. "Afterwards, however, the guests all left and he [Jean Vanier] found himself alone with his three new companions." The phrasing was left unchanged in her 2005 revision, *The Miracle, the Message and the Story*. In 2014, Jean named the little household who launched L'Arche on August 5, 1964, "Mrs. Martin came with her accountant. There were also Dr. and Mrs. Préaut, Fr. Thomas, and Jacqueline d'Halluin, the secretary of Fr. Thomas; I was there with Jean-Louis Coïc,

Dany, Raphaël and Philippe. Coïc—it is a Breton name—knew Fr. Thomas who had asked him if he would give me a hand. He cooked fish really well. However I don't think that Jean-Louis liked the lifestyle, and he left as soon as he possibly could!"[29]

Pause here: that founding story of three men in the house the first night, Jean, Raphaël, and Philippe, had expanded nearly thirty years earlier to include Dany. But who is Jean-Louis Coïc? Is it possible that, after so many decades, the very earliest story has a new addition?

Actually, Jean-Louis Coïc was named in 1989 in Jean's long account "Our Story" in the 1989 *Letters of L'Arche*, reprinted as *An Ark for the Poor*. "After a festive meal that Dr. and Mrs. Préaut and Fr. Thomas shared with us, I was left alone with Raphaël, Philippe and Dany. We were all a bit lost. Jean-Louis Coïc, a long-time friend, was there to help out a bit." In that issue of *Letters of L'Arche*, Jean-Louis is even identified in an early photo.[30] The narrative of Jean "left alone" with his three new housemates is engaging and vivid, and it certainly presents how that day felt to Jean, who knew that he was now committed and could not easily change his mind. He alone carried full responsibility for this new venture. But he was not "alone" with Raphaël, Philippe, and Dany. In his very next sentence, he identifies a friend who was there with them. Perhaps it is not surprising that the next sentence was unnoticed because that description sounds as though Jean-Louis was a casual visitor, not actually living there as part of that first household. And yet a few sentences later, Jean again mentions Jean-Louis: "Jean-Louis or I would take turns preparing the meals."[31] Jean-Louis stayed for more than a month. Henri Wambergue moved in on August 22 and lists Jean-Louis as one of the people living in the little house. In a 1964 letter included in *The Beginnings of L'Arche*, Louis Pretty listed the early members of the household, grateful for Jean-Louis's help in literally building L'Arche: "There was also Jean-Louis who was a mason and helped us a lot with the renovations, especially anything to do with stone. As there was no toilet in the house, at the back of the garden we built a shelter with a bucket in it, and that became our toilet. Jean-Louis worked hard to create the stone walls for that little shelter." The same photo with Jean-Louis is in that 2015 publication as well, but he is not named.[32]

So now we must envision that first night with five men in the house. What do we make of this? People who know L'Arche well could wryly observe that anyone who has lived in L'Arche knows the role of the overlooked assistant toiling without recognition, but most do not know that this role began on that very first night. One could chuckle a bit ruefully at this strange twist of the story because the story of the underappreciated assistant has been repeated myriad times around the world. Perhaps on the first night, L'Arche was given two important patrons: Dany, patron of L'Arche's failures and limitations, and Jean-Louis Coïc, patron of overlooked assistants. Perhaps Jean-Louis is also the patron of all the assistants who arrive and discover quickly that the life of L'Arche is not for them. Jean explains that Jean-Louis had been an acquaintance of his and a friend of Père Thomas from the time of L'Eau Vive. He was an older, somewhat taciturn man who did not warm to people, including people with intellectual disabilities. But he did not abandon Jean in his new venture. Rather, he remained, cooking and working, until there were two other assistants in place. And according to Louis Pretty, he helped L'Arche deal with its crap, literally, by building a shelter for the bucket that was used as a toilet.

In forgetting to include Jean-Louis, did the story of the first night also launch a reductive myth of a single, heroic founder alone, rather than a story of mutual support? Even if Jean-Louis was not entirely thrilled with his new housemates, there was support for Jean in having another assistant in the house. How else could Jean have gone to the pay phone in the village to make the call about Dany? In the 1980s, the addition of Dany to Jean's story gave L'Arche members a sense of possibility, even permission to fail. But it would be absurd to suggest that retrieving the name of the forgotten first L'Arche assistant gives permission to overlook the work and contribution of assistants in building L'Arche. This is important: not only the founding story but also its readers and participants have been evolving. In his 2007 collection of letters, *Our Life Together*, Jean announced, "The myth of the perfect founder who does everything inspired by God is evolving in our communities into a more collective ownership of the founding story."[33] Jean was suggesting that in the decades since adding Dany to the story, L'Arche has matured enough to look to its founding story as a shared story that helps understand its vision, origins, culture, and assumptions. This shift from seeing Jean's story as "the myth of the perfect founder who does everything inspired by God" to "a more collective ownership of the founding story" became essential in 2015, as L'Arche struggled to incorporate another layer into its founding story.

THE 2014–15 CANONICAL INQUIRY INTO PÈRE THOMAS

By the time L'Arche began in 1964, Père Thomas had resumed, in a limited way, the sacramental ministry, personal accompaniment, and spiritual direction that Rome compelled him to give up at L'Eau Vive more than a decade earlier. But he had a problem. Accusations of inappropriate sexual behavior with women who entrusted themselves to him for spiritual direction had caused his superiors abruptly to terminate his ministry and leadership at L'Eau Vive in 1952. While the results of the ensuing investigation have remained sealed, the alleged abuse was made public in Paul Weindling's 2010 biography of John W. Thompson. Weindling concludes starkly, "The images of Père Thomas as an inspirer of compassion and as a base abuser remain unreconciled."[34] Père Thomas died in 1993, but in 2015 a canonical inquiry revealed that he "was the perpetrator of abusive sexual behavior" toward women who came to him for spiritual direction during his years at L'Arche's retreat center La Ferme. The inquiry concluded, "No matter how much good Père Thomas has done, for which many are grateful, these acts and their justification are proof of a distorted conscience that claimed many known, and no doubt unknown, victims for whom justice must be done."[35]

L'Arche International leaders Patrick Fontaine and Eileen Glass shared this information in a letter:

> We are writing to you as our fiftieth anniversary celebrations draw to a close. Each celebration gave us an opportunity to re-read our story in a more in-depth way….However, the current re-reading of our story must take into account some sad news concerning Père Thomas Philippe.

They offer the conclusions of the report, then continue,

> We are grateful to these people who courageously expressed their suffering and want to offer them our support….It is inevitable that such acts call us to take a new look at Père Thomas' teaching and at his contribution to L'Arche's development….We also believe that this information will help all of us to a more authentic and less idealized reading of the story of L'Arche.

In a public letter of May 2015, Jean Vanier expressed his shock: "A few years ago I was told of certain acts, but until now I remained totally in the dark as to the depth of their gravity. Therefore the news of these revelations hit me like a terrible storm…in thinking of the victims and of their suffering, I want to ask forgiveness for all that I did not do or should have done." Two years later, in a book of autobiographical essays, Jean described his own slow process over two years of pain, anger, then deep sorrow and mourning to recognize what he had previously found incomprehensible and thus ignored.[36]

How does a community integrate news like this into the founding story that has shaped its very identity? In every L'Arche community around the world, the community leader was asked to share the results of the investigation with members of their community and their board of directors, asking every community urgently to review its policies, training, education, and reporting of sexual abuse and confirm that they had functioning protocols in place. In writing about the investigation into Père Thomas, the international leaders emphasized that the news affects the founding story. "Even if these events took place over thirty years ago, this news has truly shaken members of our communities and affected the interpretation that we had of our history. We also share the desire to integrate these areas of shadow into how we tell our story."

Listen again to how the international leaders articulate the challenge: "…how we tell our story," not how Jean will tell the story. They invite all of L'Arche to own its history together: "We pray for and invite you to pray for those members of L'Arche and those communities, who are most affected by these events…so that our history, which will only be solid if it is built on truth, can also be built in unity." Although Jean Vanier's response was crucial, the leaders of L'Arche International assumed responsibility, even authority, for the founding story of L'Arche in Trosly. It is no longer only Jean Vanier's story. The leaders take for granted that it will continue to evolve beyond him.

There could be a legitimate effort to minimize the importance of Père Thomas, but he is an integral part of the founding story. Much of the theology of L'Arche was articulated first by

Père Thomas and published for readers of *Letters of L'Arche* in multiple languages around the world beginning in 1971: a theology founded on mutuality, the body, incarnation, affection, and communion beyond rational understanding. Yet right from the beginning of L'Arche, Jean in his own unique way adapted aspects of Père Thomas's theological insights into his daily life with his new companions: respect and open acceptance of the body in life and in death; appreciation of 1 Corinthians 12 that all the parts of the body are essential; prayer as communion and presence; the physical joking of L'Arche from toy snakes leaping from mustard pots to throwing orange peels; discovering the kingdom of God by becoming like children in all the physical fun that is so foundational to the spirit of L'Arche. L'Arche remains "founded on the body" because of the physicality of daily life together, the communication through touch, and because so much of its fun, its energy, and its spirit are based on unapologetically embodied community activity.[37]

The intrinsic tension that Christian Salenson highlighted in 2008 has surely deepened with the revelations about Père Thomas in 2015. However, unlike previous new revelations that seemed to open new possibilities, Père Thomas's complicated legacy has been painful to face and thus far impossible to integrate. Perhaps over time the troubling truths made public in 2015 will both free and further open the history of L'Arche. Salenson also insisted, in speaking about L'Arche and the body, that a wound can be life-giving "for the whole body, so long as it is not covered up, silenced or hidden. Every hurt has a story to tell."[38]

JEAN VANIER: A FOUNDER, A MYTH, A MESSENGER, A PERSON

L'Arche was created because Jean Vanier and Père Thomas felt called to "do something" together to follow Jesus. That simple story has been shaken, and there could now be a temptation to emphasize Jean even more as the heroic character standing alone in his new community idea. There is some truth in that early narrative of Jean "alone" with two companions in a life to which he was now fully committed. But by noticing those very mythic overtones, we can also recognize some of the pressure and projections that Jean lived in and with for more than five decades. Is it time to think more about what power an idealized "perfect founder" has as a symbol? Myths have heroes, who succeed against great adversity: even after half a century, it is easy to be enthralled by the mythic quality of Jean and L'Arche's founding story. But even mythic heroes have limitations. That is not to diminish Jean. He worked to articulate his own struggles and peculiarities. He often wrote about his times of deep anxiety and even anguish. Even his very public 1998 Massey Lectures confessed, "Some people with disabilities call forth tenderness in me; others call forth anguish, fear, and anger....I have often come head-to-head with my own handicaps, limits, and inner poverty. I did not always find it easy, especially when my failure was evident to others."[39]

Remember how for many decades no one noticed Jean-Louis Coïc, even though he was identified in photos and text as early as 1989? It is easy to let one good story or even myth block a more complete story. In the same way, perhaps not only L'Arche but many of Jean's admirers have been so attached to Jean Vanier as a myth that they overlooked Jean's efforts to identify his weaknesses, or assumed he was speaking in general rather than personal terms. In 1979, Jean proposed a rather unexpected book:

> I have always wanted to write a book called "The Right to be a Rotter." A fairer title is perhaps "The Right to be Oneself." One of the great difficulties of community life is that we sometimes force people

to be what they are not: we stick an ideal image on them to which they are obliged to conform. We then expect too much of them and are quick to judge or to label. If they don't manage to live up to this image or ideal, then they become afraid they won't be loved or that they will disappoint others. So they feel obliged to hide behind a mask."[40]

The right to be a rotter: Is there an almost wistful quality there? Jean rephrased it as the right to be oneself. But no one ever expected Jean to be a rotter. Indeed, quite the opposite. For example, the editors of the United Church of Canada *Observer* in 1972 introduced the text of a talk Jean had given with these astonishing words: "If you don't worship him, you don't know him," and concluded, "In the glow of his words and his life, you forget everything except that this man is a saint, calling us to be the same."[41] Think about this: for over fifty years, people have looked to Jean not only to be a saint, but also to call them to be likewise. Not much leeway to "be a rotter," whatever that might have meant to Jean personally. In 2017, Jean went further, confiding his need to love and to be loved, reminding readers that he was a person like any other, who could feel empathy for some and who could also wound and discard others. He confessed that he knew that he had hurt people, and "from the very depths of my heart" asked them for forgiveness at that moment toward the end of his life.[42]

Looking back, it becomes apparent that after 1964, the influence of Raphaël, Philippe, Jacques, Jean-Pierre, and others was as significant in shaping Jean as Père Thomas had been in his earlier years. L'Arche indeed began because of the particular and unique person of Jean: his faith in God, his courage, his passion, and even his neediness as a prayerful visionary who had not had a real home for many years. The messenger and the message are intertwined, but even in the founding story there was not only one messenger. L'Arche began and evolved as it did because of who Jean chose as his companions. Think about the playfulness, the spirituality of celebration and delight in each other. Louis Pretty sums it up vividly in *The Beginnings of L'Arche*: "Jean was always very optimistic, he didn't see any problems, anywhere; everything was perfect, there was no need to worry, everything would go well! It's clear that if he had not been like that, he never would have gotten anything done, because it was really crazy in the beginning. He didn't know anything, but he had 300% faith, and thank God he was like that!"[43]

Perhaps, as Louis Pretty suggests, L'Arche could only have been created by someone whose momentum and energy moved forward, who did not focus on problems but instead lived in confidence that everything would work out. Jean could let go of failure and conflict without feeling a need to resolve them. There can be a shadow side to that optimism in its avoidance of contradictions, as was made painfully apparent in the revelations about Père Thomas. Yet the gift side of those same limitations has been the joyful spirit that Jean discovered and cultivated with his new friends and bequeathed to L'Arche. "Isn't there something in each of us which longs to become like children and to have fun together like children? Isn't this foolishness the sign of the liberation of our hearts?" Jean asked his distinguished audience at the Templeton Award ceremony, concluding, "It is for this gift of liberation of our hearts to love, that I thank from the bottom of my heart my companions of fifty years, people with intellectual disabilities, for all that they have taught me and given me."[44] As previously quoted, Jean-Pierre Crépieux rightly asserts, "With regards to Jean Vanier, it's true that it's he who opened Trosly, but I would like to say that when one opens a home, one is not alone. If Jean had not known Raphaël Simi, Philippe Seux, Jacques Dudouit and me, he could not have started L'Arche!" In other words, the unique spirit and appeal of L'Arche evolved as it did because of the early core members who shaped Jean.

Jean explains that winning the very prestigious Templeton Prize left him feeling ambivalent because he feared it would reemphasize a focus on him, on the messenger rather than the message. The message about the beauty and the value of people with intellectual disabilities that Jean announced in accepting the Templeton Prize is a message for everyone: "For peace, people must meet across differences....It is only as we meet and share together person to person, eye to eye, and heart to heart that we discover what it means to be human and to discover the joy of being together, working together towards a common mission of peace and unity."[45]

Let us return to the insight that launched this entire discussion, from L'Arche International. It reads in full,

> We need to own the founding story of L'Arche together and be able to transmit it to others. Insufficient knowledge and understanding of our founding story limits our flexibility, creativity, vision and our sense of identity. We tend to idealize the time of the foundation and as a result, we are not able to appropriate important values and formative experiences of the story and integrate them into our personal journey. This also limits the potential power of the founding story to challenge and to transform us. This is equally true for other founding stories at national and community levels.

Is the founding story of L'Arche still overidealized? And yet Jean's story of Trosly is genuinely extraordinary. Is there an alternate danger of it becoming underidealized? L'Arche perhaps will know only in hindsight. Jesuit Bill Clarke notes that a romanticized story of L'Arche, such as he presented in his 1974 book, *Enough Room for Joy*, is incomplete but not inaccurate. It brings people to L'Arche, and many stay even after they discover a more complex truth.

SIGNS OF THE TIMES

If you have read Malcolm Gladwell's book *Outliers*, you know that no individual becomes historically significant solely because of their unique insight or charisma. Many brilliant people are born into family and historical circumstances that never allow them to contribute much, while others find their particular combination of family, culture, and friendships aligns in their historic moment. Jean Vanier's founding of L'Arche in France fits this theory. In 1964, when Jean was inspired to do something unprecedented, it helped to have parents who were internationally well-connected and respected through decades in diplomatic circles. They were also willing to fund their son's adventures well into his thirties. Strangely, it also helped to have a mentor who had been marginalized, so that by 1964, Père Thomas was not a star theologian in Rome, as some might have predicted, but instead a chaplain to people with intellectual disabilities in the small French village of Trosly. It also helped that the mentor's career path had discouraged Jean from pursuing ordination so that Jean too was free to create something new. One friend led to another: for example, a coffee with Jean's friend Dan Berrigan led Jean to meet Louis Pretty, a Montreal architect who helped for the first year. The time was right to advance ideas of deinstitutionalization and of radical communal living. Jean comments on what was coming together in society at large:

> One of the reasons that L'Arche took off was that the sixties and seventies were the years of community. The Jesus People in the United States—there must

have been hundreds of these communities, a sort of liberation, the movement away from Church to Jesus. The Vatican II Council shook things up everywhere. There was rejection of law and authority, and finding new ways through community. L'Arche fit into this movement. The economy was expanding—we could get loans from the Sécurité sociale for twenty years without interest. Europe was financially zooming. So finances, community, Vatican II, lay people—everything was there.

As we look beyond Jean and Trosly to the other early founders in this book, we will likewise see that many factors came together for each new community to be born. For each founder, their desire to do something meaningful in their lives and do something for a better world coincided with a pivotal moment for L'Arche and welcoming conditions in the countries where they began new communities. For example, Jean's time teaching at St. Michael's College in the early 1960s had made him a known speaker and connected him with the bishop who issued an unprecedented invitation to a layperson to lead a Catholic retreat. Out of that Mary Lake retreat came many future leaders of L'Arche, and the offer of a large house and farm in Richmond Hill. Steve and Ann Newroth came back from Trosly with an unusual skill set in administration, human resources, social services, theology, psychology, and even farming to begin L'Arche in Canada (chapter 1). Social services were just beginning to create policy and legislation for group homes. Bill and Peter, the first two core members to join Steve and Ann, were also in the right place at the right moment to respond.

A participant at a Daybreak planning event recommended that Jean apply immediately for money from the Canadian International Development Agency (CIDA) to begin L'Arche in India. Jean wrote that application with Gabrielle Einsle, who was ready for a change after years at the Crossroads International Student House that she had founded in Montreal (chapter 2). She had experience directing that community, and also the adventurous spirit and heart needed to found the first L'Arche in India. Mira, an Indian assistant in Trosly who had known Gabrielle in Montreal, helped make connections, and people in India were moved to help.

Nadine Tokar's founding in Honduras has a mythic quality (chapter 7). Exhausted during a break in a retreat in Tegucigalpa, she fell asleep on a local bus, woke up she-knew-not-where, and recognized that this was where L'Arche was called to begin. But she was also at a turning point in her life, open to find God's call after years of professional administrative experience in high-level sports competitions for people with intellectual disabilities. Jean's older sister, Thérèse Vanier, was a well-established medical doctor and pioneer in the palliative care movement when she began L'Arche in the UK (chapter 4). She insisted that L'Arche would become mature when it really engaged the biblical (and medical) challenge that when one part suffers, the whole "body" suffers. Perhaps L'Arche's founding ideals continue to resonate now in the twenty-first century as we become more aware of the value of diversity and interconnectedness, multiple faiths, and ecosystems.

A COMMUNITY IS MADE OF STORIES

It might help to think of each of these early communities not just as a physical place, but also as a collection of stories through time. Cultural geographer Doreen Massey suggests, "If space is a simultaneity of stories-so-far, then places are collections of those stories, articulations within the wider power-geometries of space."[46] Massey helps us to see two things. First, each community is made up of stories of simultaneous experiences. Those include multiple stories within each director as their experience was unfolding on many levels: their complex role in their community, their relationships with the larger community of L'Arche, their inner spiritual and psychological experience. But many other stories that we do not attempt to include in this book were also unfolding simultaneously: the stories of the first assistants who held the community together while the founders travelled to L'Arche meetings; the stories of the first core members who stayed and those who left; the stories of the parents and families of the founders, assistants, and core members; the stories of early board members who took responsibility in the "wider power-geometries" for unique communities with no precedents. This book is also about what Massey calls the "simultaneity of stories-so-far" in that the stories take us only so far in the life of the founders and the communities they founded. Each has an ongoing story. At the end of each chapter, a small summary is provided of what the founder did next. But these communities also now have decades of history: all have survived in their own wider power-geometries of space as their societies have changed, sometimes through catastrophic ruptures such as civil war in the Ivory Coast, hurricanes in Haiti, or earthquakes in Honduras.

Massey further notes that for every place, "Their character will be a product of these intersections within that wider setting, and of what is made of them. And, too, of the non-meetings-up, the disconnections and the relations not established, the exclusions. All this contributes to the specificity of place."[47] In these founding stories are people who could not stay, painful misunderstandings, what Massey calls "non-meetings-up and disconnections." In other words, there will never be one "authentic" story that captures the full sweep of the founding of a L'Arche community, whether it is in France or any other country. So in what follows, don't look only for the story of one heroic founder; notice also how each is part of a network of people with simultaneous stories layered in a particular historic moment in a specific place. Pay attention to what moves you in these stories, what you find unexpected or even disturbing, what amuses you. While stories inspire our choices and form our imaginations, our lives are also shaped by the stories we overlook, the disconnections and exclusions noted by Doreen Massey.

SIX SURPRISES

As I started to gather and edit this book's stories of the founders of L'Arche in seven countries after France, the new L'Arche international coordinator, Stephan Posner, asked me, "What has surprised you?" Listening to these founders, I was surprised by six common themes in their stories.

First, as I've noted, these founders and their companions were having fun. In fact, Jean asserts, "A spiritual life is not just about prayers—it is about the quality of attention. So the spirituality is in the life, which is centered on the gospel and on Jesus—so it's not the amount of prayers, it's the amount of fun. Transformation is finding that the heart of the gospel is having fun together." Jean is quick to add that it wasn't easy. In community, people find themselves dropping their barriers or raising new ones for self-protection, and either way it can be painful. But community potentially allows for a deeper knowledge of oneself and each other, and a deeper hilarity. There was a lot of excitement as L'Arche expanded, even in difficult and stressful times. L'Arche had swiftly developed an embodied spirituality of shared life, intentionally choosing to celebrate, have fiestas, go on pilgrimages, and to know each other in a day-to-day way as a family dependent on God and wary of anything that would set up barriers of wealth, security, or status. Perhaps this attracted people into L'Arche leadership who were similar to

Jean, who were able to walk into new situations with faith and a sense of comedy rather than tragedy, a bighearted outrage at injustice combined with countercultural delight in eccentricity. As you read these founding stories, look for the lighthearted moments!

Second, at the center of every story is a faith journey. Looking back, it becomes more apparent that the key relationship that founded L'Arche was not initially between Jean and the men he welcomed. Prior to starting the little house together, they had met only a handful of times, and really did not know each other, as the attempt to include Dany demonstrates. It could certainly be argued that the key relationship was between Jean and Père Thomas: Jean had given up his potential academic career and community around St. Michael's College to be closer to Père Thomas. Jean framed it differently, however. To Jean, his key relationship was with Jesus. L'Arche was his response to the call of the Gospels. As he wrote in 1979, "I began L'Arche in 1964, in the desire to live the Gospel and to follow Jesus Christ more closely."[48] In other words, what launched L'Arche was an inner response to a call, and this is true also of the founders whose stories follow. While each was inspired and to some degree guided by Jean Vanier, for most the sustaining relationship as they founded communities was with Jesus. Each founder was actively seeking coherence between their faith and their daily work. Their choice of L'Arche was a response to an intimate relationship with Jesus that led to L'Arche, a call often discovered through silence and presence, whether in contemplation or while sitting with people with disabilities. As you hear these founding stories, listen for the founders' experience of Jesus.

Third, the founding core members were a diverse group. For some of the early core members, L'Arche was a transitional home between an institution and more independent living. For example, in the United States, many did not stay in the first community because they did not require the level of support that L'Arche offered, but they needed to gain confidence before moving on (chapter 3). Even the founding core members of Jean's original household moved: while both Raphaël and Philippe continued living in L'Arche, neither remained in the original community in Trosly.[49] In contrast, other core members' needs initially seemed far too complex for the community that was trying to welcome them. Dany, who returned to his institution after just one night, is now firmly part of the history of L'Arche Trosly. But unlike Dany's story, the institution in Haiti refused to take Yveline back. The fledgling L'Arche community just had to find a way forward together, and through years of patience and love and hope, Yveline grew to become a cornerstone of her community (chapter 6). As you consider these founding stories, pay attention to the founding core members.

Fourth, these are all intriguing stories of human growth. Each of these founders was accomplished and competent, coming to L'Arche from a wide variety of careers and backgrounds. Yet all had a longing to do more with their lives. Prefacing each founder's story is a short summary of the unique path that brought each to L'Arche, the combination of circumstances and personal desires that put them in the right place at the right time. Each narrative then continues in their own words. They describe how the early community members all took a risk to say yes to new companions and a style of life that was in many ways an experiment. It was not easy for anyone. Jean's original ideals of poverty and "littleness" had to be reframed in light of different cultures. Each founder negotiated cultural and political assumptions about authority, leadership, gender roles, social class, and the role of people with intellectual disabilities. Even how to pray together as a community wasn't simple or obvious. Further, I had begun the project with a fairly simplistic assumption that all the early founders were close and supportive friends with their teams. No, they were not all friends and sometimes they didn't even like each other! Jean and Père Thomas are not the only ones who struggled through significant stress and estrangement. I was quite moved to hear of the stresses between people, the perseverance and growth required to build L'Arche together. For example, Steve Newroth articulates how difficult it was for him and Ann as a married couple with children, and how their united decision-making was hard for the community (chapter 1). Gabrielle Einsle had expected to be founding L'Arche in India with her friend Mira but had to carry on alone. She describes at one point pulling her sari over her face so that her tears were not visible (chapter 2). Dawn Barraqué missed her initial team when Gus and Debbie Leuschner returned to Canada, and found her role as the authority for her new team lonely and hard to take up (chapter 5). Robert Larouche faced death-threats in a charged political milieu (chapter 6). Thérèse Vanier might have pioneered L'Arche burnout (chapter 4). Each founder had times of intense loneliness or exhaustion. More than four decades later, they look back at these struggles with humility and candor, even humor. You will be moved by the openness with which George Strohmeyer admits that he and co-founder Barbara Karsznia did not like each other initially. Their honesty with each other allowed L'Arche to begin in the United States (chapter 3). As you read these stories, notice points of struggle and growth.

Fifth, these are stories not just of the beginnings of individual communities, but of an international movement. Jean wrote, "I did not begin L'Arche because I wanted to help a few 'unfortunate' people locked up in a dismal and violent institution. My life in L'Arche is part of a larger struggle for peace."[50] L'Arche communities have spread around the world, each gathering a remarkable variety of people. As Nadine Tokar observes, a unique outward-looking global energy propelled L'Arche in the 1960s and 1970s as Jean's friends founded new L'Arche communities around the world (chapter 7). Perhaps the vision was overidealized, but the momentum was real and was also founded in the social justice movements of the time, seeking solidarity and liberation for people with intellectual disabilities. Each new L'Arche community in this book began as a very small endeavor, but each reached into a new country and linked with the network of other communities that was advancing a global movement. As you consider these stories, observe their international engagement.

Sixth, eventually each founder had to face the other side of being called to found a community, which is leaving. L'Arche Daybreak founder Ann Newroth reflects, "It's not like leaving a job. L'Arche is not the normal contract you make with an employer. You're asking people to come with their hearts and their energy and an ability to form relationships that an ordinary employer doesn't ask for." She adds that when the commitment to L'Arche has been open-ended, "the measuring stops and you've put so much in that you've gone beyond the normal limits and you're in over your head." It makes the decision to leave complex and often profoundly painful. Some founders had a new sense of call in that transition, but most had to move forward in their lives without a clear direction. Their stories include how they experienced that point of departure, which often included a difficult time of grieving and drifting without focus or purpose. A short afterword to each story describes what they did next. As you hear these stories, listen to the factors involved and the founders' feelings as they leave.

CHAOS, FUN, AND LIVING WITH

From the late 1960s through the 1970s, there was energy and excitement in the rapid expansion of L'Arche around the world. Responding to the cry of people who had been rejected, even rescuing people from oppressive or dehumanizing situations, had a real sense of urgency. In 2017, Jean recalled the spirit of those times in Trosly: "It's difficult to imagine the chaos that was here. But there were people arriving and then we could start a new house. It was chaotic but it was exciting. It was fun and we were together. We had the Monday Morning Meetings—we would laugh." While there was no grand plan, the mission was evolving rapidly. Jean continues,

> At the same time there was a whole formation in understanding and creating L'Arche. I would talk about coming back from India. I'd talk about new assistants arriving. There was a sort of togetherness, a collective unity, excitement and laughter, and serious stuff going on. Steve and Ann coming and then Thérèse entering in brought ecumenism. Dawn leaving for Ivory Coast and Robert leaving for Haiti and Nadine leaving for Honduras. There was a quality of togetherness and a whole air of excitement, sending people off, and them coming back and saying what they'd seen. I mean, right from the beginning there was the excitement of an international movement.

Steve Newroth at a public talk celebrating the fortieth anniversary of Daybreak described the underlying values that led L'Arche to grow:

> Jean would probably say he just listened to the message of the gospels and to the needs of people with disabilities. As we began Daybreak, our vision could be expressed in two words. In French, "Vivre Avec," for it came with us from France: in English, "live with!" Meaning not so much "to work for," because "living with" was the work of L'Arche, it was the therapy of L'Arche—sharing life! When you have been born into a world that rejects you, when you have been shuffled to the fringe of society and you see yourself as waste material and someone says to

you "I would like to share my life with you," that is the most life-giving therapy that can happen.

NOTES

1. In L'Arche, people with intellectual disabilities are often referred to as "core members," because they are essential, forming the core of any L'Arche community. The term *assistants* refers to L'Arche members without intellectual disabilities, or as theologian John Swinton phrases it, L'Arche is "an international network of communities in which people with intellectual disabilities live with people who do not share that life experience" (John Swinton, "Introduction," Stanley Hauerwas and Jean Vanier, *Living Gently in a Violent World: The Prophetic Witness of Weakness* [Downers Grove, IL: IVP Books, 2008], 17).

Jean-Pierre Crépieux quotation from Association Jean Vanier and L'Arche Canada, *The Beginnings of L'Arche: Recollections of the First Years in Trosly 1964–1968*, published as an online PDF in 2015, www.larche.ca/publications/the_beginnings_of _larche_1964-1968.pdf, L'Arche Canada, 172.

Jean-Pierre Crépieux arrived in December 1964 (Kathryn Spink, *The Miracle, The Message, The Story: Jean Vanier and L'Arche* [Toronto: Novalis, 2005], 65). In 2014, Jean-Pierre Crépieux was the first person with an intellectual disability to receive the Legion of Honor—the highest honor in France.

2. Philippe Seux, quoted in *The Beginnings of L'Arche*, 33.

3. All quotations from Jean and other founders are from my recordings of personal conversations unless otherwise noted.

4. Throughout this book all members of L'Arche, with and without intellectual disabilities, are referred to by their first names, as they are called in their communities. Thus, I refer to Robert and Nadine in this paragraph. Jean Vanier is Jean, and his cofounders Raphaël Simi and Philippe Seux are called Raphaël

and Philippe. An exception to this is Père Thomas Philippe, who was always called Père Thomas in the community. All persons in this volume are identified by their accurate names. Each has earned their place in L'Arche history. We saw no reason to diminish anyone's contribution by using pseudonyms.

5. Jean Vanier with François-Xavier Maigre, *Un cri se fait entendre: Mon chemin vers la paix* (Montrouge: Bayard, 2017), 191. Translated as *A Cry Is Heard: My Path to Peace* (London: Darton, Longman and Todd, 2018), 139.

6. Canadian Broadcasting Corporation, "Jean Vanier Opens First L'Arche House," Jean Vanier interviewed by Bill McNeill, broadcast on January 26, 1965, www.cbc.ca/archives/entry/1964-jean-vanier-opens-first-larche-house, CBC Digital Archives.

7. Jean Vanier in Peter Flemington, narrator and director, *If You're Not There...You're Missed: Jean Vanier at Trosly-Breuil.* Produced by Religious Television Associates, the cooperative production unit of the Anglican, Roman Catholic, and United Churches, 1967, YouTube: published March 6, 2014, www.youtube.com/watch?v=XBXAjc_ZbZA.

8. *Jean Vanier, Our Life Together: A Memoir in Letters* (Toronto: Harper Collins, 2007), 15.

9. Jean Vanier, *From Brokenness to Community* (Mahwah, NJ: Paulist Press, 1992), 11.

10. Père Thomas Philippe, "Unless You Become Like Little Children, You Will Never Enter the Kingdom of Heaven," *Letters of L'Arche*, no. 1 (January 1971): 16–17.

11. Jean Vanier, *The Poor at the Heart of L'Arche* (Trosly-Breuil: Les Chemins de L'Arche, 1991), 19.

12. Vanier, *The Poor at the Heart of L'Arche*, 18.

13. Vanier, *Our Life Together*, 13.

14. For a description of the Val Fleuri on pilgrimage, see esp. Vanier, *Our Life Together*, 19–20. For an entertaining account of a pilgrimage to Fatima in 1967, see also ibid., 35–37 and 42–43.

15. Jean Vanier, "Our Story," *Letters of L'Arche*, special ed., nos. 59–60 (March–June 1989): 2.

16. Kathryn Spink, *Jean Vanier and L'Arche: A Communion of Love* (Nepean, ON: Meakin and Associates, 1990), 39–40.

17. Jean Vanier, "Introduction," *The Challenge of L'Arche* (London: Darton, Longman and Todd, 1982), 1.

18. Association Jean Vanier and L'Arche Canada, *The Beginnings of L'Arche: Recollections of the First Years in Trosly, 1964–1968*.

19. Vanier, *Our Life Together*, 19.

20. Vanier, *Un cri se fait entendre*, 82 (*A Cry Is Heard*, 61).

21. Vanier, *Our Life Together*, 63–64.

22. Vanier, *Our Life Together*, 3.

23. Spink, *Jean Vanier and L'Arche*, 6; and Spink, *The Miracle, The Message*, 8.

24. Vanier, *Our Life Together*, 445.

25. Kathryn Spink observed that L'Arche "was founded not on one but on two complimentary but different vocations. Its history would be very largely determined by the tension between the two" (Spink, *The Miracle, The Message, The Story*, 78–79). Spink offers a detailed exploration of the differences and tensions between Jean and Père Thomas on pages 78–82. Jean himself explores the difficulties between the two men and the turmoil within himself in *Un cri se fait entendre*, 97–99 (*A Cry Is Heard*, 71–72).

26. Christian Salenson, *L'Arche: A Unique and Multiple Spirituality* (Paris: L'Arche en France, 2009), 64–65, 68, 71.

27. In 2018, these biographies have been moved to a Members Only section of www.larche.org. The online book, *The Beginnings of L'Arche*, is publicly available—see citation above, in n. 1. It also quotes Jean-Pierre Crispeux describing his arrival at L'Arche and being greeted by the third core member Jacques: "I don't know where Jacques came from, perhaps like me he had come from his family home" (Association Jean Vanier and L'Arche Canada, *The Beginnings of L'Arche*, 5).

28. Philippe Seux, quoted in Association Jean Vanier and L'Arche Canada, *The Beginnings of L'Arche*, 33.

29. Suex, *The Beginnings of L'Arche*, 30.

30. In the March–June 1989 issue of *Letters of L'Arche*, Jean-Louis is identified in an early photo (Vanier, "Our Story," *Letters of L'Arche*, 6).

31. Jean Vanier, *An Ark for the Poor: The Story of L'Arche* (Toronto: Novalis, 2012), 25.

32. Association Jean Vanier and L'Arche Canada, *The Beginnings of L'Arche*, 56.

33. Vanier, *Our Life Together*, 551.

34. Paul J. Weindling, *John W. Thompson: Psychiatrist in the Shadow of the Holocaust* (Rochester: University of Rochester Press, 2010), 239.

35. This quotation and those following from L'Arche International are from letters that are publicly available at http://www.larche.org/news/-/asset_publisher/mQsRZspJMdBy/content/-pere-thomas.

36. Vanier, *Un cri se fait entendre*, 99–100 (*A Cry Is Heard*, 72–73). Several women abused by Père Thomas have shared their experiences at www.avref.fr, in sections about "L'Arche" and "la Congrégation Saint-Jean." More questions emerged after the French documentary "*Religieuses abusées, l'autre scandale de l'Église*," by Marie-Pierre Raimbault, Elizabeth Drévillon, and Eric Quentin, was broadcast by the French-German television channel Arte on March 5, 2019. How does a founding story integrate ongoing revelations about sexuality, abuse, and power? L'Arche continues to work on the meaning of its history and founding story.

37. See Vanier, *Community and Growth* (Toronto: Griffin Press Limited, 1979), esp. chap. 9, "Celebration," which asserts that "celebration expresses the true meaning of community in a concrete and tangible way" through music, dance, song, meals, liturgy (201). Sometimes the best celebrating is spontaneous, such as Jean's famous after-dinner delight in flinging orange

peels across the room at his friends (207–8).

38. Salenson, *L'Arche*, 97.

39. Jean Vanier, *Becoming Human* (Toronto: House of Anansi Press Limited, 1998), 100.

40. Vanier, *Community and Growth*, 14–15, and later repeated in Jean Vanier, *Community and Growth*, 2nd rev. ed. (London: Darton, Longman and Todd, 1990), 42–43.

41. J. T., "A Gentle Hallelujah," *United Church Observer* (December 1972): 22. The magazine's introduction of Jean concludes, "In the glow of his words and his life, you forget everything except that this man is a saint, calling us to be the same" (ibid.).

42. Vanier, *Un cri se fait entendre*, 190 (*A Cry Is Heard*, 138).

43. Louis Pretty, quoted in Association Jean Vanier and L'Arche Canada, *The Beginnings of L'Arche*, 106.

44. Jean Vanier, "Jean Vanier Templeton Talk," May 18, 2015, jean-vanier.org/f/nf91jv, Jean Vanier.

45. Jean Vanier, "Transforming our Hearts," Templeton Prize News Conference, British Academy, London, March 11, 2015, www.jean-vanier.org/f/nf82jv/vanier__news_conference_statement.pdf, Jean Vanier.

46. Doreen Massey, *For Space* (London: Sage Publications Ltd., 2005), 130–31.

47. Massey, *For Space*, 131.

48. Vanier, *Community and Growth*, xi.

49. Philippe moved to Le Levain community in Compiegne after it opened in 1982. A few years later in 1985, Raphaël moved to La Rose des Vents in Verpillières. Spink, *The Miracle, The Message, The Story*, 217.

50. Ian Brown and Jean Vanier, "Your questions come, I sense, from your loneliness," *The Globe and Mail*, September 27, 2008, updated March 25, 2017, www.theglobeandmail.com/news/national/your-questions-come-i-sense-from-your-loneliness/article1062901/.

Chapter 1

"THESE ARE OUR FRIENDS"

L'Arche Daybreak in Canada, 1969

STEVE AND ANN NEWROTH

INTRODUCTION

Steve and Ann Newroth were the first married couple to found a L'Arche community. They began the first L'Arche outside of France when they started Daybreak in 1969 with their child Jean-Frederick on a farm property near Richmond Hill, just north of Toronto. Prior to coming to L'Arche, both Steve and Ann had established business careers. Ann studied merchandising at Ryerson and worked as a buyer for Simpson-Sears, Canada, travelling often to New York City. Previously, she ran her own business buying women's wear for client stores across Northern Ontario. Steve studied at Royal

Roads Military College, Victoria, B.C., and at the Royal Military College, Kingston, as a member of the Royal Canadian Air Force. Further studies at the University of Western Ontario included transportation economics, leading to work with Air Canada in Montreal in the Industrial Relations department. While completing Anglican divinity studies at Trinity College, University of Toronto, Steve met Jean Vanier in 1964 when he chaired a theology students' conference in Toronto that invited Jean as guest speaker. In 1965, Steve and Ann married, and then met Jean together when he was visiting Toronto again. Steve now takes up the account.

LOST AND FOUND

I'll start with a story. When Ann and I began Daybreak, the inspiration to *vivre avec* (live with) and share life together with handicapped people was our motivation. One moment stands out as emblematic of both the vision and the sometimes madcap, nitty-gritty of shared life in those early days. One day, tragedy loomed! The accounting ledgers went missing from Ann's office. We looked high and low for them. By the end of the week, we were in panic mode. We questioned everyone because the accounts were Daybreak's financial lifeline and losing them could imperil our government funding. Saturday morning was cleanup time when everyone changed their linen and tidied their rooms. We used this occasion to go desperately through everyone's wardrobes. There in the bottom of David Harmon's chest, hidden under a pile of clothes, were the missing ledgers. David had taken them and even entered some figures as he had seen Ann do many times. While David did get a bit of a blast, we were so relieved to have the ledger books back that this incident became one of Daybreak's historic moments of levity.

JEAN VANIER AND OUR YEAR AT L'ARCHE TROSLY-BREUIL

How did we end up in such a business? It all started in 1965 shortly after Ann and I were married, when Jean Vanier spent an evening at our Toronto apartment and suggested "out of nowhere" that we join his team in L'Arche in Trosly-Breuil, France. A year later, as I was finishing Anglican divinity studies, I won a scholarship to study at the Ecumenical Institute near Geneva, Switzerland. Now we had two reasons to head for Europe.

We got to L'Arche Trosly-Breuil in 1966. Jean assigned me to lead a maintenance team with a long list of repair jobs including an old village house, Les Rameaux. Later we built a chapel behind the house. Ann and I moved into Les Rameaux with three young men with intellectual disabilities, with whom we established a wonderful friendship and learned much of our French, some of it unmentionable! Our maintenance team was later joined by Brian Halferty. He and his wife Mary-Lou were Canadians who had also discovered L'Arche and later joined us at Daybreak. Ann's work involved two jobs. In the early part of the day, she helped in the kitchen at L'Arche, and in the afternoon, she helped Philippe Seux, a founding handicapped member, do a type of needlework called "pic-pic." Ann and I recall that year in France as a year of learning the therapy of L'Arche and exposure to Jean's interpretation of scripture and faith. It was also an exhilarating cultural experience full of personal growth.

Our second year in Europe was spent with me studying at the Ecumenical Institute of the World Council of Churches in Switzerland. The program pulsed with all the hope of Vatican II for better relations between churches. When Ann and I were leaving Canada for France, my bishop arranged for me to be ordained to the Anglican priesthood the following year in London. However, during our year at L'Arche, I started to reconsider. Jean arranged for me to go on retreat at a Cistercian abbey. The idea of starting L'Arche in Canada was already under consideration, and I found through the retreat that my heart and mind opened to this option rather than ordination. When I notified my bishop, he wrote me a blistering letter of reproach. He wanted me to take a parish served by plane along the Labrador coast where my dual qualifications as pilot and priest seemed ideal. When Jean and I discussed my bishop's letter, Jean shared that he had also received a scathing letter from his bishop five years earlier in similar circumstances. That exchange has remained an intimate point of shared experience between us.

From our time at Trosly, Ann and I sought to take its community model of care back to Canada. Jean was totally supportive and readily made his Canadian contacts available. The prospect of working with Jean on such a groundbreaking project was immensely motivating. For further preparation, we spent three months working in the Camphill Villages in England and Scotland, helping people with intellectual disabilities produce beautiful art. By the time we left Europe in 1968, Ann was pregnant and Daybreak was also an emerging reality! Jean-Frederick was born September 21, 1968. That fall, I began a master's degree in psychology and special education at the Ontario Institute for Studies in Education (OISE) in preparation for my future role.

THE RESIDENTIAL SITUATION FOR PEOPLE WITH INTELLECTUAL DISABILITIES IN THE LATE SIXTIES

When we prepared to begin Daybreak, there were no group homes and no government policies supporting integration.

Almost the only options available to parents for care for their handicapped offspring were big institutions holding up to five thousand people with intellectual disabilities. There was Pine Ridge Institution, quite close to Daybreak, with about three hundred residents and another institution sixty kilometers north in Orillia that was the biggest in the province. Thousands of people made their living in those institutions, and whole communities depended on their payrolls for their economic prosperity. To try to establish community-based housing options meant facing the enormous resistance of such vested interests. Of course, all the government money for mental retardation was budgeted to the large institutions, and without enabling legislation, it was impossible to get provincial money for new programs. Also, many parents of people living in the big institutions were very skeptical that new, small nonprofit organizations could replace the professionalism and permanence of the government-funded institutions. Nonetheless, many of these parents also knew of institutional problems such as bullying and abuse, violence and injuries, nonconsensual sterilization of young women, and excessive drugging to control behavior. By the time Ann and I returned to Canada in the summer of 1968, there was new legislation known as The Homes for Retarded Persons Act of 1966. This act provided a new structure for funding homes instead of institutions for handicapped people. It ushered in a new era of community-based services, but it took some time for the government to actually allocate new funds.

PREPARING: A BIG HOUSE, AN EXCELLENT BOARD, AND READY FUNDS

The formation of a board of directors and obtaining a property were our immediate goals. With Jean's help and various Vanier connections, we gathered a really fine board. It also felt providential when, after being inspired by Jean Vanier at his 1968 summer Mary Lake retreat, Sr. Rosemarie and Our Lady's Missionaries gave their old, fully furnished novitiate house and property in Richmond Hill to our new board. Having been raised an Ontario farm boy, I soon felt that this was an ideal place for a L'Arche community. As a city girl, Ann may have taken a bit longer because the property was a real farm with fields, fences, horses, cows, and chickens. The house was huge! It was originally built as a men's novitiate, later converted to a sanitarium for nuns with tuberculosis, then converted again to a sisters' novitiate. The well-maintained building had three floors with a large basement recreation room, and above ground, an enormous kitchen and dining room, several offices and a chapel, many bedrooms and quite a few bathrooms. Ann and I moved in with one-year-old Jean-Frederick on Labor Day, 1969.

FIRST BOARD OF DIRECTORS

Daybreak's first board of directors was truly remarkable. Professor Robie Kidd, a great intellectual and head of the adult education department at OISE, hosted the first meeting at his home in Toronto. Arthur Stone, a corporate lawyer from Toronto, was the first chairman of the board and the author of our incorporation. Among other members were Madame Pauline Vanier, Robert Lavallin, Jim Puxley, Stephen and Adrienne Clarkson, Mairi Macdonald, Ronald St. Jean Macdonald, and myself. Ann also became a board member after the ministry approved of both executive directors being on the board. Then there was the venerable Don Benson who came along a bit later. His wife, Freda, had a daughter from an earlier marriage who had a mild intellectual disability. Don was the owner and chairman of Vickers and Benson, one of the largest advertising agencies in Toronto. With his many connections in the business world, he recruited

Pete Little, Pete Scott, "Swatty" Wotherspoon, Charlie King, and Vince Reid to the board.

The strength and growth of Daybreak in its early years stemmed directly from the sense of responsibility of those early board members. Jean cautioned me, "Be careful of the people you put on your board because they'll control you." But what Ann and I found was that with the quality of people on our board, they were not controlling but always there for us. These board members had become leaders in industry and commerce because they were so good with people. Vince Reid, in particular, gave me valued mentoring and personal advice.

FINDING FUNDS

Daybreak's capital fund began with Madame Vanier giving me a check for one hundred dollars and advising me to "call Mr. Royce and he'll help you open an account." It turned out that Mr. Royce was the president of the Bank of Montreal! I went up to his forty-fifth–floor office in downtown Toronto to meet with him and another senior executive just to open a bank account! The Vanier name really opened doors. To augment our capital fund, Madame Vanier loaned us her Christmas card list. She had it broken down by categories, one of which was "horse people." These were wealthy people who owned horses, and she told me, "They always wanted to be invited to everything at Rideau Hall, but they never gave any money." I wrote thirty-five letters for her to sign and send out as an appeal. We raised $55,000! That initial fundraising gave us some much-needed working capital. I always felt that the finances of Daybreak were in the hands of Providence because we never had to worry about money for our various expansions and projects. Because of their influential contacts, the board was able to access the coffers of major corporations and banks. Ann remembers that one time a substantial check arrived in the mail from the *Reader's Digest* paying Prime Minister Pierre Trudeau for an article he had written. He told them to send it to us, totally unannounced. Apparently, he and Jean were old friends.

Our board also applied, over Madame Vanier's signature, to the Ministry of Community and Social Services to operate under the new Homes for Retarded Persons Act. But Minister John Yaremko wrote back saying there was no money allocated to the legislation. Madame Vanier declared, "What a stupid letter!" Premier Davis appropriated new money to fund the act, and three months later, the "Friends of L'Arche" (our corporate name) was at the top of the list for approval.

BEGINNING WITH BILLY: OCTOBER 16, 1969

Daybreak was officially born on October 16, 1969, with the arrival of sixteen-year-old Billy Van Buren. He came because the Lawson Residence in Scarborough, where he was placed, had to discharge its handicapped children when they reached sixteen. After weeks of planning and preparations, we remember Billy arriving proudly wearing a brand-new green suit. In the months following, he went through a growth spurt but insisted on wearing his green suit at every opportunity, even when the sleeves were halfway to his elbows.

Billy, himself, was something special, but his personal cleanliness left a bit to be desired. He was quite unkempt and needed constant hygiene monitoring. He was an immature and frail sixteen-year-old with unclear speech. Ann remembers the story of the first Christmas at Daybreak when she asked him what he would like for a gift. He came out with a word that sounded like "pflatergraf"! For weeks we kept asking what he meant until he got so exasperated that he wouldn't speak to us anymore. In the end, we discovered that he wanted a Spirograph, a 1970s art kit for drawing cards with lots of spirals. It took him weeks to get his tongue around that word, but eventually he did, and he got one for Christmas!

Years later, just after Billy had died, I spoke at Daybreak's fortieth anniversary. I focused part of my talk on Billy because his personal growth over those forty years was a metaphor for Daybreak's own growth. Ann suggested entitling my talk "From Billy to Bill." It was a perfect title because this very young sixteen-year-old matured into a man who came to represent Daybreak publicly, even on trips far away, as Henri Nouwen's speaking accomplice. Three cheers, Bill!

FIRST PEOPLE WELCOMED AT DAYBREAK

Peter Rotterman was driven to Daybreak in November 1969 by his family, including his grandmother, who loved him deeply and hosted splendid picnics at her home on the Grand River for all members of Daybreak. These were events that made Peter very proud of his family. Peter and I were very different kinds of people. He was a gentle young man raised in the city. He loved music and eventually sang in the choir at St. John's Anglican Church. Unfortunately, his clubbed feet were unsteady on rough ground. I'm more of an active, outdoors person. My idea of a summer holiday was camping in Algonquin Park, and Peter gamely went along in spite of being anxious with uneven surfaces. Our first year, Red Foster, CEO of Foster Advertising in Toronto, made a substantial donation for us to dig a pond behind the Big House. This summer project involved removing half an acre of densely packed sapling brush. Just imagine Peter wearing boots and coveralls and being asked to cut down trees. He was a wit with a fine sense of humor, but even he lacked any smart comments at this point! Even so, Peter sure gave all he had.

David Harmon was also among our earliest residents (as we called them at that time). He and his mother, Muriel, were quite a package. As a lifelong Pentecostal, his mother was making a big step in associating herself with the ecumenism of Daybreak. David and I were good friends, and whenever I had maintenance tasks to perform, David assisted. He also enjoyed foraging in my workshop looking for things to repair. In the mid-1970s, David was the author of a classic moment that became legendary at Daybreak. Once while Joe Egan was away, he made a collect call to Daybreak, and David answered the phone. When the operator asked David if he would accept the charges from a Mr. Joe Egan, David quite logically replied that Joe wasn't there! The operator then quickly explained that the call was not for Mr. Egan but from him and would David accept the charges. Joe was overhearing all this and he blurted out, "David, it's me, Joe, accept the charges!" Immediately, the operator said, "Sir, you can't speak until the charges have been accepted." There was a moment's silence and then David said, "Oh Joe, I'm glad you called because someone is trying to phone you!"

Frank Sutton came to Daybreak in 1970 from a family of musicians. He could compose at the piano. He loved to entertain and would copy the classical style of his sister then switch to the more popular style of his brothers. One evening, a well-known psychiatrist, Dr. John Fotheringham, who was director of a research and parental support agency in Toronto, came to dinner. From his research, he only knew institutionalized residents. After seeing our folks setting tables, eating with manners, and then hearing Frank play, he left truly astounded. Frank spent most of his time working at ARC Industries in Richmond Hill. When he returned from work, he would walk directly into my office, patronizingly pat me on the head, and say, "Did you have a good day, Steve?"

David Gray was the brother of a friend of mine, Patrick Gray, from my Trinity College days. When he heard about

Daybreak, he put his family in touch, and David joined us on November 3, 1970. David had been working on a farm east of Toronto, so he fit right in with us, caring for chickens, gathering eggs, and grading them for sale. In 1971, Robin Hurst and I took five of our young men, including David, across Canada. While in downtown Vancouver, we found the streets and pubs full of farmers who were in town for a poultry convention. David was in his element with men of similar interest. One farmer asked what kind of chickens David raised. "White ones," replied David! The farmer knew exactly which breed David meant.

Helen Humphries was well known to us long before she came to Daybreak permanently in May 1971. She was Ann's youngest aunt. Despite her sister Lillian's prohibition, Helen was a closet smoker. We would find her cigarette ashes in the washrooms and were always worried about fire. When she was short of cigarettes, she would help herself to anyone's. This led to a showdown one day when Ann and I summoned her to the office. We expected her to be contrite. She came in, sat down in a very ladylike manner, arranged her various bags around her feet, and with her purse in her lap was perfectly self-composed. She listened to our allegations with incredulity written all over her face, and then with all the sincerity she could muster, replied, "I'm not that kind of person, Mrs. F."—Mrs. F was a name she used for Ann. We never understood where it came from.

John Smeltzer lived with his Uncle Fergie on a farm a few miles from Daybreak and joined us in 1971. John's farming experience was a real boon to Daybreak. He loved to gather eggs and wash them. Later, as the farm developed, his talents were put to good use feeding and mucking out livestock. John was also a party boy who loved music and played the spoons at every coffeehouse. He also had a serious side and could be found making copious notes in his omnipresent scribbler.

John Bloss was a Toronto boy who knew nothing about farming or country living, but a more enthusiastic individual you will never meet. He loved socializing and was a major player at every party and coffee house.

In 1972, Bill Rouse came to live at Daybreak and became one of our iconic personalities. He was such a well-adjusted, mature gentleman. Like Helen, he too was a smoker and had a tendency to "borrow" from others. My most endearing memories of him were his frequent evening visits to us in the bungalow to read bedtime stories to our children. He also knew that Ann had cigarettes!

Annie Kingsmill arrived in January 1972. She was a sweetheart! When she and her father came for a second interview at Daybreak, they sat on a chesterfield on one side of the room and I on the other. Mr. Kingsmill, a big and very proper gentleman, was "negotiating" for his daughter to come to Daybreak when suddenly Annie got up from her seat, sat down beside me, ran her fingers through my hair, and said, "What lovely brown hair you have, darling!" Her father was apoplectic and made profuse apologies, implying that Annie had blown the interview. I smiled to myself because I witnessed Annie's freedom overcome her father's buttoned-up, Victorian code of conduct. I've loved her ever since!

FIRST ASSISTANTS AT DAYBREAK

Jean and Louisette Dorr were the first assistants at Daybreak. They were a retired French couple in North America looking for an adventure. Jean was very handy and helped with the maintenance. Louisette was a warm and charming person who took care of everyone including our young son Jean-Frederick.

Geoff and Ann Morgan came next from the UK, where Geoff and Jean had served in the Royal Navy together. They came to gain experience because they planned to return to England to start L'Arche near Canterbury with Thérèse Vanier. Ann Morgan had to care for their toddler, Duster, but helped as much as possible in the kitchen. Geoff pitched in everywhere, and I enjoyed having another person with similar interests. Debbie Andrews was a Richmond Hill girl who came after earlier visits to stay in the fall of 1970. Still a teenager, she was a quiet but very positive force with the residents. Her parents had a swimming pool and an invitation was always welcomed. Debbie was better known as "Angrews," a name imposed on her by Helen.

FINDING OUR NAME

A young "flower power" volunteer who called himself Matthew Mark came up with the name "Daybreak," probably because he had just read the new memoir of Joan Baez with that name. We just let the idea sit for a while and eventually the name moved in with us and stayed. In hindsight, we realized that the name implied a new beginning, a new dawn, for so many of us. Not long after, a woman called me on the phone and said, "Hello, is that Heartbreak House?" I remember replying, "Well, sometimes, some days!"

DEVELOPING NEW MODELS AND LEGISLATION

When Daybreak was approved by the Ministry of Community and Social Services for funding under the Homes for Retarded Persons Act, there existed only a handful of other similar centers. Mental retardation had for decades been seen as a health problem. Consequently, a medical model of care evolved in the form of hospital-like institutions staffed by nurses and doctors who ruled the roost. But stories about poor care in large institutions circulated, and associations and legislators began to realize that there had to be a better way. As one of the few new residential centers, we were often directly involved with developing appropriate regulations. We would all just sit around the desk of Gwen Davenport, coordinator of homes at the Ministry of Community and Social Services, learning what government expected of us, working out issues, and working on legislation. Gradually, over the 1970s, with more careful thought and research, mental retardation became viewed as an educational and social problem to be dealt with through schools, workshops, and homes that were integrated into regular communities. Community integration really caught on, and we were active with government, social services, nonprofits, and researchers in fostering that change and growth.

OUR LEADERSHIP

Our roles as founding directors of Daybreak drew on our earlier formation. Both Ann and I had had a fair bit of business, managerial, and leadership experience. Serving as directors of Daybreak was one of the most challenging and rewarding jobs we have ever had. However, at the time of starting Daybreak, neither Ann nor I had much experience of either living in a Christian community or caring for people with intellectual disabilities. After a few years, I made the following list of what a director of a L'Arche community has to do:

- Maintain good relations with assistants
- Understand the dynamics of life with people with intellectual disabilities
- Know how to train and form assistants
- Relate sensitively to parents, many of whom are deeply wounded by their experience
- Relate to the wider community into which the L'Arche community is integrated

- Work closely and communicate well with a board of directors
- Maintain an ongoing relationship with professionals (social workers, physicians, etc.)
- Maintain a positive relationship with the funder (i.e., government) through liaison and accountability
- Engage in fundraising
- Stay connected with the International Federation of L'Arche

Ann was codirector with me. She served as accountant and innkeeper. Managing the finances was a complex job that required careful organization, including getting documentation from every assistant who spent money for Daybreak but often lost track of receipts. The receipts were essential for monthly financial reporting that had needed to be accurate and on time or you didn't get your government operating check the next month. For the Big House, Ann often cooked for thirty people twice a day and organized the running and cleaning of a huge house. The young assistants who came to work with the residents weren't thrilled about cleaning washrooms. In addition, there was laundry for twenty people with beds changed every Saturday morning. Ann managed all this work of the finances and the house. She still remembers her blood just boiling when I would come through the house with visitors who just wanted to look around and she was on her hands and knees scrubbing a floor!

As a couple, Ann and I maintained pretty good relations with assistants, but we were also a formidable team because we were close and more mature. For young assistants to challenge us required a lot of guts on their part. Consequently, we invented the Monday morning all-member meeting as a forum for planning the week, but also for clearing the air and dealing with contentious issues. Everyone was expected to attend. Ann will never forget one occasion when she complained, "How do you expect me to attend—I've got a kid." Joe Egan quickly said, "I don't see why we couldn't take turns looking after him." So the next Monday morning meeting, Joe had a sign on a nearby door that read, "Babysitting here." On many occasions, assistants like Alva Gane took care of Frederick. Then when the Halfertys came along with Erin, Daybreak became more child-oriented.

NO MODELS FOR MARRIED COUPLES AND FAMILIES

At the time Daybreak was established, there were no models in L'Arche of communities accommodating married couples, especially with children. We developed a habit of putting Jean-Frederick to bed with a babysitter most evenings and going to meetings. This became so much of a regular routine that Jean-Frederick ended up calling me a "meeting man." We were so fortunate to have such a good supply of reliable babysitters. We found the workload and my travel schedule very stressful, while at the same time I was trying to complete a master's degree. As a father, I will always remember how Jean-Frederick as a boy turned to Ann and said, "Mommy, why doesn't Daddy answer me when I talk to him?" Talk about being preoccupied!

THE DIRECTOR WHO WAS NOT JEAN VANIER

Jean Vanier is a hard act to follow. Ann and I felt we had the educational and managerial skills for Daybreak, but I often felt my inspirational skills and charisma were in short supply.

In the first years of Daybreak's life, young assistants often came after hearing Jean at their universities. They arrived expecting us to be a reflection of Jean's inspiration, but instead they would be asked to scrub floors, clean toilets, get people ready in the morning, and drive them to workshops, while expecting certain standards of care to be met. In later years, when we started to attract nuns and religious, they would arrive full of Jean's books, expecting this idyllic environment of spiritual nourishment and service. With my military background, I probably wanted things done thoroughly and on time, but that wasn't exactly where the young "flower power" recruits or the women religious were coming from! Eventually, to meet the demand of inquirers, Ann and Bernie developed a two-week live-in, low-budget orientation program. During the mornings, there were lectures, films, visits, and discussion groups. The afternoons or evenings involved placements on the farm, in the houses, in the bakery, or in Daybreak Publications. The participants stayed in the "Crash Pad," a humble dormitory in the basement of the Big House. During the year, we offered four of these two-week programs and many participants returned as house assistants.

RAPID GROWTH

From our various work experiences and leadership, Ann and I enjoyed the confidence of our board of directors. Consequently, Daybreak was able to grow rapidly, and we opened a new house every year for the first seven years. Initially, one of my best-laid plans was never realized. We should thank Providence for that! I designed a "village" consisting of ten identical houses built in a circle around a central commons with connecting tunnels. Over time, this plan became a stern warning to me of the dangers of one-size-fits-all institutional thinking rather than community, integration, and responding to individual needs.

By the end of 1970, Daybreak had grown to ten residents—nine men and one woman—all living in the Big House. In 1971, we designed and built a new home on our property for five men and five women. Known simply as the New House, it opened December 21, 1971. Meanwhile, in our farm operation, Brian Hayday took charge and put our egg business on the map. It started with five customers and ended up with eighty-five, to whom we delivered eggs weekly. Now we were becoming entrepreneurs!

Another big highlight of 1971 was our community trip to join the French L'Arche communities and Jean Vanier on a pilgrimage to Lourdes. The pilgrimage featured several gigantic liturgies, and it was also the first celebration together as an international organization. Our residents took to it with such openness and joy.

Ann was unable to join us on the Lourdes pilgrimage because we were expecting our second child. She had a very difficult pregnancy, and when Timothy Peter was born prematurely, he lived only two days, leaving a shroud of sadness over our home.

George Beatty joined us early in 1972. He was one of the biggest and strongest men I have ever met. He came from Acton, where he had worked at the local feed mill unloading hundred-pound sacks of grain. How were we ever going to employ those muscles? Fortunately, the nearby Pickseed seed company took on George. He thrived there but, coming from a high-status family, he thought it quite acceptable when work was slack to walk into the executive offices and make himself at home!

The pond, finished during the summer of 1972, became a favorite recreation spot on the property for swimming, canoeing, and skating. Having been a regular visitor to Daybreak, Sue Mosteller joined in 1972 and became head of the Big House. The Halfertys made a couple of summer visits and then arrived permanently in October as heads of the New House. By this time, we completed a bungalow at the back of the property that became our family home. In addition, the workshop was remodeled with a work kitchen that became a bread bakery toward the end of the year and subsequently served for canning the produce we grew.

One of the best social programs we developed was a weekly event called the "Coffee House" that began in September 1971 and carried on through our time at Daybreak. Friends, families, and many visitors were hosted by our residents for music and dancing in the huge recreation room in the basement of the Big House. Frank Sutton's brothers and sister, Gwen, contributed significantly to the music. John Bloss was the greeter-in-chief. Our board member, Don Benson, gave us a coin-operated soft drink machine for the Coffee House and our guys quickly learned how to jimmy bottles out of the machine without paying!

A key event of our whole time at Daybreak was the pilgrimage to Canterbury and France at Easter time in 1974. We were often asked why we spent money on big events rather than operations or facilities. My answer was twofold: first, our fundraising for trips and vacations was entirely separate; second, if life is based on powerful, moving experiences of adventure and exposure to new cultures or spiritual insights, then one's relationships and values will be informed by these experiences. Such opportunities do not come so readily for people with intellectual disabilities, so we should be vigilant to offer them.

One such opportunity was actually the idea of Peter Rotterman. Lotta Dempsey was a well-known Toronto journalist with a column aimed at helping people achieve things. Peter wrote to Lotta telling her that he and his friends at Daybreak were going to England and France, but many had never flown before. Could she write to see if Air Canada would take us for a short flight for everyone to practice flying? Thanks to Air Canada, the trial flight was a great success! Ann and her committee, in coordination with Thérèse Vanier in England, succeeded with the mammoth task of organization and fundraising so well that a group of

219 of us went on the pilgrimage. A bus drove us from the south coast to a point on the old pilgrimage road, and we walked the final two miles to the Canterbury Cathedral, singing and praying and ringing our pilgrim bells. We participated in the cathedral services from Maundy Thursday to Easter Sunday, celebrated by the archbishop, who encouraged us to ring along with our pilgrim bells. Afterward, we went on to Taizé in France and met up with the European houses of L'Arche—bringing our numbers to 750 in all! Together we celebrated the tenth anniversary of L'Arche.

By 1975, Daybreak had come to a point of maturity. We had recently constructed the Green House, giving us two comfortable and manageable homes including the New House. We also made offices and a meeting room at the Big House. Not only had we created fine facilities, but we had become a stable organization providing a valued service, and the "therapy of L'Arche" was creating development in people we had not expected. We realized that there was also a need for more vocational training and self-help skills. So we contracted two job stabilization counselors, and after only three months, they had worked with fifteen residents and made ten placements. At this time, another important discovery was seeing the reality of early-onset Alzheimer's Disease affecting our residents with Down syndrome. When Bill Rouse began to decline in this way, we were able to bring in nursing care and maintain him in his home at the Green House. Caring for Bill taught us how to deal not only with growth and development but also with gradual regression and ultimately death.

WORK: THE FARM, THE BAKERY, AND DAYBREAK PUBLICATIONS

The farm was now a productive entity with cattle being fattened for market, chickens laying dozens of eggs, and over thirty acres of wheat sown. Len Lomas, the farm manager, was joined by John Smeltzer and George Beatty, who both returned to it from outside placements. Meanwhile, the bakery was also growing, now that it had been equipped with some real commercial equipment that allowed Manager Kathy Jamin to increase production. "Daybreak Pubs" was a project aimed at distributing the books and pamphlets of Jean Vanier and other writing about L'Arche, such as "Letters of L'Arche." It was located in the Big House with Peter Rotterman and Annie Kingsmill happily pitching in.

DAYBREAK CHURCH INVOLVEMENT AND WORSHIP

The early residents at Daybreak came from a mix of Anglican, United Church, Pentecostal, and Roman Catholic backgrounds. For many years, we took the Anglicans to church at St. John's, Jefferson. Peter Rotterman sang in the choir and Peggy Hopkins, Alva Gane, Frank Sutton, and Brian Turner, along with a few others, attended regularly. The Big House contained a beautiful chapel! We used it for so many special occasions: the official opening of Daybreak, Christmas celebrations, Easter liturgies, and masses when priests who were friends, both Anglican and Roman Catholic, visited. One of our most memorable services occurred under the ecumenical encouragement of Vatican II when Fr. Colin Maloney, a Roman Catholic priest, and Fr. Keith Gleed, an Anglican priest, concelebrated the Eucharist. When the priests came, there was an empty cruet and no wine. Just as the service began, our two-year-old son Jean-Frederick lurched down the aisle, curled up in front of the altar, and went to sleep. We knew then where the wine had gone! Some of our residents also went to St. Mary's Roman Catholic Church in Richmond Hill. Often those who attended were not Catholic, but they participated in the Eucharist anyway. One day, I had a visit from a very agitated priest, anxious that he had been giving communion to non-Catholics!

ECUMENICAL ISSUES

In the late 1960s, ecumenical hope was in the air everywhere. I had come from the Anglican seminary when suddenly with Vatican II, we were mingling with Catholic seminarians. We were not so naive that we expected reunification of the Anglican and Catholic churches, but we did hope for intercommunion. My ecumenical understanding deepened at the Ecumenical Institute in Bossey, Switzerland, where we observed the common ground of the Anglican-Roman Catholic International Commission. It was into this tsunami of ecumenical optimism, so close to my heart, that Daybreak was born. In France, L'Arche's origins were clearly Catholic, but in Canada, Daybreak's origins were very mixed denominationally. Only one of the original ten residents was Catholic, the founding directors were Anglicans, and of the founding board, only three members were Catholic. To the public and to the parents of prospective residents, Daybreak was presented as an interdenominational organization. I affirmed Daybreak's ecumenical origins, and I believe I had Jean's support in that, but the fact that we had a former Catholic property and a lot of Catholic volunteers as well as the high profile of the Vanier family may have given a public impression of a Catholic organization.

At Daybreak, on the one hand, there was the immensely positive aspect of so many people of different denominations working together for a common cause. On the other hand, the separation at the eucharistic table caused hurt and division because Catholics priests could not invite non-Catholics to participate. During our tenure at Daybreak, we sensed a sort of unspoken vibe that Ann and I would eventually convert because others had done so. The interdenominational issue became a problem for us at a North American Federation meeting in Winnipeg in 1973. The local committee organized a glorious mass in the chapel. At the same time, a retired United Church minister led a rather mundane service in a hallway without even chairs, for the few of us who were non-Catholics. We felt left out and separated off. Ann and I called for a meeting with Jean. We demanded, "Are we part of this organization, or are we not?" His reply was so reassuring. He said, "I will not answer that question, because there is no question that you are part of this organization." Jean could handle tense situations with such sensitivity that he really turned the problem around and we resecured our sense of belonging. That security was shaken again when Jean floated the notion of L'Arche becoming a Catholic order, an idea that never came to fruition. It was contrary to everything that I had thought L'Arche in Canada was destined to be—a local expression of grassroots ecumenism.

PROFESSIONAL DEVELOPMENT

There were two aspects to professional development at Daybreak. First, there was our own need for education in intellectual disabilities and in developing remedial responses. Second, as our experience grew, we were called upon to share that experience with others. To educate ourselves about the mental illness issues of some of our residents, we established weekly meetings for all assistants with Dr. Maridene Johnston, a physician with experience in intellectual disabilities and psychiatric issues. She spent time not only with the "patient" but also with the assistants, training us to be able to provide her with relevant observations about behaviors and how to respond appropriately. In addition, we visited larger institutions like the Ontario Hospital, Orillia, and the Ontario Hospital in Cedar Springs. Such visits reminded us by contrast of the importance of our shared life at Daybreak. Some assistants also attended events at the National Institute on Mental Retardation (NIMR) and the Ontario Institute for Studies in Education (OISE), where extensive research into mental retardation services was being conducted. Pursuing my master's degree at OISE also kept me in touch with the important personalities and advances in psychological research. By 1973, Daybreak was making regular input into NIMR and began providing internships for its graduate students. Brian Halferty, while head of the New House, was seconded in 1974 to NIMR where he wrote "A Proposal for a Comprehensive Community Services Project for York Region." This put Daybreak clearly on the cutting edge as we set out how to connect residents with essential services needed at various stages of their lives.

Assistants were also called on to share about our experience at Daybreak with church, school, and professional groups. We presented the reality of our shared life—the therapy of L'Arche! Often assistants remarked on how they had come to Daybreak intending to help and instead found themselves being helped to mature by the openness and directness of our residents. We shared how this called and touched the deeper areas of our being. At a certain point, the Ministry of Health arranged for us to serve as a training site for younger staff. For Ontario Hospital, Orillia, and Ontario Hospital, Aurora, we designed and conducted both daytime training sessions and live-in programs. On one occasion, I remember the institutional staff asking how we prevented fighting among our residents. I had to admit that to date we hadn't had a fight! Two formative staff conferences were held yearly. The first, in June, was a government sponsored, two-day meeting at Queen's Park of almost all the staff of residences across Ontario. The second, held in November at the Anglican Conference Centre in Aurora, was for Daybreak's assistants alone. Besides discussion around problem areas, the staff deepened the bonds of friendship and planned the next year's events together.

OUR INVOLVEMENT WITH WOLF WOLFENSBURGER

We began to see that the Daybreak farm property was not the best setting for some of our more independent individuals. Consequently, we began to look at developing homes in Richmond Hill and Toronto. In pursuing this, we drew upon ideas of Dr. Wolf Wolfensberger about integrating people with intellectual disabilities into normal society. Dr. Allen Roeher, the director of NIMR, brought Wolf in as a visiting scholar and put him in touch with us. Soon after, Wolf met Jean and they discovered their common interests. Wolf was promoting his "Normalization Principle," which developed a set of secular values to guide the growth of community-based services within an integrated regional service system. Jean's influence made Wolf appreciate the human and even poetic dimensions of caring for people with handicaps, and Wolf's ideas became more humane and therefore more attractive and realizable. Eventually, Wolf produced his ideas in a book called *The Normalization Principle*, which became our guide for guarding against vestiges of institutional abuse in our practices. NIMR also published a monograph in which Wolf and I each wrote about L'Arche Daybreak. Wolf was so profoundly affected by Vanier that when he returned to Syracuse, he established a L'Arche community there.

EXPANSION IN TORONTO

In mid-1973, the United Church of Canada gave us a house that they owned in downtown Toronto for a very nominal rent.

What became known as "Avoca House" was a home for those who needed an urban lifestyle and greater independence. David Grey, for instance, was eager to come to the city after living in the country. He made friends with the owner of a local cocktail bar serving mint juleps that were much to his liking. David was very sensitive to being seen as "different" and would sometimes weep with frustration, wondering aloud why some people would treat him so rudely. Jim Hyrnchack was a wonderful teenager with a girlfriend named Eileen, who loved his work at Goodwill Industries on the loading dock. Shy and soft-spoken, he wore cowboy boots and loved country music. Larry Dyer worked cleaning the inside of TTC buses and spoke proudly about his days during supper. Janice Dillon was the first head of house, supported by Ken MacLennan who taught school during the day. His comfort and skill in the kitchen helped the guys join in meal preparation and homemaking. Janice recalled that once there was a petition that tried to discredit and prevent group homes in neighborhoods, but when the petitioners reached Avoca Street, our neighbors opposed it saying, "Those are our friends; we go there on Friday evenings for coffee and to sing."

COMMITMENTS TO PARENTS

A key concern for parents of a person with intellectual disabilities is a secure future beyond the parents' lifetime. One of my most moving experiences as director of Daybreak was to meet with John Smeltzer's mother in her last days. She was deeply anxious about John's future care, and I assured her that he would have a lifetime home at Daybreak. The same thing happened a couple of years later at the bedside of Freda Benson, Peggy Hopkins's mother, and the wife of Don Benson, a stalwart on our board. I could see she was in anguish and sobbing, so we held hands and recited the Lord's Prayer. Then she asked what would become of Peggy, who was already a unique fixture in Daybreak, bringing the humor, sophistication, and gossip of North Toronto. This time I felt much surer of myself telling her that Peggy had a home for the rest of her life. I could feel Freda slowly relaxing—one of those moments when heaven touches earth!

I have often pondered those promises because, while the mothers needed assurance, Daybreak was relatively young at the time and I had no idea of what control I would have over its future. We had laid the foundations of Daybreak on the solid rock of biblical values, competent administration, hard work, and personal commitment. In subsequent years, the dedicated work of future generations of assistants at Daybreak fulfilled my promises to those mothers. That is the grace of L'Arche communities. There's a fidelity that continues, not always in the same person but in the same vision and commitment. Ann affirmed, "Yes, as much as you may have made those commitments yourself, there was also the awareness that the community had the capacity to keep that promise as well."

NORTH AMERICAN REGION AND INTERNATIONAL FEDERATION INVOLVEMENT

In the early 1970s, I became chair of the North American Region of L'Arche, adding to my workload but drawing me closer to my fellow directors across Canada and the United States. I also provided advice and support to several new L'Arche communities as they started such as L'Arche Erie, L'Arche Vancouver, L'Arche Stratford, and L'Arche Antigonish. Once I assessed a community in Montana and had to recommend that it wasn't suitable for L'Arche because its director was a very dynamic but controlling priest who had no experience in a L'Arche community. At another point, I provided outside counsel to deal with divisions in L'Arche Shalom in Edmonton. Sorting out such problems helped confirm the policy at the International Federation of L'Arche that anyone wanting to start a L'Arche community had to gain real experience by spending at least a year in an existing community.

I was also involved in the second International Federation, held in 1973 at Little Ewell, near Canterbury in England, with the directors of all communities. At the time, Jean's control of the agenda and removal of a contentious item became an issue. Many directors felt they'd been cut off at the knees by Jean, but now I see that just as we were building the International Federation, it was probably not the time for a donnybrook! Jean had good problem-solving skills, and we knew he took decisions prayerfully. I think Jean liked to have things happen the way he envisioned them, but his judgment was pretty remarkable on most issues.

TAKING A SABBATICAL

After seven years, Ann and I approached the board in 1976 with the idea of taking a sabbatical year. We both felt we needed it for ourselves and for our kids. At this point in our L'Arche careers, we were experienced and we knew the life of community, of L'Arche, and of the federation. But the workload was very heavy, and we were still having to put the kids in bed early to go to evening meetings or events. I was also travelling a lot in my role of North American coordinator, as I was often required to meet with other communities and help them work out a range of issues. We arranged for Bernie Van Rooyen (later Cormier) and Sue Mosteller to be the codirectors in our absence. We had by this time bought an old house in Port Hope, which we renovated during that year, and we wrote a book on

Alzheimer's Disease. NIMR published it, and to our surprise it was reviewed all over the world. Thérèse Vanier once sent me a very positive review that had shown up in an English journal. We wrote about different stages of the disease and included various charts on how to care for people at each stage. During that year, Ann and I also started a consulting company doing work for provincial organizations and for the federal Central Mortgage and Housing Corporation.

LEAVING L'ARCHE

The most painful issue we ever dealt with at L'Arche was toward the end of our sabbatical year when we had to decide whether to come back to Daybreak. Eventually, we felt we had made the break, and fortunately it was a mutual decision with Ann. We never had arguments about it. We probably harbored a sense of ambivalence that made it possible to consider leaving. I think that was always the life of L'Arche—one of ambivalence. You're living a life in which your basic sense of security is being challenged because the life of handicapped people and the life of community are always pulling you away from the conventional norms society sets for us, leading into the insecurity of commitment to others. We were also at a mature age where we knew ourselves, knew what our family needed, and recognized our strengths and limitations. That seems to be part of the Christian journey—learning to know and accept ourselves. That journey of growth and change is always with us.

We didn't go back to visit Daybreak for a long time afterward. Ann reflected, "There's a feeling of discomfort and disharmony to go into a situation if you're not part of it. It's like a marriage that doesn't work out. The feelings are very complex, very interwoven. I don't see how leaving L'Arche can ever be a clean break. I just think there are too many ties." When it became clear that we weren't returning to Daybreak, we really scrambled to get established in other ways. We both took up work and leadership in social service organizations for people with intellectual disabilities.

Looking back over our Daybreak years, I remember feeling the strength of our experience in L'Arche as mature leaders. We achieved a lot! We started seven houses—one every year—and in that process established the credibility of L'Arche with academia and with the Provincial Government. We expanded to Toronto, developed a working farm, started Daybreak Publications, a job stabilization project, and the bakery business. Daybreak was also put on a firm financial footing. Because of that experience, we were able to help other communities get started with policies and practices. The crowning achievement of those days was learning how to live with wounded people and how to implement the therapy of L'Arche.

CONTINUING TO SERVE

After Daybreak, Steve and Ann served on the boards of community service organization and continued to work in services for people with intellectual disabilities. Ann worked as executive director of Access Community Services in Port Hope, then for twelve years as executive director of Catulpa-Tamarack Child and Family Services in Orillia, Ontario. Steve became administrator of Muskoka Centre, tasked with closing it and finding homes for its three hundred residents over a seven-year period. For two years after that, Steve helped to close two institutions in Alberta as CEO of Alberta's Provincial Mental Health Board. For more than a decade, they have aided the small

Mexican L'Arche community of El Arca Querétaro, offering practical help on visits to Mexico, and fundraising through Steve's local Rotary Club in Bracebridge. Ann and Steve have remained connected to Jean Vanier and L'Arche and were honored guests at the fiftieth anniversary celebrations in Trosly in 2014.

Chapter 2

"GATHERING INTO ONE"

L'Arche Asha Niketan in India, 1970

GABRIELLE EINSLE

INTRODUCTION

Gabrielle Einsle founded L'Arche Bangalore, the first community in India, in 1970. Born in 1930, she grew up in Germany during World War II. After the war, she gained international experience in England as an au pair in a family with four children, then in Brussels, where she studied theology as a member of an international society of laywomen called the International Catholic Auxiliaries (AFI), who subsequently sent her to study sociology in Montreal, Canada. Next, she went to South Korea to become the secretary of foreign correspondence for the bishop of Seoul and to teach

German at three universities. At the end of 1961, she returned to Montreal, where with a group of AFI members, she started the "Crossroads Student Centre" that provided support and programs for foreign students. This experience inspired her to complete a master's degree in sociology.

Gabrielle also developed a strong interest in India during the mid-1950s when she met a group of Indians in Munich, and later an Indian priest in Rome. This interest increased when she became friends in the early 1960s in Montreal with Mira Ziauddin, an Indian doctoral student at McGill. Another good friend at Crossroads was Canadian architect Louis Pretty. On a 1964 sabbatical, Pretty had joined Jean Vanier in Trosly shortly after he opened L'Arche. Pretty stirred Gabrielle's interest through weekly updates about Vanier's new venture that he wrote to his Crossroads friends. In 1965, Vanier came to Montreal and met Gabrielle and other friends of Pretty. Over the next few years, her connection with Jean deepened. She recalls, "During Jean's subsequent visits, twice a year, to Canada, I became quite familiar with what was going on in L'Arche and with Jean's growing discovery of his call, as I attended many of his Canadian talks."

Gabrielle also got to know the Vanier family. She was invited by Jean to visit at Rideau Hall when his father was governor general and became close to his mother Pauline. On a trip to Europe in the summer of 1966, Gabrielle went to Trosly to visit Jean's community and her friend Mira who had moved there in 1965 to become an assistant. She was deeply touched by the unity and spirituality of

the community: "I attended evening Mass, sur-
rounded by an incredibly united group of people,
who expressed their faith in Jesus with a devo-
tion and liberty quite different from the chapel
of the Université de Montreal." A few years later,
in 1968, Gabrielle went to the first retreat that
Jean Vanier gave at Mary Lake. She decided that
within a year she would leave Crossroads and go to
L'Arche in France with the possibility of later going
to found a new community in Africa or India. In
1968, Gabrielle also took up volunteering in a
Montreal hospital for paralyzed and incurably ill
men. Attending to their suffering opened her to a
reality so different from Crossroads and confirmed
her sense that it was time to leave for L'Arche.
Gabrielle now takes up the account.

CAFÉ TABLE GRANT

I have a vivid recollection of the moment at the end of January 1969 in Montreal when I told Jean that I was ready to leave Canada for Trosly, adding, "Yet I cannot forget India!" It was then that Jean told me of Mira's plans to return to Madras, where her father was sick. She was thinking about the possibility of L'Arche in her own country. Mira had not shared such plans with me. Jean was quick to combine all this and asked me on the spot to join him on January 25th in Toronto, where he hoped to find ways of financing the foundation of a community in India. His contacts informed him that the Canadian International Development Agency (CIDA) was ready to grant $30,000 because of a surplus in last year's budget, provided we submit the details of our budget the next day. This agency was actually somewhat familiar to me as I had previously obtained a grant for Crossroads from them. So, on a little table of a café in Toronto, we concocted a budget as best we could and we got the grant. Fortunately, this kind of boldness in Jean would be blessed, especially in India.

LEARNING ABOUT L'ARCHE IN TROSLY

In late February 1969, I came to Trosly for nine months to learn about L'Arche. Once in Trosly, my involvement in the planned foundation in India became quite serious. There was an immediate need to acquaint myself with some basic insight into the running of a L'Arche community the way it was organized in France in 1969. I took part in the meetings of the community council as an observer. Together with Mira, I listened to the questions of new assistants and tried to help them integrate their views with the needs of the community. In the mosaic workshop, I learned to crack colored tiles with pliers into various shapes and to put them together to make doves, Madonnas, and hot plates. I belonged to the home of L'Ermitage. Dr. Franko, the psychiatrist, was an invaluable eye-opener for me, helping to understand people's behaviors and the underlying reasons for them, both of the "boys" and of the "assistants."

July brought an event that helped me to take a firm footing in L'Arche in a more basic way: we went on pilgrimage. What helps L'Arche not to stagnate is to move! The whole community of Trosly set out for Fatima in a bus and various cars. Later that summer, I took charge of a holiday group of twenty-five men with intellectual disabilities from Trosly and twenty-five assistants who all camped for a month at a nearby farm called "La Merci." This chaotic experience of camping with fifty people—including Mira, Adriano, and Tom from America—was my "baptism of fire," preparing me for what the beginnings of L'Arche in India would be like.

FIRST DAYS IN INDIA AND A
DONATED PROPERTY

On October 30, 1969, I left with Mira for India. It was assumed that Mira would stay in L'Arche, so we were sent for three months on a reconnaissance mission for L'Arche in India together. We had money, but we didn't know if India wanted L'Arche. We went to find out, and Jean joined us about a month later. Before Jean arrived, we began contacting people. Mira knew how to contact Dr. Reddy, the superintendent of the biggest mental hospital in India that is in Bangalore; Dr. Subrahmanyam, a psychiatrist; Mr. Saldhana, administrator of the biggest hospital in Bangalore; and Mrs. Sudha Reddy, a Hindu lady of high class who was a member of parliament in Delhi. These were powerful people in Bangalore, each of whom Mira and I met individually.

When Jean came, seventeen days in a completely unknown country were enough to secure the essential requisites for the opening of a L'Arche community in India (and for the justification of the CIDA grant from Canada): a place to start and a legal body to be recognized by the local authorities. This is how it happened. The place was obtained through a godsend, in the person of Major Ramachandra, whom Maria, the Italian assistant replacing Mira in Trosly, had known in India, and to whom Jean had written. For this disciple of Gandhi, all men were brothers and he was happy to see a project for handicapped people start in Bangalore. There his friends, dedicated followers of Gandhiji, were running a school and homes in a slum area behind the station called Deena Seva Sangha. For a symbolic rent, they offered us a two-acre property at the outskirts of Bangalore, which had not been designated for any particular use. I will never forget the visit of the good Major when he came to show us the place. As he was eagerly hastening with Jean across that piece of land, Mira and I followed more pensively, now plucking one of the little blue flowers still growing on the dry, stone hard ground during the long, dry season, now glancing apprehensively toward an ownerless house on the property, invaded by seven families. Two deep wells, one equipped with a pump, were showcased as a special feature of the property—rightly so because our life here was to depend on their depth!

THE GOVERNING BODY

The first governing body to manage the affairs of the future L'Arche community consisted of ten members. This is how it was founded. After Jean had met a number of people, following up Mira's initial contacts and his talks in Bangalore, he invited eight of them, with Mira and me, to consider the foundation of a society responsible for future L'Arche India homes. We gathered them in a little place, and Jean talked to them about our project for handicapped people. He asked them if they would be ready to form a governing body so that we could be recognized in the country and they said yes—it was amazing! The men and women present, persons with important positions in society, opted for a registration under the Mysore Societies' Registration Act, providing also for the creation of local boards of management in other parts of India. The way that Jean had described the genesis and spirit of the little L'Arche in Trosly made them confident to accept the responsibility of such communities in India.

Jean returned to Trosly in December 1969. I accompanied him to Bombay on the plane where we finalized some documents for the registration of Asha Niketan in India. There we met Mother Teresa for the first time, of whom people were starting to talk. After Jean left, we wrote the rules and regulations with Mr. Saldhana to be presented to the Indian government so that we could be recognized as a registered society. Mira went to see her parents in Madras while I stayed in Bangalore.

THE CHARTER

Then Mr. Saldhana said, "I think we should have in these rules and regulations of our society something like a charter which says exactly this idea of community that Jean Vanier expressed." He saw that we needed a charter to safeguard the vision of L'Arche so it would not become an institution. So the society passed a motion to include a charter written by Dr. Vanier in the Memorandum of Association, outlining the spirit in which these future homes were to be run. This was a wise proposal indeed, to ensure that the particular gifts of the intellectually disabled people to be welcomed would be recognized and allowed to blossom. In India, as anywhere else, one can easily be taken over by the legal authorities and rendered an institution for the disabled or beggars or fools.

I can still see the airmail sheets, sent by Barbara Swanekamp from Trosly, on which she had typed a "Charter for Asha Niketans," written by Jean on December 27, 1969, to be discussed and accepted by the new governing body in Bangalore. It was approved unanimously, but for the change of one little word concerning the assistants: those who "serve" was replaced by those who "minister." This was the first charter of L'Arche, and it would give rise over the years to new insights and guidelines in living together in communities that welcome people anywhere in view of their needs and search for meaning rather than on grounds of their caste, creed, or race. It was an important early root for the guidelines articulated in the "Charter of the Communities of L'Arche," which were adopted in 1993 by the International Federation.

IMPORTANT NAMES

A very beautiful name for the Indian communities was chosen with Jean when we participated in a "social seminar" in Bangalore attended by delegates from all over India. Following his description of how we wanted to live in our homes, Jean offered a prize for the best suggestion of an Indian name. The Sanskrit expression "Asha Niketan" (Abode of Hope) won. Next, we needed a name for the new association to be registered. Mira was visiting her family in Madras, so it fell to me to accept (or not) a proposition made by the governing body. To get around the proposed term, "Institution for the Retarded," I came up with "Fellowship with the Mentally Retarded" (inspired by "Fellowship with the Holy Spirit"). After insisting on the "with," which the board wanted to replace by "for," the name passed.

MIRA'S DEPARTURE

Two of the three months' reconnaissance mission on which Mira and I had been sent by L'Arche had passed very quickly, full of events, birthing the project of L'Arche in India. After Jean's departure, I started to feel the weight of responsibility resting on us. This was underlined because I began to realize that Mira, for personal reasons, had doubts about whether she would continue after our three months. I expected to launch the community with Mira, but then she got all these letters from the United States from a certain Tom. Tom had discovered L'Arche in 1969 and participated with the large holiday group at La Merci that summer. Tom was an assistant in Trosly when I was there with Mira.

In January 1970, Mira told me that she would not stay. She told me that I could found the community on my own in

Bangalore because I was not from that country. She said that sometimes foreigners have more ways to access money to start something. Sometimes they're allowed more freedom and have greater possibilities at their disposal in new and unusual undertakings in a country not their own. Mira left in February 1970, went back to Germany to complete her studies, and went on to marry Tom. In 1972, they came back to India as a married couple to found a community in Kotagiri, but Mira had health problems and Tom had visa difficulties so it had to close after nine months. We ended up driving there to get the two handicapped people it had welcomed to bring them to join our Bangalore community.

CARRYING ON MYSELF

I stayed in Bangalore until the beginning of March 1970. After Mira's departure, the sisters we had stayed with kindly continued to put me up, but my impatience to move into our own place grew from day to day. I kept myself busy, spending my mornings at the big mental hospital, where I was free to move around thanks to its superintendent, Dr. N. Reddy, who had become a most appreciated member of our governing body. The "wake-up" veranda, where the patients were lined up on the floor after their electroshock treatment, still a routine at the time, remains one of my vivid memories. I preferred the occupational therapy workshop, where I could sit with a group of women, weaving. My decision to learn how to drive a car allowed me to acquaint myself with various corners of Bangalore.

Following Mother Teresa's recommendation in Bombay, I had the joy of meeting Sr. Claire in Bangalore. Before my departure for France, Sr. Claire accompanied me on a visit to the future Asha Niketan property. It was still occupied by several families, whom we would need to dislodge. In the reassuring presence of Sr. Claire, I allowed myself to suddenly burst into tears, feeling incapable of embarking on the adventure of starting a L'Arche in India. Putting her hand on my shoulder, Claire comforted me: "All will be well!" This is when I had the desire, without sharing it, to see a little hut put up at the far corner of the property, where the Blessed Sacrament could be sheltered. I was far from Trosly! Behind our premises there was a very popular ashram whose loudspeaker attracted many followers, and from nearby one could hear the regular call for prayer from a little mosque. Five minutes away, Sisters of the Apostolic Carmel had their convent and a school where Catholics among us could find the possibility of attending the celebration of the Eucharist.

TRUST AND FAITH

What gave me the confidence to launch the foundation of a L'Arche in a foreign culture? It was the experience gathered during my few months in Trosly, that mutual trust could grow between "them"—people with intellectual disabilities who are frequently kept apart, and "us"—the so-called assistants. Thus far this experience had always gotten the upper hand in our relationship. The few occasional encounters with "them" in various institutions in Bangalore or in families I visited had confirmed my presentiment that although in a culture different from mine, we could still find mutual trust. All I know from my experience so far is that God's compassion for his little ones is intense.

The moments of discouragement, even despair, with the moments of hope and resurrection that confirmed in me and in others the desire to stay, are hidden in each one's heart and hardly allow for comparison. They are moments that each one is free to accept and assume, trusting our yes to a particular call, inviting us to let ourselves be transformed in the company of our handicapped brothers and sisters. Yet without my faith in Jesus, who knows my fragility and stubbornness better than anyone else, and who even uses it in his mercy, I would not have been able to stand up to what I felt was awaiting me. I shared that faith and weakness with those who knew me and trusted me, and on whose prayers and friendship I counted.

BACK TO TROSLY

I left for Trosly in April 1970. It was a wonderful time because the Faith and Light Pilgrimage to Lourdes that was to happen in 1971 was already being prepared and I was able to help. I became very involved in the preparations, and I even went to Rome on a pilgrimage with Bill Clarke and Andre Petit. By July, the Fellowship with the Mentally Retarded Governing Body in India had put through my visa application. I received a long-term visa, which was quite unusual. It showed that we had big shots in the Indian society.

TRANSITION AND PREPARATION

When I came back to Bangalore in August 1970, I set out with some apprehension to revisit the land of the future Asha Niketan, five miles from the city center. To my surprise, the sight of the place, where nothing had changed in the meantime, reassured me. This filled me with a joyful peace and new courage to start work. To decide about the first men to be admitted to Asha Niketan, the governing body set up an admission committee consisting of Dr. Reddy, superintendent of the All India Mental Hospital; Dr. Subrahmanyam, psychiatrist; Dr. Joyce Siromoni; and myself. A mixed home was out of consideration in the Indian culture at that time. It was resolved that we start with four or five men, a number to be increased up to ten in the first year, to favor harmonious growth. Yet the day of their arrival was quite unpredictable while the place to welcome them was not habitable.

Still stuck in my rather comfortable room at the French sisters, who had kindly welcomed me again on my return, I forced myself to start moving by asking Sr. Claire for a temporary shelter at the Missionaries of Charity. To my surprise, she had been instructed by Mother Teresa to help me out with a bed (it was huge and apparently a "gift of the pope") placed in a corner outside the cloister of the sisters. Such a transitory solution compelled me to get things going to be able to move into "our" place.

GETTING THE PROPERTY READY AND MOVING IN

My plan to start living there, without waiting for everything to be ready, set the governing body in motion as well. They started to contact masons, carpenters, and electricians to make the existing old house habitable. To protect the remote property, they hired a watchman for the nights, a Gurkha. He also served as a human telephone. The families occupying the land illegally had taken shelter in some dilapidated outbuildings, refusing to give up their *pied-à-terre*. Their situation pained me deeply and left me helpless until the owners of the land were able to persuade them to leave peacefully. When I met them subsequently by chance at a spot where they had settled, the friendliness of their greeting touched me.

It was a time of great loneliness for me. As I travelled the five miles back and forth into the city in an auto rickshaw to follow up the work of the contractors, my sari proved a helpful dress, allowing me to pull it over my face to hide my tears. I tried to live up to the confidence that the members of our governing body put in me, because they had committed themselves to carry our project, touched by Jean's vision. But, aware of my inadequacy to be all that they expected me to be, their very trust crushed me at times.

As soon as one room of the house under repair was in tolerable condition and lockable from inside, I decided to settle into it, armed with a mosquito net, which I fixed with long strings to the four walls to protect me on my mattress on the floor. This seemed the only way to speed up the workers during the day, who were not interested in spending less paid time on the site. Even if they knew that I was under the auspices of the well-known people of our governing body, they must have been astonished as the "memsahib" (as foreign women in India were called) started to check the proportion of cement powder to be mixed with the (much cheaper) sand to prevent future walls from collapsing. At night, the Gurkha reassured me with his songs and whistling that he was on duty.

JEAN COMES TO ACCOMPANY THE FIRST DAYS OF THE COMMUNITY

Jean came on October 18, 1970, to accompany the first steps of that little L'Arche that God let us start in a culture we did not know. He came with Ronald Pickerskill, a Canadian who had spent seven months in Trosly. Our president was surprised to hear that the assistant to live with me in the same house was a man. At that time, Jean wrote in a letter, "We arrived in Bangalore at 6 p.m. Gabrielle was there to meet us. She looked so happy and relaxed....She has accomplished much work: the electricity, sanitary system and bedrooms are all ready. The house has been repainted." Around the same time, I sent a letter to my parents on October 16, 1970, and wrote, "After tomorrow, Jean and Ronald will arrive. I could not find beds for them yet. The pump is still not working. I have to draw the water from the well, which is very dirty. It has to be boiled on a little kerosene stove. Yet, I am absolutely sure of God's help at the right moment, since it is He who wants this Asha Niketan." Our two letters make for rather different perspectives. When Jean believed that it was God who inspired his moves and entrusted a project to his care, he tended to minimize the obstacles. His faith in God made him very pragmatic. My tendency is more retrospectively to magnify the snags, to make a point of what has been achieved through my trials and endeavors. But I know too that the real obstacles are within us. Maybe this is why God channels his grace through his little ones, who help him to gather his children, who otherwise would remain dispersed. What a job they face, to bring us up to their level of efficiency, which is quite mysterious and divine.

FIRST HANDICAPPED MEMBERS: GURUNATHAN AND JOE-BOY

The first two men, selected by our admission committee, were Gurunathan and Joe-boy, for whom I had prepared a temporary place next to the prayer room while we waited for seven bedrooms to be arranged along the downstairs veranda. They arrived three days after Jean and Ronald.

Gurunathan came from an orthodox Hindu family. He came with his brother, an ex-army officer. His widowed mother cared for him like for a little child needing to be fed, even at his age of twenty-five. He was in excellent health and well capable of looking after himself. He seemed happy to be with us, a man of great kindness whose benign smile made it difficult to guess what was going on inside of him. At home he used to go from temple to temple, spending long hours in silence and performing the rituals of a devout Hindu. Gurunathan returned to his brother after two years with us.

Joseph was called Joe-boy by his Catholic mother, a doctor. He was possessed of all the resources of a man with Down syndrome, catching us unawares with his hilarious and obstinate games. With him, Ron had an immediate chance to deploy the whole range of strategies learned in Trosly to get Joe-boy out of the toilet. After a couple of years, Joseph also moved on when his mother needed him on her chicken farm.

Guru and Joseph were privileged to benefit from Jean's personal initiation into the way we like to relate to each other in L'Arche. Similarly, Jean and Ron had a chance to practice a certain way of eating, greeting, and praying with them. While they played football or dug in the garden to sow carrots, I struggled with the Indian way of preparing rice and vegetables on a tiny kerosene cooker on the floor. When I was spotted in this exercise by visitors who came to see Jean and "the place," I felt like dissolving under their scrutinizing gaze focused on this sari-clad memsahib on the floor!

DAILY PRAYER TIMES

Following supper, we gathered in the prayer room, the best room upstairs under good shelter from the heavy monsoon rains, unlike the temporary bedrooms next door. After his weekend with his family, Guru brought back a framed picture of his favorite god, Murugha, placing it proudly next to the icon of Mary and a little cross, my gift from l'Ermitage in Trosly, and Joe-boy was keen to add a picture of St. Anthony. Questions about interreligious arrangements in L'Arche came later. For the moment, Gurunathan, Joe-boy, Ronald, and I were simply sitting, mornings and evenings, on a mat in front of some symbols known in our respective traditions, which helped to create the space to meet God.

Soon followed the admission of Srinivas, Mohanraj, Lenny, Shyamsunder, and Ravi. Then the space in front of us all was populated by Lord Shiva, Ganesha, a glittering rosary, and Lord Krishna. God in his mercy—and probably with a great sense of humor—certainly did not lose his bearings in such a pious collection of symbols, supposed to honor him. I am sure he was more interested in our hearts that longed for him, certainly more so than in some manmade "idea" of togetherness. It is not the little symbol of a boat with some people of L'Arche, surrounded by abstract symbols of nine religions to be found in India, that will work the miracle of making us one—L'Arche not being a super religion!

I believe that our utterly unpredictable and humble beginnings praying together in Bangalore were God's gift. The people who called us to cherish this gift up to today in Asha Niketan are the Srinivases, Shyamsunders, Gopals, and Aramudas, who remain faithful to the grace received of praying together at Asha Niketan. It is important that those we call "assistants" allow and facilitate each one in the community to frequent his or her traditional place of worship or choose one—or not, if they don't have any. For me, it has always been vital to find an accessible place where the Eucharist is celebrated daily. And for Srinivas or Somasundra or Gopal, it was unthinkable not to celebrate Diwali or Ganesha Festival.

During his month with us in 1970, Jean was keen to compose a common prayer for Asha Niketan, expressing our trust in God's compassion and tenderness and our desire to be true, humble, and nonviolent, welcoming those God sends us. The final sentences of it are a direct translation of the French prayer, said in Trosly and other French-speaking L'Arche communities, from their beginnings:

O Lord, bless us with the hands of your poor!
Lord, smile at us through the suffering faces of
your afflicted!
Lord, receive us one day in your eternal abode,
Where you live in bliss with your beloved
children!

DILIP

One of God's beloved joined Guru and Joseph quite unexpectedly two days after their arrival at Asha Niketan. His name was Dilip. He accompanied Sr. Maria-Delores from the Cheshire Home to fetch Jean and Ronald at the Bombay airport. Sr. Maria-Delores had met Dilip on a train, naked and starving. He spoke little and in Hindi (not spoken in Bangalore), and he loved to sing—and to slip away to the Bombay cinema. In his letter of October 22nd, 1970, Jean said of Dilip, "I am happy that Asha Niketan is beginning with him. He is the poorest of the poor, without any family, without anything. Nobody wants him. He is rejected everywhere he goes. If we were not there, he would be on the streets."

Dilip was soon hospitalized for an intensive Largactil treatment to help us and him to control his unpredictable gestures (one being to swallow the fragments of glass bottles he enjoyed breaking). I remember a long moment at his bedside in the hospital when Dilip was in a coma. Feeling no movement of life in his hand that I had held for some time, I started to pray, thinking of Jesus on the cross. After a while, I noticed something like a breath circulating through our joined hands, like the movement of a brother I had always known. A few weeks later, Dilip disappeared from the mental hospital. I remembered that we had been told of his past escapes, but I did not find him at the cinema in Bangalore, nor at the station where he might have taken a train to clear off into nowhere. I was simply left with the hope that we shall meet again in God's eternal abode, where he lives with his beloved children.

WORK AND PLAY

Our little garden team, consisting of the gardener Haroki-osamy with his little son Tony, Jean, Ronald, Guru, and Joseph had planted the first little shoots of carrots, beans, and radishes that appeared. There was no diverting Jean from his main raison d'être on that little piece of land on Bannerghatta Road in Bangalore to put down the roots of the new home. The increasing number of visitors, attracted by his talks in the city, who came all the way out to meet Dr. Vanier, had to content themselves with a brief greeting, concluded by, "Would you excuse me, I have to get back to our work." Jean's hands, covered with earth and some blisters, gave ample proof of his occupation.

What was happening in Jean's presence, over barely one month, was truly amazing. To my parents I wrote, "This whole affair here is a miracle of our faith in God's providence, bought with some suffering. Imagine, we started to work for a well-known factory, 'International Instruments' in Bangalore, whereas so many people are unemployed!" Our subcontract work consisted in placing little screws into so-called tank units, destined for car engines. In the absence of any other facilities to handle the job, we rolled up the mattresses on our wooden beds, using the beds as tables. An even bigger event than the factory contract was the purchase of a record player, thanks to the generous gift from our brothers in Trosly. What a gadget it was, in the big box, with its detachable lid, serving as loudspeaker, to involve everyone in a continuous flow of newly improvised dances!

FIRST ASSISTANTS

Jean left us on November 11th after having launched with us the new little L'Arche and putting in place the daily maneuvers to keep it afloat. Jean had left a crew of three assistants on Bannerghatta Road after Regina had joined Ronald and myself two days before Jean's departure. Regina was from Sri Lanka, but had lived for some time in France and spent a few weeks in Trosly before coming to Asha Niketan. Regina was to stay for eight months with us. Her knowledge of Tamil, English, and French was a help and a screen to hold back some of the reality from me as a foreigner.

Over Christmas 1970, we took a break before the crew increased by three new Indian members. Ron spent ten days with the brothers of Mother Teresa in Kolkata, Regina at her uncle's place, Guru and Joe-boy with their families, and Srinivas—quite reluctantly—at the mental hospital. I stayed alone at Asha Niketan, guarded by our watchman at night. By January 1971, Saroja arrived to be our cook. She was a widow of nineteen, recommended by Deena Seva Sangha. She stayed several years with us and became a sister for all. When I met her one-and-a-half-year-old son at her family's home where he lived with ten people in a room, we decided to welcome him at Asha Niketan as well. His name was Karnagara. Jacob from Kerala stayed for several months, an expert in all the painting jobs to be done, as well as a good cook.

"LORRY TO GOD"

All these new people had to cope with my inadequacies as the director of Asha Niketan and the secretary of the governing body, who didn't speak the local language, Kannada. Concerning my civil status, I remember being instructed by Fr. Amalor

Pavadas, who was a well-known theologian in India, that a single foreign woman in my situation has to be married or be a nun. I responded, "What to do? I am neither!" Pending future plans to finance the development of Asha Niketan, our wages were paid through the grant from Canada. Some of our daily expenditures were covered through our factory and garden work as well as by donations from friends in Germany, who had opened an "India account" for us. Oxfam gave us three huge "Andhra buffalos"—cows giving very rich milk that could be sold to restaurants—and a delivery van.

Meanwhile, we continued our arrangements of fresh flowers every morning, around the cross, Hindu divinities, oil lamps, and incense sticks, as we read from the Bible, Gandhiji's writings, and Hindu scriptures and sang in Kannada, English, Tamil, French, and Sanskrit. Srinivas started to combine his Krishna and Vishnu songs with alleluias and managed to transform the song "Glory to God" into "Lorry to God," as this type of vehicle kept speeding along Bannerghatta Road in front of our gate. It was a time when nothing could stop our hope and enterprising spirit. It was also a time when Asha Niketan felt quite united in the Spirit with the pilgrimage of thousands of handicapped people to Lourdes during Easter of 1971, the founding event of Faith and Light. I had been able to slip away over Easter, to join in my heart from afar with the pilgrims in Lourdes, travelling to Velangani in Tamil Nadu, called the Lourdes of India.

SRINIVAS

Srinivas came from the mental hospital, while Jean was still with us in November, for a short trial period—just long enough to get a glimpse of what was awaiting him...and us. During Jean's next visit, a year later, Jean described him as "a little rascal who dances and plays and is terribly unstable." His gift of drawing us into his outbreaks of joy was matched by his quickness to fly into frightful tempers, caused by anything beyond the understanding of his little head, too small for his big heart. As Srinivas's family had been informed that he was to be discharged from the hospital, I wanted to reinstitute the link with his parents. My first short visit at their house with Srinivas made us consider the possibility of gradually working toward trying a longer stay. After a visit of several hours, Srinivas stayed for one day. Finally, we programmed a weekend visit, which alas marked the end of our attempts: on Sunday morning, his mother brought Srinivas back with the verdict "Never again!" The rebuff threw Srinivas into a deep depression, leaving the community at a loss as to how to face his anger and aggression.

I will never forget my walk with Srinvias to the mental hospital to decide with the superintendent whether Asha Niketan could be his home. At every few steps, Srinivas stopped to ask, "Mental hospital?" The doctor said he was ready to take him back, noting that this would mean seeing him "vegetate" again among many other patients, without hope. I tried to curb my faltering mind: we shall not forget him, we shall visit him often. At that point, we were offered some tea. A servant brought two cups with saucers for the doctor and me, and a metal tumbler for Srinivas. My spontaneous reaction was, "But Srinivas holds a cup well!" The doctor knew my hobby horse about double standards, as he was on the governing body. The impression that experience with the tumbler made on me was decisive. I looked at Srinivas and told him, "Let's go!" On our way back to Asha Niketan, Srinivas stopped every few steps to ask, "Mental hospital *illa*?" (*illa* means "no" in Tamil). "*Illa*!" That return was the true admission of Srinivas and began the slow strengthening of our hope for a lasting stay. How happy I am that thirty-seven years later, he is still there, and I am not alone in considering him as the real "founder" of Asha Niketan.

NARASINGHA

In 1971, we welcomed Narasingha. I had gone to fetch a certain Ishwara at the hospital after his trial period at Asha Niketan in 1970, but was told that he had disappeared! Without much ado, I was introduced to another patient instead by the name of Narasingha. He had lived behind locked doors for the past five years and did not speak. A guardian brought him into the office of the superintendant, where I was waiting. He was clad in the off-white uniform of a patient. The doctor asked me if I wanted him and I said yes. Maybe the unexpected event of walking alone with an unknown memsahib hand in hand to a home where "we" were expected and welcomed with joy, was quite decisive in Narasingha's taking root at Asha Niketan. He soon revealed himself as an excellent workman. After a few weeks, he agreed to change his hospital clothes for a new shirt and pants made of the material we had chosen together in a shop in Bangalore. He also stopped swallowing bananas with their skins on and peanuts in their shells. L'Arche in India published a newsletter for several years under Dorothy Day's inspiration and guidance. Its cover carried a huge smiling sun painted by Narasingha. Its title was "From Asha Niketan with love."

THE DEATH OF KANNAN

Fully welcoming Srinivas was an important "passage" for our young community. A second passage occurred several months later in June 1971. Our little brother Kannan mysteriously led us into a new and deeper unity. Here is the story in my letter of June 13, 1971, to my parents:

Since Monday of Pentecost, Kannan is present among us in a new way. On that Monday, when we took up work after siesta, we noticed his absence. Searching for him all over the premises, Ronald and Krishna discovered his towel on the little steps, leading into the well—not the one from which we draw water every day, but the well at the far corner of the garden where we rarely go. It is a well about 4–5 meters deep.

Both Ronald and Krishna dived immediately in search of Kannan without finding him. I started to pray automatically to Archangel Gabriel, feeling certain that Kannan had drowned. Trembling all over, I asked Ronald to dive again. "I am scared!" he groaned before jumping a second time. He came back with our brother Kannan in his arms.

As I ran toward Bannerghatta Road leading to the hospital to stop the first passing car, they wrapped Kannan into a sheet and Krishna carried him to the gate. Immediately a strange car stopped to come to our rescue. Reaching the hospital, I remained there to arrange for urgent efforts to revive Kannan's body and to inform his family. When Kannan's father arrived, his son's body had already been transferred to the mortuary. I took the father's hands. He gazed at me for some long moments, before simply saying: "The ways of God."

The next day I spent a trying morning at the hospital with Kannan's father and members and friends of his family, who did not want a postmortem done. We endured painful interrogations by the police, following their routine questions. At last, Kannan's body was released. We covered him with a special safran cloth and laid him in the space of a little van, belonging to the father's friend. Sitting around our brother, we drove to the family home, where Kannan's mother, his sister and all the neighbors were waiting. They placed the body on a bed, surrounding it with fresh flower garlands and incense sticks, and covering Kannan's forehead with sacred signs. Then the men proceeded with the body to the cemetery for incineration according to the Hindu rituals.

Kannan's death has united us in a new and mysterious way, just at a moment when crises of some of the guys and difficulties among the assistants were causing frictions in the community. The death of an innocent person can bring about clarity and peace among those who loved him. For me, it was as if Kannan's death has taken away all my fear, my questioning and my lack of confidence in God's presence. Since his departure, the Holy Spirit gives me much peace, rest and a new freedom and clarity for the decisions to be taken. The love of God is fathomless!

STRUGGLES AND YEARNING FOR GOD'S GIFT OF UNITY

Faced with events beyond our control, we can become more aware of situations that seem stuck. Sometime after Kannan's death, I started to feel that something was sapping the mutual confidence among the assistants and friends who had initially supported the first steps of Asha Niketan. Something was undermining the unity among us. Once the governing body started to deal with the situation, it gradually became clear that it was best for one of our members to part from the community.

Should it have been up to me to go? The governing body decided otherwise. I went through moments of great anguish, discouraged by my own weakness, impatience, and touchiness. A community is born and shaken again and again through struggles and conflicts. Such crises can open us to recognition of our failure and weakness, and lead us to pardon our challenger or ourselves, as they can lay us open to the spirit of evil and lead us into discord. In our Asha Niketan prayer, we asked every day, "Lord, give us hearts of peaceful mercy to quiet passions, discords, and violence and that we may see your presence in our rejected brothers."

OFFICIAL OPENING

By the end of 1971, we felt ready for an "Official Opening" of Asha Niketan. It took place on December 12th, in the presence of Jean, the governor of the state of Mysore, Darma Vira, and two hundred guests representing various social, medical, and educational organizations, families, and friends. Until the last minute, the attendance of the governor had been uncertain, as at that moment everybody was afraid of an imminent war between India and East Pakistan (today Bangladesh). Prior to this event, Jean had spent ten very moving days in Calcutta, visiting the camps of refugees from East Pakistan with Mother Teresa and her sisters: ten million people and several millions outside the camps.

OUR EVERYDAY LIFE

It must be said that our involvement in "public relations" with government officials and organizations had to be carried out hand in hand with our agricultural and livestock responsibilities! No rain from November until June meant every morning at six o'clock drawing 150 buckets of water from the depth of our wells and carrying 3 of them to each of the 100 banana trees we had planted. As for the three huge buffaloes donated by Oxfam, one of them was nearing the day of her labor and delivery. One morning at 1:30 a.m., I was roused from sleep by her heartbreaking clamor. Rushing to the shed, I discovered the cause of her plight: her fellow buffalo had broken loose. Criss-crossing the garden in my long dressing gown, my flashlight spotted the animal enjoying our cultivated vegetables. Holding on to her tail, indicating the direction with my stick, I let myself be dragged to the shed. However, as I was fastening the cord, the brute managed to pull off again and charged back toward the vegetables, dragging me along at the end of her tether until I gave up, my dressing gown covered with cow dung. Krishna was away that night, and Ronald, fast asleep, understandably took some time to respond to my call: "Ron, the buffalo is loose!"

So much for our animals, not to mention the crowd of thirty monkeys that chose again and again to stay on our land in the most insolent manner. There were also deadly little snakes now and again crossing the hall where we ate on the floor. Ronald acquired remarkable skills for getting rid of the snakes with the nearest tool at hand.

MEETING WITH OTHER COMMUNITY FOUNDERS AT AMBLETEUSE

Three months after the official opening of Asha Niketan, I went to France and attended a meeting of the founders of all the existing L'Arche communities, six of us by 1972: Agnes and Adriano (La Merci), Steve and Ann (Daybreak), Marcel (Amble-teuse), Thérèse (ready to start Little Ewell), together with Jean, Père Thomas, and Marie-Helene from the governing body of L'Arche France. It took place at Ambleteuse in France. We started to write a document that would become the charter of L'Arche. Later in Trosly, I met with Jean Vanier briefly before leaving. I told him of my weakness and lack of self-control. Jean felt it was not necessary to dwell on this, the sole important thing being to follow God's plans. He noted that our dejections only delay things and weaken us. As long as Jesus lives and is at work in us, our weaknesses are the best chance for God's plans to come through. His plans can be quite different from ours!

VISIT TO CALCUTTA

After the meeting at Ambleteuse in 1972 (the beginning of what was to become the International Federation of L'Arche), I returned to Bangalore. Then, in August 1972, I visited Calcutta with Judy at the invitation of Mother Teresa. In a letter to my parents on August 26, I related how deeply Calcutta touched me:

> I am on the train with Judy again, on the way back from Calcutta. I just had a strange and very peaceful dream about dad who remains very close. I am sure this journey was guided by God. Nothing was planned in advance. Mother Teresa, constantly on the move, happened to be in town. She took us to one of her homes outside the city, sitting with us in the back of a jeep on sacks of rice, vegetables and fruit, even bringing along picnics for us. We spent the day with crippled, sick and dying people as well as abandoned children. On the last day, the brothers Missionaries of Charity took us to the worst slums of the city. In the middle of the street we waded with them through black mud up to our ankles, to a home for people suffering from leprosy. In the home for the dying we helped to wash emaciated bodies, hot with fever and covered with ulcers. It is true that people die of hunger in Calcutta. At Howrah Station a bundle on the ground may be identified as a person who

starved to death only when it starts to smell. If my present commitment did not call me, I would go to Calcutta. Somehow one can't help but be compelled by this city. We talked with Mother Teresa and other people about the opening of an Asha Niketan there. I think it won't take long.

SYMPOSIUM AND CELEBRATION OF ASHA NIKETAN BANGALORE

In September, I was back in Bangalore. Our governing body had decided that it was time to bring Asha Niketan to public attention through a symposium in Bangalore, to explain what we believe and try to live. I told my parents in a letter dated September 29, 1972:

> Dr. Reddy's idea to hold a symposium on Asha Niketan, and 2 other institutions, to begin a dialogue, took place. It was announced days before by the press and was followed by a press conference with seven journalists. Ronald, Judy and I gave "talks" on "community and mentally retarded people." All went very well, followed by a discussion of two and a half hours. For us, it was a "family event." For the first time, all the guys' shirts and trousers were ironed, missing buttons sewed on, to be appropriate for the event! It was an important and successful happening for all, at a moment of real joy and peace in our family, after many a trial. God does things so well!

I did not go to India with a ready-made message to pass on. However, I was conscious of something I had not known before discovering it in L'Arche, and I was ready to share it with anyone who cared to know: I had met people who, without knowing their gift, knew how to unite people, all sorts of very different people.

It is through our encounters with new brothers and sisters in India, whose gift reminded us of our handicapped brothers in Trosly, that we found the gift of L'Arche more and more confirmed. The students at Crossroads and I did not create the same bonds as those that unite me with Jean-Claude, Andrew, Raphaël, Benoit—and now Srinivas, Shyamsunder, Kashi, Madhu, or Barun. These brothers hold the secret of how to build on our common humanity, regardless of culture, rank, knowledge, or religion. I must also say that assistants Ron, Judy, and Zizi who came later to Calcutta are simply fantastic "colleagues" who grasp the deepest sense of L'Arche. We did not set out to found an "interreligious L'Arche Community" in Bangalore. We set out to welcome and respect persons as human beings. It is the people who make L'Arche "interreligious."

AFTER BANGALORE

After Easter of 1973, Gabrielle moved from the Bangalore community to become the founding director of Asha Niketan Calcutta. Martha Gunn-Bala replaced her in April 1977, when Gabrielle became regional coordinator for the four L'Arche communities in India. In 1980, after taking part in the Second Interlude for Longterm Assistants in Courchevel France, international coordinator Sue Mosteller asked her to move back to Asha Niketan Calcutta to serve as transitional director, which she did until 1983.

Gabrielle returned to France in 1983 for a sabbatical at L'Arche Trosly, L'Arche Bogner Regis, and *L'Arche London. She moved in December 1984 to L'Arche in Belgium. After a short visit to a new project in Germany, Gabrielle met with Claire de Miribel, the international coordinator, ready to be sent anywhere, specifying that her "no-objection-to-return" visa for India was still valid. In 1985, she was asked to support L'Arche founding core member Raphaël Simi who had moved to L'Arche La-Rose-des-Vents in the tiny village of Verpillières in France. Gabrielle stayed with him, Bernadette, and Armelle in the "little house" until December 1989, then moved to L'Arche Le Levain in Compiegne. For five years she enjoyed the company of her old friends from Trosly at the workshop in a half-day job until her retirement at sixty-five. In 1993, she participated at the L'Arche Federation in Quebec and, in 2005, at the L'Arche Federation in Assisi where Gerald Arbuckle encouraged her to write the story of the foundation of L'Arche in India. Gabrielle's story in this book includes selections from her unpublished English manuscript "How to Gather into One God's Scattered Children?" ("My Way into L'Arche"). Her French account was published in 2016 as* Comment rassembler les enfants de Dieu dispersés? *Gabrielle continues to live in Compiegne, maintaining her connections with the L'Arche community there.*

Chapter 3

"WE LEARNED TO CHEW SLOWLY"

L'Arche in the United States, 1972

FR. GEORGE STROHMEYER AND
SR. BARBARA KARSZNIA

INTRODUCTION

Sr. Barbara Karsznia, OSB, and Fr. George Stroh-meyer together founded the first L'Arche community in the United States in Erie, Pennsylvania, on November 22, 1972. Sr. Barbara was a psychology instructor and counselor at Gannon University, especially for female students who were at that time restricted to evening classes. "When Sr. Barbara and Fr. George shared their desire to begin a L'Arche community, it was in the context of the early 1970s when it seemed like springtime with life just bursting out everywhere!" recalls Sr. Barbara's Benedictine prioress, Sr. Mary Margaret. She continues,

> *The community of sisters took up the spirit of Vatican II by looking to the spirit of St. Benedict, our founder, listening to the perennial message of the gospel and reading the signs of the times. Our Benedictine community had committed to a mission for peace, and had also begun a soup kitchen. Many people were coming north from Mississippi, black and white, not very well educated, but poor and looking for jobs, for a home, and for quality of life. In addition to the Emmaus Soup Kitchen, the sisters began a food pantry, the Neighborhood Art House, with lessons in dance, music, clay, and help with homework—especially reading—for children of all ages and neighborhoods. As prioress, I felt that L'Arche fit right into that, and I gave Barbara the okay. When one sister goes to do something, other sisters go to help, so I served on the board and other sisters were involved in the foundation as volunteers, especially helping to organize the formal structures required by the local and state governments and as assistants in the homes.*

Meanwhile, Fr. George was teaching sociology and theology at Gannon University with new interests in social work and in communities responding to the gospel. But he also felt like he was "missing the boat" in the academic world and yearned to experience a more vital ministry.

The account continues now in Fr. George's own words, completed on November 22, 2017, "the Day of our Forty-fifth Anniversary."

BOTH "UNIMAGINABLY SIMPLE AND MANAGEABLY COMPLEX!"

I'd like to tell the founding story of the community of L'Arche in Erie as an experience of the spirit shining through the living and breathing reality of our history, with a response of deep gratitude for the whole story including twists and turns of our life in community together. I would like to keep in view its sufferings, so that members of our community and those who are interested will feel our kinship when they too experience both the "agony and the ecstasy," especially the gulf that has always existed for each of us between the reality of our lives and our ideals. Bruno Barnhart, a brilliant, beloved Camaldolese Benedictine monk avers, "We humans prefer a manageable complexity to an unimaginable simplicity." We in our L'Arche community are learning to prefer both.

OPENING AND CLOSING (ALMOST)!

It is fundamental to the graced history of the founding of L'Arche Erie that this the first L'Arche community in the United States began just in time for that essential American celebration: Thanksgiving. On Wednesday, November 22, 1972, at 1:20 p.m., we opened our doors and welcomed four core members, John, Donna, Bill, and Shirley, in time for a late mid-day meal. Benedictine hospitality came to our rescue for the first four days. On Thursday, Thanksgiving Day itself, the rest of us braved a cold and windy day on the shores of Lake Erie for a late lunch cookout while Barbara stayed home to roast the turkey. Our yearly community celebration of the Thanksgiving feast has so much meaning for us even today because it is a double celebration for us as a founding American holiday and the anniversary of our own founding.

We began at that time of giving thanks when our hearts were thrilled and full of expectation. We missed our own traditional family feast of the day, but we were blessed to celebrate with our new community members their first of many proper family celebrations of our own. From the beginning, and throughout our forty-five-year history, we have sought to welcome persons without family ties as our priority, an important, symbolic way of beginning and maintaining our community's vision and making our decisions. Our holidays were important times because for many of us there were no other places to go and for others no other place we wanted to be. We celebrated these major holidays and holy days—Thanksgiving, Christmas, and Easter—with lots of gusto and as a family.

Within weeks of our Thanksgiving beginning someone suddenly came to the door of our new L'Arche home with a daunting greeting: "You know you are operating illegally, and I could close you down immediately!" It turned out that he was the director of the Pennsylvania state agency providing homes and services for developmentally challenged persons, and he had come to our home to see for himself just what we were up to. He walked through our home, talked with all of us, and noted that the house was woefully unfit according to state standards, all while at the same time taking photos that we feared he would use as evidence against us. He explained the requirements to meet standards and to seek approval, and agreed to overlook our unorthodox beginning and to offer us the opportunity to stay in existence if we presented a proposal for certification and approval as a Department of Welfare agency in the state of Pennsylvania.

Remarkably, we heard that after his inspection, our visitor soon was showing photos of our home in visual presentations throughout the state to illustrate exemplary service and how to make quality of life possible in small, human homelike settings! We found out much later that Dr. Wolf Wolfensberger, a well-known and respected mental retardation expert, highly supportive of Vanier's vision and indeed instrumental in the founding of the L'Arche community in Syracuse, New York, had supported our community and worked diligently to persuade his former student, this director of the Pennsylvania state agency, to permit us to continue. But much as state regulation was part of our start, before L'Arche Erie began at all, what were the most important things that came together to prepare for our founding? Put simply they were, for me, Sr. Barbara, Jean Vanier, Jesus, and the family of L'Arche.

FRIENDSHIP BETWEEN SR. BARBARA AND FR. GEORGE: NOT SO FAST!

Initially, I did not like Sr. Barbara, and soon the feeling was mutual! Our coming to know each other and value each other happened over time and only after overcoming hurdles of distrust and disrespect. Though we were professional associates at the college and would cooperate in planning the daily celebrations of the Eucharist, Sr. Barbara disliked me because she sensed I was a willing participant in the rejection of her as a counseling colleague by a good number of the all-male counseling staff of the college. I finally came to discover in a long conversation with her that this rejection by colleagues was painful and dismaying for Sr. Barbara. I was moved by her frank emotional response and scandalized by my ease of taking part in the judging and devaluing of another human being. This was a cornerstone lesson of the heart that later connected for me with the message of L'Arche.

Sr. Barbara and I began to work together in some alternate adult education classes, parish liturgy celebrations, and Benedictine community events. It did not take long for her to persistently query me about doing something larger together, something for others. She had a "holy discontent," along with a striking empathy for the suffering of others, often moving her to drop everything and do something about it on the spot. Her intense aspiration, her "pressing the issue," her willingness to be demanding of her friends, and her capacity to organize and follow through, as well as our growing commitment to do something, were all additional cornerstones upon which the foundations of a project began to form even before either one of us knew about Jean Vanier or L'Arche. There is no question we were both moving from the mind to the heart, and that it was our growing mutual affection and encouragement that supported this somewhat unorthodox journey. I admit this was a difficult step for me as an independent, young, male member of the clergy, teaching sociology and a bit filled with myself, and may I say afraid? I can say now that this journey saved me, providing an experience sorely lacking for me at the time.

YOU'VE JUST GOT TO COME TO THIS RETREAT WEEKEND IN TORONTO! OR ELSE! INSPIRED BY JEAN VANIER

The next steps unfolded in the context of the unrest, change, and new hope happening on college campuses and in the country at large in the late 1960s, namely antiwar and antimilitary fervor, accusations of racism, general discontent with government, and suspicion of all institutions. It was at the same time an opportunity for searching, a time for active renewal (and confusion) in the Church, for alternate communities to spring up, and for nontraditional ministries of peace and justice to flower. In the middle of it all and my own entanglement in campus tensions with an accompanying loss of confidence in myself, Sr. Barbara introduced me to Jean Vanier, who invited us to believe in ourselves and to enter more deeply and boldly into God's love.

By chance Barbara had met a Canadian priest, Fr. Stephen Somerville, who had attended Jean's initial retreat in 1968 at Mary Lake. Stephen urged Barbara and me to come to Jean's February 1971 retreat in Toronto, insisting, "You've just got to come to this retreat!" From 1968 onward Vanier insisted that his retreats welcome excluded and devalued members of Christ's Body, including developmentally challenged men and women. Through the retreat Jean called me in a very personal way to step out of myself and into the mind and heart of Christ, replacing *my* heart of stone with a heart of flesh.

In the retreat, Jean invited me to "stay in the chapel" to meet Jesus "and permit him to soften my heart, to break its barriers and finally to be reborn." Jean spoke of Jesus as the one who comes to liberate us in all the human conditions of vulnerability and fragility. I sat in the chapel, just sat, for long periods of time in silence, not always in inner stillness mind you! I trusted Jean, who trusted Jesus, and I fell "into the cup being held out for me to drink." I can say I met Jesus in a way I had never before experienced. That cup would continue to be my courage, my sustenance, and my suffering over these many years of community living and loving. Jesus invited me to take down the self-protective barriers that I put in place to protect my unacknowledged broken heart, to break the all too familiar chain of anguish, violence, hatred, fear, and competition so prevalent in my human relationships. I was overwhelmed in meeting Jesus in this radical and transforming communion.

I was reborn, a little bit at least, more a down payment of the Spirit promising reliable inspiration and direction, not to mention the gift of "confusion," which is by the way a little acknowledged gift of the Spirit. All I knew at the moment was that I trusted the invitation and wanted to let Jesus break through the barriers of my heart and the limitations springing from my inexperience in human relationships. I became absolutely convinced, "This is it; this is what I have been looking for!" This meeting with Jesus inspired a radical turning point in my life.

GETTING TO KNOW THE FAMILY OF L'ARCHE

Sr. Barbara and I met a number of members of the L'Arche Trosly community in August 1971 at Jean's retreat at the Cenacle Retreat House in the Chicago suburb of Warrenville. There the charism of the communities of L'Arche began to reverberate as a concrete possibility in my life and ministry. After the retreat, Fr. Jim O'Donnell in Cleveland invited the two of us to join in the yearlong planning process for Jean's "Let's Celebrate Jesus" retreat in Cleveland in August 1972. The little group from Erie who had attended the Cenacle retreat confirmed that Barbara and I would do well to visit the Trosly community for two weeks at the end of December 1971 into 1972. So we travelled to Trosly to take part in the daily life, work, prayer, and celebrations of the founding community. Celebrations, liturgies, the time at meals were simple, honest, human, and intentional, revealing a communion deeper than the barriers of culture and language that left me a bit outwardly disoriented. My most clarifying moments were in the adoration chapel.

Through our visit to Trosly and further contacts, Jean invited us take part in a planning team that he convened twice each year to pray, to be renewed, to listen to one another, to read the call of the Spirit, and to plan his growing number of activities in North America. This experience was a continuing discovery of life and spirit, and deepened in us a foundation of universal family never before experienced or imagined, and a sense of Christ alive in all our hearts together.

THINGS CASCADED RAPIDLY INTO OUR LAPS. OR WAS IT WATER RISING UP FROM WITHIN?

One evening, soon after returning home from Trosly, I happened to be reading one of the early Letters of L'Arche, in which Jean writes of the growing family of L'Arche and asks in the letter, "Where will the next community of L'Arche come to be?" I was moved reflexively to say aloud, to myself, "Here, right here! Why not here in Erie, Pennsylvania!" My forceful emotion was uncharacteristic for me. At that moment I remembered some advice I heard upon leaving Trosly, that you should give time for this next step to come clear and not do something big, but make a change of something small, maybe even just change your place of residence. I continued my full-time work at the college but left my faculty residence to take up residence with an emotionally fragile, older pastor of a small parish where I eventually ministered for thirteen years and discovered the joys and sorrows of being a parish priest.

Adding to the foundations I described earlier, three further essential steps led to L'Arche Erie's founding. These were desire, formation, and the personal blessing of Jean Vanier. As my shout, "Why not here?" demonstrated, I felt a strong urge for L'Arche. So the desire was clear but not the circumstances. At least not yet! Jean Vanier walked with us in our growing desire and impatience to take a next step. Sr. Barbara, at this time, was simply feeling a desire for change. She was eager for deeper formation in L'Arche. Thanks to Sr. Mary Margaret, the community prioress, and to the intuition of Sr. Joan Chittister, OSB, and other Benedictine advisors, she gained support from her religious community for a year of "sabbatical" to deepen the relationship with Jean Vanier and experience L'Arche communities in Ontario and France, open to the possibility of extending her mission as a Benedictine sister into the context of L'Arche. Barbara was invited to attend meetings with Jean in Canada and was also welcomed to Daybreak for a few weeks, a time we both acknowledged was too short.

Steve and Ann Newroth, the founders of Daybreak, offered practical advice and encouragement. Steve came to visit us in Erie and to give presentations at Polk State School and elsewhere. He shared his broad knowledge of the world of disability and institutions as well as his experience in Trosly and beginning the first L'Arche community in North America. With Steve's advice we proceeded to follow the Daybreak model, first gathering a group of twenty-five to forty friends and professional persons to form the "Friends of L'Arche," out of which a smaller group served as an executive board of directors. Sr. Sue Mosteller, who had taken up leadership in Faith and Light and had close connections with Daybreak, also provided vital friendship, direction, and confidence.

The other kind of formation that we needed was with people with intellectual disabilities. We were fortunate that we had a fine local center for day programming for people with developmental disabilities in Erie. The Gertrude A. Barber Center was founded by a woman who for twenty years made groundbreaking strides in recognizing the basic human rights of developmentally challenged persons for education, health, and wellness. The center offered programming and mustered the support of the wider community for these gifted but often overlooked people and their families. As Barbara and I shared news of Jean Vanier's message and communities, Dr. Barber was attracted to the vision and welcomed us to volunteer with the center. The core group preparing for L'Arche included Barbara, Paula Simon, Cheryl Ott Rink, Charlene Matson Serfozo, and myself, among others. We volunteered each Sunday evening at the Barber Center for a year before, during, and after we opened our L'Arche home. We organized times of prayer and song, friendship, snacks, a bit of dancing, some tears and laughter, becoming friends with the people we served and supported while discovering their beauty, gifts, and diversity, and the one human heart that we all share. It was from this group that the "second wave" of core members like Leroy and Mary chose to join our community when we had openings in our homes in the first few years.

The Barber Center provided us with vital formation and vision, but also with a community without walls that was a prophetic precursor to the L'Arche community soon to be born. Our involvement with the center continued long into the life of our community. Barbara and I and the core team who would eventually become the first assistants of L'Arche were not well versed in the whole professional area of mental retardation. Unwittingly, perhaps a bit naively, and yet in retrospect, wisely, we did not proceed according to acceptable standards of operation. This was partly with advice of others who were concerned that, if we applied according to standard procedure, we would have likely been denied permission by government authorities to begin our L'Arche community.

As we started to prepare for our first L'Arche home, Barbara and I became close to Sr. Peter Claver, a Trinitarian sister, and Sr. Rita Panciera, a Mercy sister, both leaders of the Erie House of Prayer community. They supported us through our initial discernments, visits to Trosly, engagement with the Barber Center and the Polk Center to begin making friends with our prospective founding members, working with Steve Newroth and Jean to focus our plan, developing our organization with the help of the Sisters of St. Benedict, and relying on Mel Ott to find our first home. With Rita and Peter around their dining room table, we experienced one particularly striking time of prayer, a time of deep unity of heart and mind in the Holy Trinity. It was something too deep for words, confirming our call and our readiness and giving us the courage to take the final steps to begin the L'Arche community!

JEAN'S FIAT

I will never forget the way it happened, in October 1972, on the second floor of L'Arche Daybreak's Big House in Richmond Hill, Canada, with Barbara and I sitting on the floor with Jean. We were all there for the Daybreak ribbon-cutting ceremony to open its second home, the New House, later that afternoon. But for now, we were updating Jean about our project for a community in Erie. We met to reflect with Jean on the preparations of the last year and a review of our plans to welcome core members in one month's time. We reiterated with Jean our commitment and readiness to begin the community in Erie. After sharing news of progress, Jean asked, "Are you keen on being part of L'Arche?" We responded, "Yes, we are." Then Jean said, "I am keen on having you." Right then and there he accepted our community into full membership in the federation, to take effect with the arrival of the first core members.

The moment was intoxicating, charged with an emotion of quiet joy, expectation, and sense of privilege (never mind the yet hidden challenges unlike any I had ever experienced to date!) that we were being entrusted with a mission requiring our own human and spiritual growth while joining a supportive and growing movement of worldwide significance. At the ribbon cutting after our meeting with Jean, we felt like we had "cut" the bonds of the past and took an irrevocable step in our personal journeys and in our commitment to others.

Thus, with Jean's fiat, by late November we began as a full-fledged L'Arche community. Less than a year later at the second International Federation Meeting in October 1973, we were presented as full members of the L'Arche Federation. We were welcomed warmly but not without a deliberation and agreement that, hereafter, full acceptance of a community into the federation could no longer be "proliferated" with such charismatic abandon. This was not to crimp the work of the Spirit moving through Jean, but to highlight that procedures for welcoming communities must come from a deliberative and consensual agreement of the entire International Council. Of course, this was the way to go forward, but it in no way diminished the stunning entry of our little community solely upon the approval of Jean.

CONNECTING WITH THE REGIONAL INSTITUTION

At the same time our bond with Jean and L'Arche was growing, a Benedictine sister with whom Sr. Barbara was living presented us with an invitation to a clergy open house at the regional institution for developmentally challenged persons. We were thrilled to attend, and we met a small group of residents preparing to leave the overcrowded institution and move directly into a number of local community settings. We shared our news of the beauty of L'Arche and our excitement that this vision could be rooted here, and the staff member was excited to introduce us to the residents he was preparing to leave the center. Some weeks later, after further visits with members of this small group, they were ready to come live with us if we were ready to welcome them. We confidently said that we were willing to provide them a home, and welcomed them on November 22, 1972, though not without some fear and trepidation.

FIRST CORE MEMBERS EVENTUALLY LEAVE

The first core members who began L'Arche Erie did not stay for the long term. However, even if it was not permanent, these founding members sensed that they belonged to a community for whatever time they stayed. Soon after he arrived, I remember Bill Kohler sitting in the living room saying, "Boy imagine this—we used to see people on TV in their living rooms and now here I am in my own living room watching TV!" While the first four core members in our community found an initial home with us beyond the institution, they were not interested ultimately in long-term community membership and stayed with us only long enough to prepare themselves to live more independently. They probably should not have been placed in the institution in the first place, and of course they accepted our invitation to be free of the institution.

John, angry that he was put in an institution, didn't want to be with us so much from the beginning and left us soon after arriving. Donna, an original founding core member, came, left, stayed close at times, and finally returned to celebrate her forty years in L'Arche. She was determined, independent, faithful, and creative: an imaginative and impressionist artist who belonged to many groups and volunteered in several places. She built relationships, walking everywhere until she could not walk far and needed rides, including to Pittsburgh to visit her family. She needed to have her independence encouraged and respected in order to be fully herself.

Shirley, who held a nurse's aide certificate, was quickly hired for a good job in a nursing care facility. She was so capable but was wounded by the circumstances of her life. Our support prepared her to live in her own apartment, eventually marrying and becoming a mother. Bill, who likewise was gainfully employed, soon expressed his desire to move on to live at the local YMCA in his own apartment. Floyd, a later arrival, who was a "road addict" and could not be prevented from hopping trains in search of parents (as well as to avoid commitment to daily work), finally went off and did not return. Archie was released to us from jail, patently unwise for us in retrospect, but he didn't belong in jail and he had nowhere else to go. Archie was a delight to welcome, but his fragile alcoholism and need for other relationships could not be supported in our young community setting. And there were others who chafed more at the discipline of community living than they valued the mutuality of a common life, and so left us for independent living, marriage, or simply to return home with family.

Their desire to see their aspirations come to reality in no way defeated our sense of purpose, though it was not easy for any of those first residents to leave, nor for us sometimes to approve their choices. We were a willing alternative for persons who needed a place to live and a transitional home. We welcomed those who were institutionalized unnecessarily and enjoyed the common journey of living in our community. We blessed them and supported in every way to help them succeed. And yes, we experienced their failures along the way to achieving their aspirations.

FINANCES, FUNDING, AND ACCOUNTABILITY

When our community began, we had not sought government approval or funding, desiring to live simply and without much fanfare. We were also not very aware of government regulations, financial support, or needing to be certified to function as an agency. Barbara, Paula, Cheryl, and I would volunteer a lot of time and contribute all or some of the money we were earning, and we would make sure that everyone had enough money to be well. We ate a lot of onions and apples, and from time to time, had some great meals given to us from a local Catholic rectory where Benedictine sisters were the cooks. In reality, ever since approval and funding from our first months in 1972, we have been held to very high standards set by the state of Pennsylvania with the oversight of strong consumer advocacy. The local county authorities overseeing all treatment programs were supportive of our community but that did not exempt us from demanding standards for fire safety, health, wages and staffing, record keeping, and accounting for all progress plans for core members, their financial holdings and budget expenses, as well as rigorous yearly inspections and recertification that were introduced in 1980 to the present day.

COMMUNITY AND COMPETENCE

There was an uncontainable excitement in beginning the first L'Arche community in the United States, a natural, home-like setting for all of us, including myself, a place to enjoy a common life and to discover our call and mission together. One of my priest brothers told others, "This time, George and Barbara bit off more than they could chew!" I was at first offended by the remark but can admit that his statement was not so far off the mark. We came to learn how difficult it can be for human hearts, minds, and characters to share life in community. And we made mistakes along the way. But the saving grace will never be undone! I was in a real human community and suffered the difficulties of these relationships with others as surely as I was asking others to hold me in the complexity of my character.

It's true our reach exceeded our grasp, but we learned to

chew slowly and to tread the water of this onrushing river of fruit-bearing life barreling through us. Yet while we were naive in many ways about our new adventure, Barbara and I were also comfortable professionally in the world of education and social action, as counselors and administrators, teachers and organizers. Barbara had a well-developed relationship with many professionals in Erie. Even before the local support network for developmentally challenged persons was as fully developed as it is today, Barbara took advantage of her numerous contacts, many of whom were her former students, in the business world, medical field, and counseling networks to gather in support for our first core members. Enormous respect for Barbara among educated women in Erie garnered not only support for us but hands-on collaboration. And, of course, we took courage from Jean, who would remind us and other community leaders of what is essential with his telling question following our community reports in the early federation meetings, especially when we felt the weight of difficulties: "Are the core members secure and are they growing?"

LONG-TERM CORE MEMBERS: LEROY, MARY, FRANK, AND FRANCES

Leroy and Mary, while living at the Barber Center, made it known quite clearly when we began our community that they preferred to come to live with us. They had come to know us from the Sunday programs of prayer, singing, and fellowship that we organized as volunteers at the Barber Center the year before starting L'Arche. Leroy, severely physically compromised, spoke of earlier times of being placed in cages while institutionalized and of being locked up so he couldn't move around, which didn't help him to learn to walk. Mary would say, *"They took my doll, they took my clothes, and would steal my food."*

In fact, Mary learned in the institution to survive by hiding her food at mealtime in order to eat it later. Mary chose quite strongly to come to live in our community because she had gotten to know us and wanted to live with us. Mary was prayerful and, for some time, was capable of living with us in one of our smaller homes, reading the newspaper out loud, checking out all the obituaries, reading her Bible. She loved to socialize and dance at the nearby community center where she was a prolific artist. Mary could cook meals, care for the kitchen, do needlework, and became the elder in our community. Having been taken from home when her mother died and placed in an institution, Mary often lamented that she was not permitted to go to her mother's funeral. Mary, aged eighty-six, was proud to live so long and to experience a healing from so many years of being in the institution.

Frank never tired of relating with glee how many times he ran away from the institution, always following the railroad tracks out of town, easily followed by his finders. When Frank first came, he hardly spoke at all, but eventually his stories and vocabulary were amazing. He never once stopped cherishing that we "got him out of the institution." Frank would say, "Oh you know I can have my own room. I can go shopping now. I am in charge of my own money." Frank was thought at first by a professional to be lazy but, in reality, was probably never taken seriously or given responsibilities that matched his capabilities and interests. Frank worked every day as the chief worker in a greenhouse at the Barber Center for many years when living with us. He at first walked everywhere, and his keen eye was adept at discovering everything from old lamps, tools, and even money on the way home. He had a fully functioning "workshop" in his bedroom, turning down our invitations to take it to the basement. He was always building or remodeling his own furnishings and was our go-to electrician to repair a lamp, a cord, a clock—our very own electrical engineer! He was strong and capable even in his seventies and eighties. Frank would never turn down an invitation to have fried chicken and a beer and loved to "shoot the breeze," especially with Joe, with whom he had been friends since they were in the institution. Frank was motivated by love and would do anything for anyone—as long as you did not mess with his money, or even be perceived to be doing so!

Frances discovered L'Arche as a place where people cared for her and where she and I discovered the value of being friends. She remains a capable woman, caring for others, caring for fellow apartment dwellers, visiting others in institutions, babysitting for neighbors. It was obvious from the beginning that L'Arche could not easily limit Frances. She was very impatient and "unreasonable" in the face of our "programmatic" plans for her. For example, she left our home for the first time during the middle of the night and got on a bus to visit a friend who lived far away long before we had worked out the plan for her to travel such a distance. Eventually, Frances lived with Carol in their own apartment. She has a spiritual heart and appreciates the spiritual value of L'Arche and its mission of presence and friendship but, mind you, as an equal rather than a dependent. She has proven herself to be a faithful caregiver to so many persons of all walks of life, including her mother, her severely disabled twin brother, and her sister. Yes, Frances remains a member of our community in her love for us and in her freedom to choose us freely as members of her family. In the meantime, she is present to many others who are not members of our community but who respond to her compassionate heart as she steps forward in complete confidence to meet them as equal and capable. Frances is unique.

It's always been a practice that all major decisions in the community regarding the characteristics of our homes or where one would reside in our homes were based on the needs of those who came to us. We moved, we began new homes, we expanded activities whenever there was a need for our people to be satisfied in their basic needs and fulfilled in their capacities to live more freely and fully.

CHALLENGES OF COMMUNITY

We were a small community at the beginning, off the beaten path. Neither Barbara nor I had experience living in another L'Arche community before we began. We were pretty naive about how to welcome assistants and include them in the direction of the community or nurture them in their potential long-term development. Our homes were small and could not accommodate larger teams of assistants. We had to keep industry and employment regulations, and so we were not free to split salaries. We had to pay the exact number of hours worked as well as overtime. We couldn't even legally ask our assistants to offer their time voluntarily. Our assistants were wary of things that looked exclusionary, and there was hesitation to name things that would cause distinctions between and among us.

One of our challenges, and at the same time a gift, was our reliance on assistants who did not live in our homes. We welcomed capable and competent assistants who were not willing or able to live in our homes. In fact, I was the first live-out assistant, living in the rectory of St. Stephen parish and working full-time at Gannon College. Whatever the downside of having few live-in assistants at any one time, we have never placed undue pressure on home teams to carry on without enough assistants because we didn't want some living outside L'Arche homes. We made a commitment from the beginning never to risk hardship or diminish the quality of life for our core members or assistants through refusing to use the many fine assistants who are not necessarily living in the community.

SYMBOLS AND RITUALS IN THE BEGINNING OF THE COMMUNITY

The Candle and Silence

Praying around the candle at the table after the evening meal in our homes was and is fundamental to the end of our day. A psychiatrist, assessing one of our early core members, related how essential this time of prayer around the candle was as the one thing that held her from completely disintegrating emotionally. As a community, we liked to pray and to be silent. We had lots of community retreats, spending overnights, listening to talks, preparing crafts and signs, and incorporating these things into our prayer times. Our core members enjoyed a tradition of silence, not because they had nothing to say or because no one was listening. We practiced silence and still do through times of meditating in the John Main way, thus encouraging all of us, assistants and core members alike, to practice growing the profound capacity of our own hearts, toward the Word made flesh, beyond words, thoughts, or feelings. This contemplative practice of candle, silence, and thoughtful petitions continues today.

Adoration

While at Trosly in 1971–72, Barbara and I had spent many hours in adoration before the Blessed Sacrament. We continued this practice daily when we returned home to extend what we experienced at Trosly, even being joined each morning by the president of Gannon College, Msgr. Wilfrid Nash, who supported me so strongly in each stage of our discernment. Having a chapel with the reserved Blessed Sacrament was the foundational symbol for our L'Arche community, strongly rooted as we were in the Roman Catholic tradition. Our adoration practice was at the heart of our stability and endurance in the beginning.

The Waterspring

Eventually, the chapels we always maintained somewhere in one of our houses found its home in the spiritual center of our community, named the Waterspring, from a verse in the Prophet Isaiah referring to the spring of water gushing forth, and the words of Jesus promising that a river of living water would spring up and overflow from the one who believes. We were grateful to have an adoration chapel, a chapel for liturgy, two bedrooms for retreatants, a library area, and an office for me. Many persons passed through the Waterspring for days, for rest, for reflection, for longer Ignatian retreats led by me, varying in length from a weekend to thirty days for some. The center no longer exists, but the Waterspring lives on in the hearts of our community members.

The pastoral volunteers in our community go two by two to our homes once monthly to spend time visiting, sharing a meal, and planning a prayer. The prayer every Tuesday at noon includes a sharing on scripture and prayerful reflection about those who need our support. Early on in our community, and for some time thereafter, thanks to the encouragement of radical spiritual "elders" Fr. Bill Clarke, Tony Walsh, and Colin Maloney, reflection times for assistants once monthly—reflecting on "How am I?" "How do I love?" "Where is God in my life?"—though not always easy, were helpful to us to build a spirit of community and caring with each other. There is currently a scheduled meditation time in the journey home on each Sunday afternoon, a tradition begun when the Waterspring closed. Our long-standing tradition of prayer, reflection, and meditation seems to me to meet the criteria of Jesus who promises that the spring of water continues to flow through our community members.

Celebrations

We were greatly taken with the striking way that L'Arche expresses deep realities in very graphic, sensate ways, and its unique way of bringing laughter to affirm our mission in a joyful and profound way. Barbara researched celebrations and learned a lot about fiestas, skits, and celebrations, which we used when planning the closing fiesta of major L'Arche gatherings. Rather than host workshops for clergy or professionals on the importance of welcoming persons of disability, we joined with an ecumenical church group to bring people of all abilities together to create "Peace Festivals"—daylong gatherings to enjoy each other, to paint our faces and clown, to dance, to mime, to pray, to sing, and to celebrate together, at times around a campfire. We had New Year's Eve sleepovers, we did community retreats, and we went away for Labor Day weekend as one last fling for summer and to do planning for the year. We took off for picnics at the beach or in Cook Forest, and had meetings at Camp Glinodo. We all added our enthusiasm to each other's lives.

Singing, Taizé Vigils, Chat and Chews

Singing was always a favorite way of spending time together and of worshipping. Even not knowing the words or tunes did not dissuade us from prayer and celebrating through song. Our community loves to sing! Every Friday evening for a while we welcomed friends into our home for prayer, singing, and dessert. Since experiencing the Vigil of Taizé each Friday evening during the Assistant Renewal in Scotland in 1986, I returned home to begin this practice of keeping vigil around the cross, and it remains a regular practice in our community, at first every Friday, then eventually every Friday during Lent. This practice has continued now for over thirty years. In our L'Arche homes, there's also a unity between everyone because we do come together weekly for things. One of the favorite activities, still happening after many years, is the Tuesday noon "Chat and Chew," a time for naming and holding people in prayer, signing and sending out huge greeting and prayer cards for them, followed by a longer time of prayer and scripture or silent meditation and a happy time of lunch together.

Reaching Out

We have been blessed by many years of connection with the Erie House of Prayer from the earliest days of starting to prepare for the community. The friendship between our communities continues, more faithfully since 1988, the year Jean Vanier called all of L'Arche to a Year of Prayer in preparation for its twenty-fifth international anniversary. We took that invitation seriously and committed ourselves to join the House of Prayer community in prayer for L'Arche and to become regular members of the House of Prayer for Saturday liturgies and the joy-filled brunches after.

We were also active in St. Stephen's Church, where I was the acting pastor, and rented a home next to the church as one of our residences. We provided some work training for individuals who cared for the church and home, and many parishioners supported us strongly. It was in this time that L'Arche and the parish cosponsored a Hmong family from the refugee camps in Thailand to the United States for eventual citizenship in our country.

FIRST DEATHS IN THE COMMUNITY

Sr. Barbara died in 1982 at fifty-three years of age, the first to die in the Erie community. Knowing she would not live to attend the first U.S. covenant retreat, she announced the L'Arche covenant before us in our own community in a striking celebration in Holy Week not long before she died. The opening of our Oasis home on November 4, 1980, was something born directly of the covenant relationship between Barbara and Mary.

For the last couple of weeks of her life, Barbara returned to the Benedictine Priory to live, but Mary remained with her and we stayed close to her, prayed with her, and loved her until the end. We celebrated the Eucharist as a community in the monastery shortly before her death, and we all went to her room to say our goodbyes. Jean Vanier and many L'Arche brothers and sisters from international communities came from the federation meeting in South Bend to join us for Barbara's funeral. Her death has been one of the cornerstones of our community, the stone of loss and grief, a bit of a weight to bear but just as surely a rock-solid and stable foundation stone of the community going forward. Even today, Barbara's parting gift to me shortly before she died, a framed colorful floral design inscribed with the words of Mother Teresa: "Let's do something beautiful for God," remains on my wall not only as a grateful memory but to serve as my first inspiration upon rising each day, an echo of the primary movement of the Spirit in our lives.

Five years later, Carol Wills was the first core member to die in the community. She was institutionalized directly at birth. She knew she had parents and family but, for years, imagined they must have thought she was dead, until her father unexpectedly appeared to visit her in her teen years. Eventually, we contacted her parents, who came to Erie where Carol met her mother for the first time. Carol had a full-time job as a health aide and lived in an apartment with Donna. Later, sensing that Carol would die young, Barbara encouraged her to partner with Frances in establishing a fully autonomous home with minimal support provided. Finally, a year or two before Carol's death, her parents welcomed her to stay for a week with them in Florida. When Carol got sick, her family started coming here to visit and were touched by how her L'Arche home was truly hers. When Carol fell ill a second time, she moved to our Oasis home where the hospice nurses were sometimes frustrated by her many outings and full schedule. Her purse was at the ready, filled with paraphernalia for bingo! For most of her life Carol rejected her own image because of her distinct features, which she considered deformed and an object of scorn by others. She routinely broke any mirrors given to her, until, as she never tired of saying, Barbara taught her to look at herself in the mirror and see herself as beautiful. Carol literally died in our loving embrace while gazing at the icon of Christ held out before her beholding her iconic beauty!

After Carol, when somebody died, we tried to work with whatever church they belonged to. Some of our people even chose their own caskets. We preplanned funerals and asked if there were certain things they particularly wanted. We always looked at their favorite songs, or if they had a special reading. We made great efforts, even for those no longer in our community or just friends, to plan a real celebration, whether of memories at the time of viewing or a church celebration.

A few other early deaths: When Madlyn died, we were moved by the amazing transformation in her family's regard for her. They really didn't see her beauty until the night we shared memories in the funeral home after her death. I think her family was grateful beyond measure that L'Arche discovered the gift of Madlyn and shared her with them. Joe used to become agitated by the attention given to others during their illnesses, but in his own last days he became filled with sensitive care for everyone who gathered around his bed. This was Joe: strong, resolute, refusing chemo, brain damaged, suffering devastating seizures, yet at his core a fully adult man of light and peace. Frank kept his workshop in his bedroom, and in the end culminated his life by dismantling his workshop piece by piece, giving away his tools, his pictures, and his wall hangings to those who had loved him through the years. As he weakened, he spoke his quiet and personal farewell to each of us with words I will always cherish: "George, I love you!" Frank revealed my beauty to me, and I miss him sorely!

Finally, let me honor Mary's death. When Mary was coming to the end of her life and bedridden, we moved her bedroom into our prayer space where she could also be close to our kitchen and the activities of the home. Her failing health was painful for her and for all of us because as Mary became ill and incapacitated, she would tell one of us, "I hate you!" or refuse to speak or look at me but allow me to hold her hand, a marked change in the precious Mary we all loved. At the end of her life, she found her way to express her affection for us all. Many community members and friends of Mary gathered in her room and sang her favorite community picnic songs. I will never forget the way she looked at each of us gathered around her bed, "taking us into her heart" and speaking volumes in her silence. Mary was embracing each of us, maybe to take part of us with her only a few days after that precious time of song and prayer. When Mary died early one morning, all her housemates gathered around as we prayed.

In my time as an interdisciplinary hospice team member, I have had the privilege to attend to many individuals and their families at death. Nowhere have I experienced the spirit that is so palpably present and the quiet, prayerful heart of those gathered at the bedside of someone actively dying as I have in our L'Arche community. It is often our core members who lead the way in knowing just what to do at the mortal sickness of our dear ones. Nor have I experienced such quiet and celebration-filled presence to the mystery of death as at a L'Arche funeral. I will be honored to follow them when my time comes.

AND NOW? LIKE A PEBBLE DROPPED IN THE WATER!

The earliest movie made of L'Arche, *If You're Not There, You're Missed*, has a scene at the pool in the Val Fleuri garden in Trosly. The water is moving in expanding concentric circles. This is an apt image of our L'Arche community's journey, which is not linear but concentric. At the second federation meeting in 1973, our Erie community reported on the demands of the state for accountability and the resistance to L'Arche from local professionals. Jean Vanier commented, "It is not the state that is or will be your problem, it is the challenge of community." Challenges in community for all of us, vexing as they may be, bring us to the "poverty of spirit" that is the source of our energy to listen deeply, believe in the beauty of each one, and to have endless patience in calling forth the beauty of one another. I recently had the privilege of working with university students in their philosophy of ethics class as they formed groups to digest and make group presentations on Jean's book *Becoming Human*. I was touched by the good-hearted students, Christian, Jewish, Buddhist, and Muslim, as they wrestled with the very issues of our L'Arche community and of the human community at large to be fully human, fully alive!

AFTERWORD: LEAVING HOME AND RETURNING AS IF FOR THE FIRST TIME

In the mid-1990s, George began distancing himself from L'Arche, both emotionally and in his role as a priest in L'Arche. He explains, "This movement did not come out of the blue, and involved some circumstances that were difficult to experience, for me and for others. I was no longer involved in structures of L'Arche at North American or international levels. I was content with my region's initiative, entrusting the spiritual animation of communities to lay members, something I have championed in L'Arche at every level. I resigned membership in the international priest fraternity and distanced myself from the L'Arche practice of celebrating the Roman Catholic Eucharist given the restrictions around reception of communion. There were other tensions, some of which were created by my lack of tact and patience. But more important, it was just time to step down as the pastoral leader of the community after twenty years of exercising substantial authority from the beginning, one that could be strong and independent, not so subject to accountability, somewhat characteristic of an ordained minister in an essentially lay community." With a new community leader in place, and his Roman Catholic bishop's urging, George realized, "I can just live L'Arche, just live it simply." He moved from the L'Arche home where he had lived for fourteen years to take an apartment on Gannon University campus and returned to full-time university ministry. He remains linked to his home in the community, taking part in major community events and praying with the community. "I am present when I can be present, I try to accompany core members as they come to the end of their lives, and I offer spiritual support and pastoral presence when appropriate."

George's spiritual journey continues to unfold. "For a long time, I have been practicing contemplative prayer with wonderful teachers and communities. The Christian mystical tradition and contemplative Zen tradition opened an unexpected door within me so that I am being reborn in L'Arche. Mystery is available to us. Jean Vanier insisted that a contemplative mystical perspective, *rooted in prayer, is essential if we are to see the face of the crucified but risen Jesus in our own disability, in those who are more obviously labeled as disabled, in those abandoned, indeed in our disabled church, and in our divided world. Monastery without walls! L'Arche community living!"*

Chapter 4

"GIVE THE BREAD THAT YOU ARE"

L'Arche in the UK, 1974

THÉRÈSE VANIER

INTRODUCTION

Thérèse Vanier was born in England in 1923 to Pauline and Georges Vanier. She had four younger brothers, including Jean, who founded L'Arche. During World War II, Thérèse was a member of the British Mechanised Transport Corps and even sailed in an Atlantic convoy. At the end of the war, she served in the Canadian Women's Army Corps in France and then Germany.

After World War II, Thérèse studied chemistry at the Sorbonne and medicine at Cambridge University. She completed clinical studies at St. Thomas's Hospital in central London and subsequently spent two years at Great Ormond Street Hospital for Sick Children in London, and another two at Tufts University in Boston with research fellowships in pediatric hematology at each. In 1962, she returned to St. Thomas's Hospital for a decade, with a one-year secondment to the pediatrics department of Makere Medical School in Uganda. At St. Thomas's, she became the first woman consultant physician, serving as senior lecturer and consultant clinical hematologist from 1965 to 1972.

In the late 1960s, Thérèse became friends with Cicely Saunders, the founder of St. Christopher's Hospice, who had pioneered a whole new field of care for the dying. Thérèse remarks, "I was a clinical hematologist and I found myself moving into palliative care initially because I was thoroughly unsatisfied with the way I was caring for children particularly who were dying of leukemia." To learn more about palliative care, she arranged to come to St. Christopher's on weekends. It was soon after that time that Thérèse also got involved with L'Arche.

Thérèse died in 2014. The following account in her own words is selected from three conversations we recorded in 2010 combined with selections from her book, The Founding Story of L'Arche in the UK, *and a small selection from Tim Kearney's 1999 interview in* A Prophetic Cry.

GOD'S CALL AND THE 1971 PILGRIMAGE TO LOURDES

I believe the extraordinary sequence of events that brought L'Arche to England and to Canterbury was truly God-given and a clear call from God. It has been said that if you seek to follow God's call you must expect to be surprised. I was very surprised indeed to find myself in L'Arche.

At Easter 1971, I was in Lourdes as doctor to one of the groups on the Faith and Light pilgrimage. Something in the region of seven thousand members of Faith and Light converged on Lourdes for Easter from all parts of the world. I was there, not only to care for the pilgrims but to find out what my brother Jean was up to! He had become involved in the planning, and he made the running of this pilgrimage a personal concern. It was my experience of being powerless in front of some of the handicapped people in the pilgrimage that really shook me. I spent a lot of time with a man named Billy Saunders of about fifty, who had the most awful attacks of asthma and probably should never have gone on a pilgrimage like that, and his mother who was eighty something. I pushed one wheelchair. They were both grossly overweight and his mother had terrible arthritis, so I saw a lot of them.

I realized that the prayer of Billy's mother was quite clear: she wanted Billy to die before she did because she was convinced that if she died first, there would be nobody to visit Billy in the hospital. Billy's prayer was very simple, "I don't want to go back to hospital. Don't let me go back to hospital." Confronted with these two people for nearly a week over the Easter period, I just felt completely helpless. I really wanted to do something, and so the thought almost exploded within me and I said to Jean in the evening while we were still at Lourdes, "You know if you want, if it would be possible to set up L'Arche in the UK, I would really like to help do that." Jean never missed an opportunity, and so that was really how it started. What brought me into L'Arche really was Billy the handicapped man and my sense of powerlessness.

Sometime later, a priest who'd been in my pilgrimage group rang me up and told me Billy had died. Apparently after I had seen Billy and his mother off on their train to South Wales, they had gone to her house because they got back too late to take him up to the hospital. So he spent the night at her place. There he had an attack of asthma that killed him, so his prayer was answered, and he never went back to the hospital. It took her a long time to realize that this was an answer to Billy's prayer, because she blamed herself for taking him on the pilgrimage.

In addition to meeting Billy and his mother at the pilgrimage, I also made an important connection with a man named Geoffrey Morgan. Geoffrey had come to the 1971 Faith and Light pilgrimage as a representative of the Daybreak community in Canada, where he and his wife, Ann, and their son Christopher were living. He told me that he and Ann had decided that they were going to stay in L'Arche. The thought of L'Arche in the UK appealed greatly to them.

For me, the death of Billy, alongside my meeting with Geoffrey and Ann Morgan, seemed to be a sign from God. Billy's prayer not to return to hospital and his mother's prayer that Billy die before she did had both been answered. My sense of powerlessness in front of their need had, it seemed to me, received a response from God—as if I was being told, "You know you do not have to do everything, and here are companions on your journey!" Between Geoffrey, Ann, and myself, supported by Jean, the idea was born of establishing L'Arche in Britain. At this point I made the decision to leave St. Thomas's hospital where I had a very responsible job as senior lecturer and consultant running the clinical hematology department.

ST. CHRISTOPHER'S HOSPICE

Two things reassured me and gave me strength. The first was having met Ann and Geoffrey Morgan, and the other was an invitation to work two days a week as consultant physician at St. Christopher's Hospice, caring for dying people. Here I realized that I would learn much from those I cared for and from those I worked alongside, which would stand me in good stead in L'Arche. I decided that I could live on the salary they offered me and accepted the appointment at St. Christopher's with the idea of "doing" L'Arche at the same time—whatever "doing L'Arche" might involve.

USE POOR MEANS

I was now faced with a decision. Was L'Arche to be my destiny or not? This was no easy decision. I went to see an elderly priest in Liverpool, Fr. Pownall, who listened very carefully to my story and then said, "You know, Thérèse, I can't tell you what to do because I don't know. I can see your difficulty in deciding. All I have to say is, whatever you decide to do, use poor means." I thought about this while going back to London: "use poor means." The wheels of the train were saying to me over and over and over again: "Use poor means, use poor means, use poor means…!" It went round and round in my head until I was getting giddy! Later, when I asked myself what it all meant, I realized that it meant only one thing. At St. Christopher's, I would become totally involved in an area of medicine in which I was competent, which I liked, and which I knew I would be good at. If I went to L'Arche, I felt that I wouldn't have a clue as to what to do. So where or what were the "poor means"?

I think the answer was already becoming obvious when I was with Billy Saunders and his mother in Lourdes on the 1971 Faith and Light pilgrimage and I had felt so powerless. I knew that I was now experiencing "God calling." Gradually it had become clear to me that my future was bound up with L'Arche, to which I did not feel at all suited! I had no knowledge of mental handicap. I certainly had no experience of founding a new charity and all the paperwork and meetings with new people required. My "conversion" to L'Arche had been very gradual and was highly resisted for quite a long time! But gradually it became clearer and clearer to me. By that time, I was in L'Arche, whether I fully realized it or not.

FOUNDING COMMITTEE

In 1972, while I was still at the "vision stage," Jean and I were building a wonderful committee (or board) for L'Arche in the UK, and the necessary steps were being taken to establish a legal identity. Besides Jean and myself, the committee included Tim Hollis and Lord Hylton. Lord Hylton had worked with my father when he was governor general of Canada, so there were connections between his family and mine. We had much help from Raymond Hylton, who recruited Richard Carr-Gomm, who had founded the Abbeyfield Society for homeless elderly people and had gone on to found the Carr-Gomm Society. Next was Leonard Cheshire, who had founded the Cheshire Homes for disabled people. Another member was Fr. Michael Garvey, headmaster of the Catholic St. Edmund's School where Jean had given his first retreat in the UK in 1971, and Francis Wigham, one of the organizers of the UK Faith and Light groups that went to Lourdes in 1971. Finally, there was John Stitt, an ex-naval man who was now a solicitor. John was the first chairman, and he was extremely helpful and efficient. The committee met in Chelsea where I had a flat in those days. I remember John arriving on a moped, dressed like a spaceman and wearing a huge helmet. He would bring the moped into the garden, cast off the helmet, and then get on with the work. He was great fun. In many ways the members of the committee were the "founding fathers" of L'Arche in the UK. The skills and expertise of the various members meant that before long L'Arche had both a legal identity and a bank account.

FINDING A HOUSE

Meanwhile my brother Jean had a surprise—a telephone call from someone in France wanting to dispose of a house in Sturry in East Kent near Canterbury, followed by the advice that he should see the archbishop of Canterbury if L'Arche was to work in that area. Ann, Geoffrey, and I were certainly surprised at the offer of a house in East Kent. We hoped to begin L'Arche in England and thought of many possible areas, but East Kent was not among them. As it turned out, the house was quite unsuitable, but nevertheless Jean and I went to see the archbishop of Canterbury, Michael Ramsey, on New Year's Day 1972. He welcomed us warmly and was very interested. He said we would be given first refusal on any property in the diocese that came up for sale. He added, "You are doing God's work, but you are doing something very difficult." Subsequently, L'Arche acquired the Old Rectory in the village of Barfrestone, about ten miles southeast of Canterbury. The house opened in 1974.

LITTLE EWELL

At Barfrestone, we decided to call the Old Rectory "Little Ewell." We liked *Ewell* because Ann and Geoffrey had found a spring and *Ewell* is an old Kentish word meaning "spring." "Little" was necessary because there was a neighboring village called Ewell. The idea was that the little L'Arche community would be fed by a greater Source, becoming a source or spring of nourishment flowing out to many people in a quiet and hidden way.

It was not until January 1974 that the first handicapped people moved in; three men from nearby Eastry Hospital who we had invited to join us: Bill Armstrong, John Boorman, and David Turnham. Soon after, Geraldine and little John and later Jane, Yvonne, and Betty joined the community at Little Ewell. The establishment of L'Arche at Barfrestone had not been without controversy. We had needed permission to turn the house into a care home, and I had met the local inhabitants at the pub. They were evenly divided between those in favor and those against. Those who were against believed our clientele would be a source of violence in the village. I firmly dispelled uninformed notions of what we were about and invited local people to come and visit us.

Ann and Geoffrey really got the community going. We didn't bother with who was in charge. It was obvious that it was me who was responsible, but the daily life of the house was in their hands. Geoffrey suffered a chronic illness, which he learned to live with. Ann was a very powerful person, like me in many ways, and she was more than capable of running a house and coping with her own children. She already had a young child and then had another one. Just the arrival on the scene of Ann and Geoffrey gave me a certain amount of support. At the same time, I was obviously the sort of person who had many contacts and was able to make use of them. Jean, too, because of his naval connections, was in a position to call on a lot of people for help, so gradually things got into gear in the UK. While the rectory was still being renovated, I was involved, with Jean's help, in looking for assistants. Letters from Canada and from the UK began to arrive from people who had heard Jean speak. One in particular came from Celia Heneage, a young English girl who had just left school. She became one of the first assistants at Little Ewell.

I developed a rhythm of living at Little Ewell for two, three, or sometimes four days a week. The rest of the time I had to be in London because I was earning my living by working at St. Christopher's Hospice. Working in the palliative care set up there actually kept me sane because I knew what I was doing and felt fully competent in that sphere even if I was feeling quite incompetent in L'Arche. It was at this time that the little community of Barfrestone—Geoffrey, Ann, and me—decided together to make a very simple request: that we go to an Anglican monastery and a Roman Catholic monastery and ask them to pray for us. We went to Minster, a Roman Catholic Benedictine abbey, which was about fifteen miles away. Then we went up to St. Mary's, West Malling, an Anglican Benedictine abbey, and asked them to pray for the new little L'Arche community.

BILL ARMSTRONG'S LESSONS

When we opened, new residents arrived quickly, and within six months there was a full house. Bill Armstrong had been born in Tyneside in North East England. He was proud of his mining stock although he had never been able to work as a miner himself. He was a tall man who was quite good-looking, and he had a strong temper. Bill and I used to meet very often over a cup of tea at about six o'clock in the morning. By that time Bill would have fired up the Aga cooker. He would be sitting there with the cooker behind him, having a cup of tea and the inevitable cigarette.

Bill was quite a character, and he taught me two important lessons. The first was on an occasion when the community was having an important meeting. Bill was in a foul mood and decided he wasn't coming. Some fifteen minutes into the meeting, he appeared at the door—still in a foul temper—came in, and sat down. Nobody said anything. Then Bill said, "I want to know if anybody wants me to stay here." I remained silent. David was another handicapped man and was the butt of Bill's anger and unpleasantness. David said, "Bill, I want you to stay." David had triggered off something. People began going around the room, in turn, and saying to Bill, "Bill, I want you to stay." Then it came to Geraldine's turn. Geraldine had a strong sense of who was in charge. She looked at me and said, "Thérèse, I want Bill to stay." Whereupon David looked at Geraldine and said, "Don't talk to Thérèse, talk to Bill." I never forgot the sequence of events; it was such a lesson. The second lesson I learned from Bill related to money. In the evenings, I would have a bite of supper and then go off to this or that organization to talk about L'Arche and to beg for money. There was one occasion when Bill looked at me and said, "You won't forget to smile, will you, Thérèse? Because if you smile, people will know you are happy." He was used to my rather serious disposition.

THE 1974 EASTER PILGRIMAGE TO CANTERBURY

Little Ewell had been open for barely two months when a phone call came from Canada asking if we could arrange for two hundred pilgrims, half of whom would be handicapped, to attend Easter Sunday Eucharist in Canterbury Cathedral. Surprisingly, there was a warm response from the cathedral authorities to our extraordinary request. They went to endless trouble to give us whatever we asked for. So it was that on Easter Sunday, two hundred L'Arche and Faith and Light pilgrims processed into the choir of the cathedral. Each one carried a small bell that they rang at the Gloria. The presiding archbishop of Canterbury joined in the ringing, the same archbishop, Michael Ramsey, who had welcomed Jean and me two years before. As the congregation left at the end of the service, they met the pilgrims singing and dancing and were quickly caught up in the continuing Easter joy. This remarkable event was made possible by our already close relationships in Canterbury, the cradle of the Anglican Communion. It was this totally unexpected pilgrimage from Canada that helped us, and a great many others, to experience some gifts that many people with learning difficulties can offer to the churches.

WALSINGHAM PILGRIMAGE

A year later in 1975, Tim Hollis suggested that we make a pilgrimage to Walsingham. Tim and I were very sensitive to the ecumenical issues at stake, and we were determined that the sixty or seventy pilgrims should visit every shrine of every denomination in or near Walsingham. On the first morning of our stay, we visited the Slipper Chapel, the Roman Catholic shrine, where we prayed and lit candles. In the afternoon, we went to the Anglican shrine where we were invited to go down and drink from a spring. We enjoyed that and we had the two symbols of water and light to remind us of our own Christian baptism. We sang and prayed, and then set off for the Orthodox shrine in the old railway station that was no longer used. We asked the Orthodox priest, an icon maker, if he would say some prayers with us and bless us with oil. The oil was the third Christian symbol, which we wanted to receive. The priest said that he would be very happy to arrange this, and he prayed a very long Russian prayer, but we were okay, and we were all blessed with holy oil. These three visits happened on the same day. The fourth day we visited a Quaker family who lived in the house in Walsingham where the original apparitions are said to have taken place. It was a beautiful day and we had cups of tea on the grounds. When asked, the Quaker family answered, "Of course, you can dance, and you can sing, and you can do what you like." So we danced and sang in this beautiful Quaker establishment.

ECUMENICAL CHALLENGES

Also within the first few months of Little Ewell's opening, a Roman Catholic priest from Western Canada came on a sabbatical to help as an assistant with us. Not long after he came, he asked if we would like him to celebrate the Eucharist every day. His offer made us confront the implications of our interdenominational community, including the important fact that our five handicapped members at that time belonged to the Church of England. This brought up the whole question of eucharistic hospitality and whether our non-Roman Catholic members could have special permission to receive Catholic communion. In search of advice I went to see Richard Stewart, the ecumenical adviser of the Roman Catholic Diocese of Southwark, who explained that such a permission would not be possible and added, "Don't you think your first responsibility to your handicapped members is to enable them to become full members of their own church if that is their wish? In any event is there not a danger that their families and others may see any such special permission for your people as a Roman Catholic take over?"

This led to our (perhaps I should say my) decision to obey the rules of the Roman Catholic Church and thus live with the reality of division between our churches. This may seem an obvious outcome today, years later. At the time, of course, we had no experience of things ecumenical. I came back with a clear message from Richard Stewart, the ecumenist that I'd gone to see. I'd thought I was going to get some sort of advice about special permission for our Anglican people to receive Roman Catholic communion. But when I came back from consulting the ecumenical advisor, I told Ann, Geoffrey, and the others about our conversation and how I now realized we should abide by the rules of the Roman Church. This didn't please me at all, but it seemed that it was the only thing to do and that we should not break those rules right at the very beginning of our community. Instead, everybody should accept the fact that they do belong to different churches. Ann and I were soon at loggerheads over this because when she and Geoffrey had been at Daybreak, initially getting to know L'Arche, Ann had been caught up in the fact that everyone had been going to Roman Catholic communion, regardless of their denomination. She couldn't understand why now at Little Ewell she couldn't receive Catholic communion. So I was seen as a sort of authority figure, which I was of course.

CONFIRMATIONS

Following Richard Stewart's suggestion, I contacted the local Anglican rector, who had two churches to look after, one of them being the lovely old church in Barfrestone. My request was extraordinarily difficult for the rector, but he never refused anything he was asked. All the people who wanted to be confirmed met together. The rector saw them as a group and then met each one individually. The bishop of Dover was an elderly man, and he was perfectly willing to administer confirmation, although the confirmation of handicapped people was something completely new to him. In the past there had even been a question about allowing handicapped people into a service lest they disrupt it. All turned out well. The bishop came to meet the handicapped people, and in due course, he confirmed them in their lovely little church at Barfrestone. This series of church events involving our handicapped people and the choices they had to make about confirmation led us to ask ourselves questions about the best way to discover exactly what our handicapped people wanted. How were we to involve them in the decision-making process?

ALTERNATING EUCHARISTIC CELEBRATIONS IN THE COMMUNITY

The next step came when the Anglican rector of Barfrestone and Basil, our visiting Roman Catholic priest, agreed that it was probably important for each of them to celebrate the Eucharist in the community. They started to do this on alternate weeks, which turned into alternate fortnights. This arrangement continues in the community with an Anglican Eucharist once a month and a Roman Catholic Eucharist once a month. We lived reasonably peacefully with the new arrangement except for Ann's evident distress. It was not until 1986 that Ann and I "made it up" at the first ecumenical covenant retreat, which was held at Park Place Pastoral Centre. A few days into the retreat, she asked my forgiveness for her attitude and I asked her forgiveness for my attitude. We forgave each other for having been at cross-purposes for such a long time and that was really good. But it had been a long twelve years.

COMPETENCE AND DEALING WITH STRESS

My part-time work at St. Christopher's Hospice allowed me to continue in a professional role in which I felt comfortable. St. Christopher's broadened my understanding of the place of vulnerable people as teachers and "formers." It also taught me about the need to acquire appropriate skills, including the skill of good management. In St. Christopher's and L'Arche there is both the need for love and for competence. I used to feel frustrated at what I felt to be a lack of competence in L'Arche. At the same time, my "professionalism" was sometimes suspect to people in L'Arche. But it also encouraged assistants to recognize the help we need from "professionals," in the fields of medicine, psychiatry, psychology, or social work. I was keen to ensure that assistants had professional training and some understanding of the dynamics of community life.

I was very much aware of an unacceptable degree of stress among L'Arche assistants. In that connection, I remember a French member of L'Arche who carried major responsibility telling me that there was no such thing as stress in L'Arche! I never heard Jean say that. I spoke to him about stress and, as always, he would listen to what I was saying. But for him there were other priorities; hence this was an area of real disagreement between us. It was a time when I was pretty stressed out myself. Every time I heard that Jean had been giving a talk on the joys of living with mentally handicapped people and their tremendous gifts of community, I used to get exasperated because he never spoke about how hard it could be at times.

SEEKING PROFESSIONAL SUPPORT

One of the things that Jean did bring to the whole business was the sense of what he lacked—that he was not a professional psychologist, or psychotherapist, or somebody who knew anything about the sort of professional attitude to take with people who have intellectual disabilities. You have the fact that Jean was capable of both giving lectures on the Gospel of John on the one hand and wanting to work with somebody who's a real expert on caring and nursing for dying people with intellectual disabilities on the other hand. I think that for all his enthusiasm, Jean also had this other element in his mind that said you've got to do this properly, you've got to do that properly, and somebody else has got to help you professionally.

A friend of mine was contrasting the way Jean and I each went about things. She said that Jean tackled things because he knew there was a worldwide, monstrous need on the part of people with intellectual disabilities, and the more people you could get involved in that and the more handicapped people you could get in your community, the better. Soon they had a bed, some food, and someone who really loved them. My attention, however, had been turned by my medical qualification to focusing on the individual I was with at that particular moment, who necessarily takes my full attention. Otherwise I'm going to make mistakes, and you cannot make mistakes with medicine.

EARLY DEATHS IN THE COMMUNITY

Deaths of people with learning difficulties have a kind of ripple effect, not just on the immediate community but throughout the whole region. This is clear from the vast number of people who turn up at funerals. Nick's death in the Lambeth community was such a powerful experience. People came to his funeral from all over L'Arche. It was exactly like a family funeral. People came to the funeral who I did not know at all. They offered condolences because they knew what we had been living and what we were still living.

My favorite story is about Betty and Yvonne at Little Ewell. Yvonne knew that Betty was slowly dying, and she would sit next to her and do her knitting—a lovely little lady with Down syndrome sitting next to a dying handicapped person. At this stage, Yvonne knew that Betty could die at any moment, but that didn't seem to worry her. She knew that Betty would occasionally stop breathing and then would start up again. On one occasion, Yvonne came dashing out to find an assistant because Betty had stopped breathing for longer than usual. But, of course, when they reentered the room, Betty had started breathing again. Yvonne remarked to the assistant, "Oh well, God will just have to wait, won't he." They also say something about us. Betty's funeral in Little Ewell had a real sense of celebration. We were all asked to dress in summer clothes, bright colors. There was a real sense of gathering. These early funerals are models of the way L'Arche should bury its dead.

We developed a kind of tradition regarding death and funerals. We ask the undertakers to bring an open coffin, and it's put in the room where the person has lived. Then people who want to do so, come and say goodbye. Not everybody wants to, but lots of people do. When this started happening, I was initially in some doubt about how good it would be for some people, in particular for the handicapped people. However, it has proved to be the right thing to do, and it is appreciated. Somebody like Doris in the Lambeth community would never have gone to a funeral. But she went to Philip's funeral because she had lived with Philip and loved him. Doris didn't want to hear anything about death. She had been in a hospital for the mentally handicapped for forty years or so and had not been told of the death of her parents until long after the event.

NEW UK COMMUNITIES

Within four years, four other communities were founded in the UK. Each new community gave us the opportunity to live another stage in our ecumenical vocation. In Inverness, our people were members of the Church of Scotland for the most part. The next year, 1976, it was Liverpool Catholic Social Services who offered us a house. There are a high proportion of Roman Catholics in the population, and this is reflected in the numbers from that church in the Liverpool L'Arche community. Liverpool is also the city where three church leaders—the Anglican David Sheppard, the Roman Catholic archbishop Derek Worlock, and John Williamson, church moderator representing the Reformed churches—worked together in every possible way and in particular on civic occasions, whether these were of celebration or of grief. Then, it was with the strong encouragement of a trust interested in supporting care in the community for people with learning disabilities in Lambeth that L'Arche Lambeth opened in 1977. The following year, L'Arche Bognor Regis opened a house in a housing estate, following an invitation from Servite Housing, which is interested in including disabled people among "ordinary families" on such an estate.

TIM AND MARION HOLLIS

Somewhere around 1976, Tim Hollis became general secretary of L'Arche UK, and his wife, Marion, became company secretary. In the course of time, the L'Arche office grew around them. The office or secretariat was first based in the Hollis's own home. It became the hub of the life of L'Arche, and the discussions and findings of the various committees were filtered through it. Marion as company secretary had previously worked for a number of years in a solicitor's office, so she was able to work with the legal side of what was happening in the various communities. Tim and Marion also started formation programs for assistants in their house. New assistants would go up for a weekend from Thursday to Monday, and Tim and Marion would put them up and feed them. The quality of those formation programs and the people they invited to take sessions was so high that not only new assistants benefited, but older ones as well.

PAT AND THE PARADOX OF STRENGTH IN WEAKNESS

There's a man called Pat, who is one of the most anguished people I have ever met. Some time ago, I went with Pat and other people to the confirmation of another mentally handicapped man. Pat is terrified of certain things, stairs being one of them, and coming out of the cathedral are very shallow stairs. Pat was about to embark on a panic attack, and I firmly took his hand and distracted him as best I could. Then, a man on the other side of him nearly knocked him over. Pat righted himself and realized that the man was going to fall. So he took the man's hand. At that point I realized that Pat was completely distracted from the stairs, so I let go of his hand. He then helped this man, who was drunk, to come down the steps. Then the man sat down on one of the steps, so Pat sat next to him and just looked at him and said, "My name is Pat, what's your name?" The man didn't answer, he was past it. So Pat went on chatting to him. I didn't think this could go on indefinitely, so I said, "Pat, we're going to miss our bus, I think we'd better be off. You know you have helped this man down and he's okay now on the steps." And then Pat turned to the man and said (and sometimes he gets his genders mixed up), "He's in a hurry, sorry, I've got to go." Pat here certainly embodied something of L'Arche's practical application of the paradox of strength in weakness.

EXPANDING ROLES

I was the first director of Little Ewell, the first house of what became L'Arche Kent. I tried to spend two to four days at Barfrestone each week. But by 1976, the Liverpool community was starting and there was now Lambeth where I was organizing the opening of L'Arche in West Norwood. I had to attend national committee meetings, and there were four communities on the books: two in reality, Kent and Inverness, and two hopefully about to be born, Liverpool and Lambeth. Looking into the future, there was Bognor. At this time, I was also a trustee of Faith and Light, which was trying at that time to get legal status in the

UK. In addition, I was giving talks on L'Arche during Faith and Sharing retreats.

At St. Christopher's Hospice where I worked part-time, it didn't take long for them to discover that I was the only fluent French-speaking doctor involved. So St. Christopher's sent me off to talk about hospice care in France, Switzerland, Belgium, and even French Canada. I also became a L'Arche regional coordinator, covering Inverness, Liverpool, Little Ewell, and soon Lambeth, Oslo, Helsingor, and by 1978, Kilkenny, Ireland. As a regional coordinator of what became the Northern Europe region, I was also a member of the International Council of L'Arche.

CHANGING LEADERSHIP

In 1976, it seemed obvious to me, and to others whose advice I sought, that someone else should take responsibility for Little Ewell. This would enable me to concentrate on Lambeth. We were caught up in a sense of real mission to people with mental handicaps so that events often overtook the capacity of individuals and groups. One had a sense that God was talking to us in those events. Jean had even said and written, "God makes use of our mistakes and our inadequacies."

Sometime after Little Ewell opened, I was invited to speak to the Dover Rotary Club of which Jack Holdstock was president. Subsequently, Jack joined our local committee and in due course became chairman. He took great interest in the house and got to know the assistants and the core people. Later on, his wife, Lois, did the same. When I realized that I must stop being director at Little Ewell, I thought that maybe Jack could take it over. I spoke with Ann and Geoffrey about this and then spoke about Jack with the other assistants and with individual committee members. In retrospect, I realize how much pressure

I must have put on people because of my own tiredness and need. There seemed no other possible solution. I got the overall impression that everyone was prepared to work with Jack. He took over as director in December 1976.

Things ended badly. While we were having a regional meeting in Denmark in October 1980, two assistants from Little Ewell asked to meet Jack and myself. They made it clear that the assistants were finding Jack's attitude hard to cope with. They felt he could not go on as leader and were not prepared to work with him any longer. The outcome was that I had to tell Jack that he should resign earlier than had been originally planned. For myself, this whole episode was part of a steep learning curve. It was a cause of deep sadness, not to say guilt. The sadness was because of the distress and pain caused to people I cared about. I am grateful for the forgiveness of those who suffered the most distress and pain.

REGIONAL AND INTERNATIONAL MEETINGS

During the 1970s, I found myself involved in three critical meetings of the International Federation of L'Arche. The first was in 1972 at Ambleteuse in France. All the early founders were present. The federation decided to hold the second meeting the following year in 1973. We met at the house in Barfrestone, which was to become Little Ewell. We used the workshop for our meetings as that was the only part of the house that was finished. We had a further meeting at Trosly, where we attempted to thrash out a charter for L'Arche that could be acceptable to all. Then we met again at the nearby monastery of Ourscamp, where we put together a draft charter. Whenever I think of the charter, I think of Jean's expression, "In L'Arche we're a bit like rabbits, we sniff our way around." We wanted to present people with a simple statement, which summed up the essence of L'Arche.

In 1975, the meeting of the federation took place in Eastern Canada at a place called Shadow Lake. At that meeting, twenty-six communities were represented and there were five observers. It was on this occasion that Jean resigned as international coordinator and Sue Mosteller took on that role. It was a time when everything tended to be dependent on Jean. This was happening, for instance, with people opening communities because they'd been inspired by something that he'd said. Well, that's fine, but what do you do when Jean decides he's not going to go on being international leader and asks Sue Mosteller to take over? She had to take over in the same sort of way but without Jean's background. She didn't have the same temperament. I mean Sue would be in tears as stress took its toll, whereas Jean had simply just ploughed through it as if the stress wasn't there.

EXHAUSTION

By the mid-1970s, I had reached a point that I recognized as being overstressed, and I stopped and disappeared for three months to the home of a friend of mine who lives by the sea. I think I reached this stage when the Lambeth community was sort of on the road to becoming. Sue Pallant had taken responsibility for getting the house itself up and running so I could just leave it in the hands of a very good local committee that was masterminded or chaired by a delightful and competent Church of England priest named John Wiltshire. I was also still trying to cope with Little Ewell and its difficulties in trying to find somebody else to look after the community.

I think the exhaustion that can happen in L'Arche is not so different from somebody working on an intensive care unit, who disregards their own health and needs because of a shortage in personnel and working too many hours. There comes a time when they just can't do that and they crack. So it's no different than that. But for me, in L'Arche it was extra intense for all sorts of reasons, simply because of its history of growing so quickly and because of the way it spread across the globe. There is a particular intensity with something growing as fast as that without actually consolidating, and instead expecting each community to be independent yet belong to an international federation and doing all the things that the federation wants you to do, like suddenly flying to India for a general meeting. So I became exhausted and took three months off. I rested, slept, and walked by the sea. I forgot about myself and about L'Arche. I just learned how to walk on sand and different stabilities. After three months, I came back to the Lambeth community, which was becoming a reality, and soon after came the offer to take regional leadership.

SPIRITUALITY COMMISSION AND THE NEEDS OF ASSISTANTS

The only time I really lost my temper was when I was representing the UK and the Northern Europe Zone on the International Spirituality Commission. I had been invited to attend the meeting to give the ecumenical aspect a voice. We sat down on the day after everybody had arrived to work out an agenda. I suppose there must have been about thirty people from all over the world. When it was my turn to say something, all I had to say was that I saw absolutely no point in talking about the spirituality of L'Arche, or in deciding what it is, if there were no assistants around to live it. It was at a time when I was very conscious of the stress that people were living with, and I said that I thought we had to look at the needs of assistants in this regard because you can't split off spirituality from being well.

That started something rolling and we spent three days talking about assistants and their needs. So I feel very proud of having lost my temper that day!

I am reminded of another meeting of the International Spirituality Commission at Trosly in 1995. The theme was "meeting the needs of assistants, especially those living in community households," a subject I had previously insisted on including. If we really wanted to have any assistants left to live the spirituality of L'Arche, we needed to do something about helping them to stay on. At that time there were real difficulties everywhere. People were getting much too tired and stressed and were giving up.

Another participant at this meeting made the link between our spiritual needs and our psychological needs. This was Anne de Bargue, a psychologist and psychotherapist who had worked with assistants in Trosly for many years. I translated her excellent talk into English and sent copies to all community leaders in 1995. The title of her talk was interesting: "Becoming an adult while sharing in the life of a community house." In a way, we were at a time of transition during which an awful lot of attention, energy, and interest were, for the first time, being put into the whole question of human resources. For instance, what Anne de Bargue was saying was that stress can overwhelm young people when they grow up and become adults in the context of a community where they are care assistants.

ECUMENICAL VOCATION

God speaks to us through people and events. Looking back, we can see that L'Arche, a Roman Catholic foundation in France, came to England, where we received the very warm welcome of the Church of England, allowing us to settle in Barfrestone. Through a series of challenges, we discovered our ecumenical vocation, stemming from the needs and rights of our people to belong to their own churches. Certain customs or traditions—the shared meal and the night prayer, for example—have become ways to share in spirit together. One of the traditions from Trosly that we enjoy is celebration whenever possible—birthdays, the comings and goings of people—any excuse for a great celebration in the community. The rituals of death and burials are also important. These domestic liturgies became immensely important in all our communities, particularly as they provide an opportunity for unity that we cannot have around the Eucharist.

Anglican Bishop Stephen Verney became a very good friend of L'Arche Lambeth and visited the community on a regular basis. On one occasion he wrote to us about community and Eucharist, "You know you are Eucharistic communities. Take the bread, receive the bread, which each of you is for the other. Give thanks and bless. Experience the brokenness within you and give the bread that you are to one another." Years ago, we started a tradition of handing out blessed bread to the different houses at the end of a Eucharist (not the consecrated bread but blessed bread). I remember I often handed out the blessed bread and quoted what Stephen had said.

In the 1970s, covenant retreats began to be organized to help members of L'Arche formally declare a covenant about their commitment to live according to the spirit and principles of L'Arche. For a long time I went to covenant retreats with L'Arche in France or Belgium. There the covenant was closely linked with the celebration of the Eucharist. The rite of announcing the covenant took place just before communion. When people were announcing the covenant or when they were talking about doing so during the retreat, I used to sit there in tears. I couldn't see how I could ever participate. This was at a Roman Catholic Eucharist and there was not anybody else there from the UK. More particularly, there were no Anglicans. By that time the UK communities were evenly divided between Roman Catholic and Anglican members. I didn't see any way out of it because I also saw how very helpful the covenant was to many people.

Not until 1986 did a group of us meet to work out the implications of an ecumenical covenant retreat in England. We sought to formulate a liturgy at which to announce the covenant, which was other than the Eucharist. Suddenly the idea of a ritual "Washing of Feet" emerged, replacing holy communion on one of the days of the retreat. In an ecumenical retreat, the "Washing of the Feet" became the central liturgy on the last day of the retreat. It was the liturgy during which people could express the desire to live a covenant with the poor and the weak. Subsequently, in many L'Arche communities the ritual of foot washing that was first developed in covenant retreats has been adopted. As a result, the afternoon of Maundy Thursday has become an important occasion on which we ceremonially wash one another's feet before we go off to celebrate the Eucharist in our own parishes. In our ecumenical reality, we were all living the divisions, not just talking about them. I believe it was this living experience that eventually led us to the healing experienced in washing each other's feet—putting into effect St. John's Gospel of the Last Supper.

AFTERWORD

In 1976, Thérèse Vanier left her position as founding director of L'Arche Kent, the first L'Arche community in the UK, moving to south London to become founding director of L'Arche Lambeth for four years. From 1975 into the 1980s, she also served as regional coordinator for what became the Northern Europe Region. Meanwhile, until she retired in 1988, Thérèse continued to work at

*St. Christopher's Hospice and often spoke about
its work at international conferences. In 1995, she
received honorary degrees from both the University
of Southampton and the University of Ottawa, in
recognition of her pioneering contributions to palliative care and work with people with intellectual
disabilities.*

*Between 1990 and 2010, Thérèse wrote several
books:* An Ecumenical Journey *(1990),* Nick: Man
of the Heart *(1993),* One Bread, One Body *(1997),
and* The Founding Story of L'Arche in the UK
*(2010). She continued to participate in the Lam-
beth community, living nearby in a flat until 2007
when she moved to St. Peter's Residence in South
London. Her insistence on the need to blend love
and competence while ensuring assistants' physical, mental, and emotional health remained constant themes. In 2013, she celebrated her ninetieth
birthday with her brother Jean and other friends.
She died on June 15, 2014. In honor of her passion
for ecumenism, the dean of Canterbury Cathedral
agreed to have her funeral there. It was thought to
be the first Roman Catholic funeral mass held in the
cathedral nave since the Reformation.*

*The continuing relevance of Thérèse's work
and philosophy is explored in a 2015 biography
by Ann Shearer, titled* Thérèse Vanier: Pioneer
of L'Arche, Palliative Care and Spiritual Unity,
*which draws on the memories of nearly fifty people
who knew her as well as her own published and
unpublished writings. In that book, many noted
Thérèse's sense of humor. Once she gave longtime
L'Arche member Hazel Bradley her own version of
the Ten Commandments:*

SHARING LIFE

1. *Thou shalt not be perfect, nor even try to be.*
2. *Thou shalt not try to be all things to all people.*
3. *Thou shalt not leave undone things that ought to be done.*
4. *Thou shalt not spread thyself too thin.*
5. *Thou shalt learn to say "No."*
6. *Thou shalt schedule time for thyself and thy supportive network.*
7. *Thou shalt switch off and recharge—regularly.*
8. *Thou shalt be boring, untidy, inelegant, and unattractive at times.*
9. *Thou shalt not even feel guilty.*
10. *Especially thou shalt not be thine own worst enemy, but be thy best friend.*

Chapter 5

"WHAT ABOUT AFRICA?"

L'Arche in the Ivory Coast, 1974

DAWN BARRAQUÉ

INTRODUCTION

Dawn Follet (Dawn Barraqué after her marriage in 1984) was the founding director of L'Arche in the Ivory Coast in February 1974. Dawn's road to L'Arche began in March 1971 when, as a psychology student in her final year at Queen's University in Canada, she met Jean Vanier. Raised in the United Church of Canada and nurtured by the Evangelical student group Inter-Varsity Christian Fellowship as a teenager, she had become dissatisfied with her studies and yearned for something that would connect more fully with her strong faith. She was drawn to a public talk Jean gave at the university because she had grown up with a cousin who had Down syndrome and had actively volunteered during her university years with people with intellectual disabilities. Dawn remembers being inspired by Jean speaking of L'Arche in India: "His message was strong: 'Who will bridge the gap between the rich and the poor?' 'How in our lives can we reach out to those in real need?' He spoke about how much he had personally learned from his life with people with intellectual disabilities: 'How much their thirst for relationship could open our own hearts.'" She recalls, "I felt that this was a very clear answer for what I had been looking for." She spoke with Jean and arrived in Trosly that September.

Her initial role was in the kitchen at the Val Fleuri and on their assistants team. All she had been looking for in her studies of psychology, sociology, and theology felt deeply unified here in a wonderfully interior and concrete way. She was struck by the suffering and thirst for relationship of the men in the Val Flueri: "Working in the kitchen was a privileged place since many came just to talk. They had suffered from abandonment by their families and years in psychiatric institutions." She found herself nourished by the spiritual life of the community and the prayer in the home together after evening meal. Her rudimentary French soon improved with such an intensive immersion. She took on a number of different roles in the community, including short periods in the new home in Pierrefonds and at la Nacelle in Breuil, and an inspiring time of helping welcome new assistants until her departure for the Ivory Coast in February 1974.

Along with gaining such a range of different experiences in Trosly, three inspiring features helped prepare Dawn for taking up the call for Africa. One was that she participated in various retreats that Jean Vanier gave in many different cultural contexts. She recalls, "I think Jean was always happy to have people from the community who would go to pray and who could share about what we lived and discovered at L'Arche." These retreats with Jean strongly confirmed Dawn's desire to stay in L'Arche. A second feature that expanded Dawn's vision of L'Arche was hearing about Jean's travels abroad and Gabrielle Einsle's stories about the growth of L'Arche in India. Dawn notes, "Progressively I felt a deep and persistent call to live with L'Arche in a poorer country and poorer situation. I wanted to talk with Jean about this growing desire but was worried that he would say, "Are you kidding?" thinking that I was not strong enough for such a challenge. But Jean took my request seriously, and said it was important to listen to this inner desire and that we would carry it together. A third feature of preparation for Dawn was becoming Roman Catholic. Despite being raised in the United Church of Canada, she went to daily Mass whenever she could and was welcomed by Père Thomas. Through her time in Trosly the mass and adoration became central to her faith and were a key concern when the possibility of Africa began surfacing. She reflects, "There was something very strong that if Africa was a call for me, I had to be sure to have the strength of daily communion." Dawn was confirmed in the Roman Catholic Church at a normal daily Mass celebrated *by Père Thomas in June 1973 with Jean Vanier as her godfather.*

The account now continues in Dawn's own words.

"WHAT ABOUT AFRICA?"

Looking thoughtfully at the map on the wall, Jean asked me rather surprisingly, "What about Africa?" I had been thinking about India. Ever since Gabrielle's talks about L'Arche in India, it had begun to seem familiar. But Jean said, "I would see you much better in Africa than in India!" When I had spoken to Jean about wanting to live L'Arche in a poorer context, two other Canadian assistants in Trosly, Gus Leuschner and Debbie Pond, had likewise seen Jean with the same sort of request. Perhaps there might be a team here. With Jean's encouragement, Gus, Debbie, and I met in a local café where we thought, shared, and above all prayed together about this new idea. We were open and amazingly peaceful although we knew it meant jumping into something totally unknown for us. Our answer was, "Well, why not? Sure! We will at least go ahead, see, discern as things advance." Each of us had confidence in Jean, in his judgement and his desire to do what Jesus wanted. Above all we had confidence in the Holy Spirit inspiring and guiding us in a very strong way.

I think Jean always had an intuition and desire for L'Arche in Africa. Over the years through his retreats, through extensive travel and the diplomatic background of his family, he had gathered many contacts with people from different African countries. Jean took out his address book and started to write to his various African contacts. It could be a doctor, a parent of a child with a learning disability, a bishop, all sorts of people in any country. He just sent letters saying, "This is L'Arche, this is what we offer, do you think this would be of interest to your country?" We received positive responses from Senegal, which shortly declined, Cameroon, Upper Volta (which later was to become Burkina Faso), and the Ivory Coast.

SCOUTING TRIP TO CAMEROON, IVORY COAST, AND BURKINA FASO

In December 1973, I set off with Françoise Cambier, who was head of homes in community of Trosly, for an initial scouting trip. Our objective was to discern the best place to begin since this would be the first L'Arche foundation on the African continent. Where did the desire of the people we met and the local needs correspond to what L'Arche had to offer? Where would we have the most support? In each country we met people from ministries of social affairs or health, doctors or nurses close to local needs and "solutions," and associations that worked with people with disabilities. We met with people from Protestant and Catholic churches and, when possible, people of Muslim faith. Each time we explained what L'Arche was—such a small thing in a way!

CHOOSING THE IVORY COAST

When we came back, we sat with Jean, Gus, and Debbie and told them all about the people we had met and the feelings we had in the different places. What were the signs of the Spirit when we listened to all that had been heard and seen? We looked at the big map of Africa again. It seemed clear that the Ivory Coast would have the people and structures to help us begin, and they had a real openness and desire to welcome L'Arche. Shortly after, we were able to meet an Ivorian bishop, Bishop Bernard Agré, who was visiting in Paris. We told him about our desire to begin a small community of L'Arche in the Ivory Coast. Bishop Agré was extremely positive, extending an invitation to come to his diocese in Man in the west of the country. His warm invitation and enthusiasm confirmed our recent choice. So all was "go" for our departure. So many questions, but also such peaceful confidence!

Gus was twenty-five, I was not quite twenty-three, and Debbie even younger. Gus and Debbie prepared the upcoming departure in their own way by getting married in Canada at the end of December! I nervously thought, "Great!" and they probably had their own apprehensions! I thought it was going to be uncomfortable, and that a team of a couple and a celibate might be tough on everyone. But it *was* great and I have such good memories of this first founding team. We had so much to live together and to share, but it was a delight to work things through with Gus and Debbie. I am sure that it must not have been always easy for them since we spent a lot of time all together.

Just a few days before we left for the Ivory Coast, I remember asking Jean two questions: "Jean, if I am not able to adjust there, can I come back?" Jean said, "Of course." The second thing I asked was, "What do you do to found a L'Arche community?" I could imagine how things might go the first day, but I wondered by the second day, "What will we do after breakfast?" Jean's answer wasn't particularly reassuring, "I can't say, I can't tell you what to do." I think more than a confidence in us, Jean had a great confidence in Providence, and that helped me also to put my confidence where it should be!

ARRIVING IN ABIDJAN, IVORY COAST, FEBRUARY 1974

The morning of our departure, L'Arche Trosly came together to see us off at the chapel. We felt really called and sent by L'Arche. As planned, Fr. Pierre Marie Coty (who was later to become bishop of Daloa) was at the airport to meet us. He took us to stay with the sisters of a local Ivorian congregation, Our Lady of Africa in Treichville, a busy neighborhood of Abidjan. Coming from the airport, Fr. Coty said, "I have spoken to Archbishop Bernard Yago, to my cousin who is director of customs and an active member of a parents' association for people with intellectual disabilities, and Dr. Max Hazera, psychiatrist and coordinator of the mental health services." He continued, "I'll come and pick you up tomorrow after breakfast and we will go to see these people." So my question, "What do we do to begin a community?" started simply to unfold. Each time we saw someone, the archbishop or the director of customs gave us new ideas of important contacts. Things just seemed to advance like this from the very first day on, starting right after breakfast! It was a question of going ahead step-by-step, with our eyes and ears and hearts open. So often, at least the "next step" seemed to be clear. As Gus said, "Things just seemed to come together."

Archbishop Yago had already found a house for us in Abidjan! He showed us a house near the school and sheltered workshop that had been created by the parents' association similar to structures that existed in France. We were happy to visit the center, to exchange with the people who worked there, and to meet members of the parents' association. We sensed the association's hope that L'Arche could offer a residential solution to their activity since all of their people came on a daily basis. The parents' association was composed of some very influential people in Abidjan, some of whom we had already met.

But soon we felt clearly that this was not the right way for us to begin. We feared that the pressure to fulfill expectations already expressed by parents and local influential people would interfere with us discovering what L'Arche should be in this new setting and on the African continent. Would we be free to discern, to "create" such a small thing as L'Arche? At the same time, we had a deep feeling that this first African seed of L'Arche would be lost in the vast urban expanse of Abidjan.

PERHAPS BOUAKÉ?

One of our contacts in the Ivory Coast had been given to us by Madame Pauline Vanier, Jean's mother, who lived in the Trosly community. Fr. Denis Martin was the abbot of a Benedictine monastery in Bouaké, and Madame Vanier knew him well when her husband, Georges Vanier, was Ambassador in Paris. Bouaké was the second city located in the center of the country and we decided to go there to see if it might be a better place for our small L'Arche home. Madame Vanier had written ahead to the monastery to introduce us as "three educators who would be coming to found a L'Arche home: Mr. and Mrs. Leuschner and Miss Dawn Follett." They came to the train to meet us but kept waiting to see if other people were getting off the train. They initially thought we were offspring of the visitors and told us later that they almost asked us, "Where are your parents?" Our "founding team" did look rather young. Fr. Denis Martin really took us under his wing! The fact that we were young, naive no doubt, unthreatening, and an almost improbable team, turned out to be at many times a real advantage. Many people felt we needed their help to be able to begin a L'Arche home in the Ivory Coast and they were indeed right! Their help as well as God's constant guidance at each step was essential.

Fr. Denis took us to meet various people in Bouaké. We became close to one of the local religious communities. Clair Logis worked with young girls teaching many practical skills and helping them to be responsible for their choices within the local culture. There was a small psychiatric center in Bouaké with a psychiatrist who showed an interest in our project and who we knew would be a resource person for us. Bouaké was a large city with the necessary resources but, on a human level, a better size to begin the community. Where in Abidjan we felt overwhelmed and even a bit lost by the size and complexity, we felt comfortable and quickly "at home" in Bouaké. We also felt the central location of Bouaké might be a future advantage if later there should be expansion to Man, where Bishop Agré had extended such a warm invitation, or even Burkina Faso.

FIRST HOUSE IN BOUAKÉ

Fr. Denis took us to meet Mr. Sounkalo Djibo, mayor of Bouaké. He made a small house available to us in Aouniansou, one of the neighborhoods of Bouaké. It was a small house, a simple one but perfect for us. We could go out to walk in the neighborhood, to the market, to our nearby church. Neighbors noticed us and had questions just seeing us. There was a back part in the yard where we could have a small prayer room and, later, two extra bedrooms. Best of all was the proximity with neighbors, especially one Muslim family with whom we became very close. Their children were always at our place, wanting to help out, to show us things, to teach us words, songs, and dances, to teach us to cook and garden—and we had so much to learn! They were enthusiastic and patient teachers! It's true that there were almost no other white people living in that area, so we were a bit of an attraction.

Clair Logis had introduced us to Monique and her family, who lived only five minutes from our new house. Monique, who was perhaps twelve years old, had a severe intellectual disability. We were able to visit her regularly. These frequent visits helped us to discover the daily life of a family who had a child with special needs, Monique's place within her family, their respective needs, and how perhaps we could be of a support to them. This contact and growing friendship was of mutual benefit. Monique was so excited each day we came to visit, knowing we were coming especially for her!

BOARD OF DIRECTORS

A board of directors was necessary, a body that would permit our legal existence and help us make the right decisions in this new culture. Our contacts were important to be able to form this board. After an initial week or so at the monastery, we realized that we needed to be closer to the city to continue exploring, so we stayed with Clair Logis for a month. One of their team members, Angele Bocciarelli, became one of our founding board members. The closeness of Clair Logis to the people and their roots in the Church and local culture helped us to learn so many precious things!

Fr. Denis Martin and Clair Logis introduced us to other committed local professional people, some of whom became members of our founding board of directors. Jean had said that to determine who would be the president of the board of directors, we would recognize this person because they would say, "Your project interests me, what can I do to help?" When Jean visited us for the first time in May 1974 and gave a talk at the local cultural center, one of our contacts, Mr. Sebastien Djibo, a pharmacist and also the mayor of Bouaké's son, stood up at the end and said word for word Jean's famous phrase, "Your project interests me, what can I do to help?" He became president of the founding board of directors!

Also during Jean's first visit at the end of May, we met for a second time with the mayor, Mr. Djibo, who promised us two and a half acres of land in this same neighborhood as our house. Our explorations in the city had shown us how houses were typically small and grouped together in a courtyard so that it would be difficult to rent a house large enough for a L'Arche community to grow, especially with room for work activities. How blessed we were to have been promised property for future growth.

FUNDING AND SUPPORT FROM L'ARCHE INTERNATIONAL

Our funding at first was from L'Arche International. Other than Bangalore and Calcutta in India, we were the only other foundation in what were then called "third world countries." L'Arche sent us and supported us financially for the foundation period. We knew that we could not ask for financial help from the Ivory Coast at that point in time. On an international level, L'Arche itself was financed mainly by donations. For many capital investments of the community, they looked for financial support from international organizations. The Canadian government's International Development Agency (CIDA) helped finance our initial capital costs, as they had in India. I realize how fortunate we were to have secure funding support so that we could focus on welcoming our first founding members and discovering our community life and call.

Later, when we came to build new projects, we did what we could to find money locally. I often travelled to Abidjan and went almost door-to-door to different embassies or larger religious communities, seeking financial support, making sure to speak of L'Arche and our community in Bouaké. The Canadian embassy, the Catholic Committee against Hunger and for Development in France, an organization in Switzerland, and many others helped us. We found capital donations for the building of the home, the funding of the chicken farm, and the building of a small school. It took time to build up a request file, to present the new project with budget and financial details, and then to report back when the project was achieved.

Running costs for daily living were more difficult to cover with outside funds. Each time we came back to France or Canada, we gave talks and shared about our small new community, hoping for interest and financial support. Later, the Ivorian government gave a very small contribution to our expenses, and we appreciated the gesture as one of recognition, knowing how many development priorities they had.

WELCOMING OUR FIRST FOUNDING MEMBER, JUNE 1974

We welcomed our first core member on June 18, 1974! Saturday had already spent a long time at the local psychiatric center, and we met him there many times. Since he was unable to speak, the center had no information on his origins. They named him Saturday, which was the day of his arrival at the center. Now we were able to welcome him. No luggage, no extra clothes, Saturday came to L'Arche riding on the motor bike with Gus! I marvel at how much trust he must have had to leave the center, which was his only security, and come with Gus to an unknown place. We were so excited, but once Saturday arrived, we realized how little we had to offer him! That day we watered a few plants together in our garden and walked in the neighborhood. For no doubt the first time in his life, we handed him a dish towel so that he could dry the dishes with us! Locally, women washed the dishes and let them dry in the sun. He must have thought we were crazy! Saturday was gentle, and certainly started to smile and even almost laugh.

NEIGHBORS

We learned eagerly from neighbors and friends about details of daily life and spent time at neighbors' homes just being there and taking things in. The children of the family just across our street spent so much time with us. We got to know each of them and saw them grow over the years. The many afternoons we spent at Monique's family were also enriching. It was an advantage to really live with the local people. An important aspect of L'Arche that surprised people was that we would live all together: persons with intellectual disabilities and those without such disabilities; people of the local Ivorian culture and people from France and Canada. Even the local religious congregations found it an almost unrealistic challenge. We knew that we needed to integrate as much as possible to avoid imposing our way of doing things. But we knew that as soon as there would be local persons with intellectual disabilities and local assistants within our L'Arche home, they would lead us with integrating and we would make our way together.

DISCOVERING OUR PRAYER TOGETHER

We counted on prayer. We were so aware that the whole thing was over and above us. Yet we knew there were many choices to be made. There was a way we needed to find, God's way. This meant listening, asking, discerning.

We had a time of evening prayer together, and in our new house in Aouniansou, we used one of the rooms as our small chapel. Weekly Mass, either at Aouniansou or at the Benedictine monastery, was nourishing. The Mass in our own neighborhood was very long and very colorful, with music, dance, and many children. The liturgy at the monastery was beautiful, with music, psalms, and a quiet atmosphere to meditate on the readings. Each brought such a depth of prayer, the possibility of offering all that was given daily in this new adventure. Days off were often spent at the monastery to take time to pray and to rest. We were faithful to these times because we really needed them.

Although at that time we did not know it, the first person with intellectual disabilities that we welcomed was of the Muslim faith. At first, Saturday had no signs of any practice of his own faith. But as his health stabilized and there was more confidence and trust between us, he started to show his own religious practice with times of personal prayer in his room. During the first few years, Saturday always attended the times of community prayer in our small prayer room or, later, chapel, but over time, he would attend only occasionally. We took him to the mosque each Friday, and we all accompanied him when he went to the main mosque at the end of Ramadan or on the celebration of Eid Al-Adha since it was a main local event in Bouaké.

The diversity of the origins and faith of the persons with intellectual disabilities that were welcomed over the years reflected the diversity of the situation in Bouaké and the Ivory Coast. All religious days of celebration—Muslim or Christian—were celebrated by all. This helped us find a way of praying together. The evening prayer around the light of our candles, with songs, short texts, or meditations, was a time of coming together, offering our daily life to God, giving thanks, and asking for his love, protection, and guidance. Occasionally over the years, there would be new assistants that would question the time of prayer and its daily practice. But since the persons with intellectual disabilities were in the chapel each evening waiting, having lit the candles (often using quite a few matches to do so), assistants soon realized that this was an essential moment in the lives of the people living in the home.

"SATURDAY" BECOMES SEYDOU

Saturday settled in little by little. Yet since he did not speak, we knew so little of him. He had a heavy medical treatment of neuroleptics that made it hard for him to control the movement of his hands. Since he suffered from mental illness rather than an intellectual disability, these medications were essential but with evident side effects. After a few weeks, we went together with Saturday to the main market place, one of the biggest open-air markets in western Africa. We came to the place where there was jewelry and products from northern Africa. To our surprise we realized the merchants seemed to recognize Saturday. We were even more astonished when they started to talk to him, and Saturday answered them! We learned that he spoke Hausa, a language from the border of Niger with Nigeria. These merchants travelled back and forth from the north to the Ivory Coast to sell jewelry and various things. From them we learned that Saturday's real name was Seydou Aousman. Seydou just lit up, and we were so excited at this discovery!

Seydou had been a jewel trader and had travelled for many years with these people. He had a wife and a child in his village in Niger. Progressively, he had become mentally ill until these friends had confined him in a building because of his aggressive behavior. But he soon escaped to Bouaké, wandered the streets, and was picked up and sent to the psychiatric center. Seydou had a whole history, a whole life story! This providential meeting allowed him to reconnect with his past, enabled us to discover something of Seydou, and opened up so many changes for him.

Another day shortly after, Seydou was with us when we went to the post office. In front of the building, Abdullah often begged. As soon as he saw Seydou, he started to speak with him. We invited him to come and share an occasional meal, and he and Seydou were able to talk and talk. He helped us again to know more about Seydou and helped Seydou come out his suffering world. After that point, he progressed a lot. He soon needed no medication. He was a good worker and became autonomous in many ways. He would walk into town and come back on his own. He was very quiet, very "wise." But even after many years, Seydou still had such a deep sadness in his eyes, despite his capacity to smile and even laugh with us. Obviously, we had not discovered everything that he had lived and endured.

N'GORAN, OCTOBER 1974

N'Goran was the second person with an intellectual disability to be welcomed, also from the nearby psychiatric center. He had been wandering, especially near the market place, finding food that had been thrown away as garbage. He had been taken to the psychiatric center a number of times, but each time, he would just leave and wander the streets again. The first day he came to Aouniansou, we all sat with Seydou around a low table for the noon meal and he said in Baoulé, "I am dirty, I cannot eat with you." So he sat on the floor in a corner with his plate. Not sure of how to react, the first day we didn't do anything, and the second day it was the same thing. One day we decided to move the table in front of him and we all sat around him on the floor. That made him laugh and was the start of a different kind of relationship.

Like Seydou, N'Goran suffered more from mental illness than intellectual disability. He had many hallucinatory periods each day, talking to people he seemed to see behind us or just next to us, shouting and hitting out at them. He never hit one of us, and he always seemed to control his gestures against these imaginary people that seemed to threaten him. When he watered the garden, he would empty out the watering can over one poor plant while he argued with the imaginary people just next to him! Despite this, one could sense that N'Goran was a gentle man. Fortunately, the psychiatric center helped us with N'Goran's medical treatment over this initial period.

Gus along with Seamus Browne, who had come from

Trosly in May to join our team, worked daily with Seydou and N'Goran. Together they watered our very tiny garden, worked on making wood beds for the home, then worked in the field and planted yams on the nearby property that the mayor had given us for future construction. We continued to visit Monique in her home setting and to benefit from all the contacts we had with our neighbors and new friends. Our life was simple.

BUILDING A NEW HOUSE

The land that the mayor had given us was in the same neighborhood as our first house. This meant we could already begin working there with Seydou and N'Goran. It allowed Gus to monitor the construction once it began and permitted us to keep our new neighbors and friends. Walking to church, to the local market, was still possible, and we could still be part of the neighborhood.

Gus worked on the plans of the new house with a Dutch architect and member of our board of directors, Frantz VonBeers. Frantz had lived many years in Bouaké, was married to an Ivorian lady, and their children had been born in the Ivory Coast. We wanted something simple, to make a home that would be like a local courtyard with the construction of "cases" built around a common open area. The construction began February 1975, and the home was ready in July. At first the house felt just too big and too new, but as it became "lived in," we realized it was wonderful—the inner courtyard with the buildings around was very unifying yet open. Unfortunately, Gus and Debbie left at that time and never had the chance to live with us in the new home! Debbie was expecting their first child, and they knew it was important for them to return to Canada.

ASSISTANTS SENT BY L'ARCHE

After Gus and Debbie left, our next assistants came from L'Arche Trosly and later from other European or Canadian L'Arche communities. Most stayed for two years and many went on to L'Arche elsewhere when they left Bouaké. First, Jean with the support of L'Arche Trosly and, then, international vice-coordinators Alain St. Machary and Hubert Allier helped to find assistants to come live in L'Arche Bouaké. Louise Cummings and John McManus were among the first to join our team. Others up until the end of 1980 included Dominique and Christiane Gilbert, Geneviève Pasquet (Kouassi-Brou), Cathy Assailly, Franck Janin, Joanne Veillette, Anne Durieux, Sue Bailey, Marie Mulliez, and Pierre Barraqué.

CHALLENGES WITH NEW TEAMS

One of the hardest things for me during these early years was being a team leader. I was the director of a small community that still had to find its way, and to feel at times my team members' lack of confidence was difficult. That was a situation that could happen anywhere and was not linked to being in Africa. It followed from being a foundation with no set guidelines and most definitely also came from my own inexperience as a team leader.

With Gus and Debbie it was different because we had been together in this call from the very beginning. It was a call and mission that we shared. I do not even think we had doubts in ourselves because we were so obviously sure of not having all the answers. We knew we needed to pray together and we needed to find the way of the community together. There was something that deeply bonded us in that and gave mutual confidence. There was something about being small in front of the daily gifts of God, his daily love and guidance.

When Gus and Debbie left and I found myself with the new teams that followed, I was still relatively young and the community was still very new. The people who just arrived looked to me for answers and did not necessarily have confidence in me, and I did not have all the answers either. It was the hard situation of trying to go forward with some members who I felt were always doubting and saying, "Are you sure we go that way? Shouldn't we go another way? Are you sure we should do that?" I started to doubt and second-guess myself. Their lack of confidence and my doubt was something that made it harder to go ahead. It was the question of finding again the "together" but also accepting a certain role of leadership. Building confidence and trust had to be part of the foundation of the new community. We needed to find together a thirst for God's will and God's way. I remember this as a difficult time but recognize that this experience deepened me and taught me a valuable lesson about taking leadership and working in a team that I have been called to use over the years.

LOCAL ASSISTANTS

We knew from the experience of the religious communities around us that it would take time for the local people to join us and stay. Our call was unique and our identity was still hard to define. "Who were we?" We did not offer the long-term security of a religious community. We lived with persons with intellectual disabilities. But was this "living together" attractive? We were growingly conscious of how much we needed local people to be the advocates of those who were touched by a "handicap," a mental sickness, or an intellectual disability, and to witness to others about sharing life with these people.

Geneviève Konaté came as our cook as we entered our new house and was an extremely important member of our community. The outside kitchen was a strategic place of the newly built house and of our community relationships. Whenever possible, people sat around the fire where Genevieve was cooking and talked. Whenever Geneviève arrived in the morning, always with her new baby attached by her colorful *pagne* on her back, she was so warmly welcomed. Her presence brought much life!

Marcelline Kanga, one or our first local assistants, came in September 1977 and is still an assistant in the Bouaké community today. Despite not having training in this area, she had a natural and well-adjusted sense of pedagogy with the people with intellectual disabilities. Her direct way of speaking sometimes helped in the community. She would clearly answer the questions that people in the neighborhood asked about living with people with intellectual disabilities.

Others came and stayed only briefly, but Adèle Kouakou, who came in May 1978, and Monique Koffi, who came in February 1979, are still with the community today. A friend in our neighborhood and local parish, Marcelline Affoué became a member of the community and one of the first Ivorian directors. She gave courageous leadership during the conflicts of 2002 in the Ivory Coast when the whole community had to exile to the south for their own safety for over six years.

DISCERNMENT AND ACCOMPANIMENT IN DELICATE SITUATIONS

Later, there were some difficulties with certain local assistants. Since the culture was so different, at first we lacked

proper discernment with the assistants we welcomed. As anywhere in L'Arche, good discernment is necessary. Here it took us
time to learn. As we had come from L'Arche in Trosly, our own
experience was that we had been quickly given much responsibility. We were aware that this had helped us to grow and to
want to continue with L'Arche. This is what we wanted to live
here. We wanted to show our trust yet sometimes we lacked
judgment. Sometimes it was too much responsibility, sometimes too quickly given.

There were two things that I learned. First, in certain situations we gave too much responsibility to local people in areas
concerning money, not realizing what a difficult situation this
put them in. Although we tried in the community to live simply, we had such an abundance of material things compared
to those in our immediate environment. There were so many
expectations from family and from village members of a local
assistant who worked "for the white people" or who even just
had a steady job. Sometimes the pressure of these expectations
and the daily contact with money or material items pushed or
encouraged these assistants to divert money. This conflict of
loyalties was in some cases extremely difficult to live.

The second thing I learned was that if there was necessarily money involved, our responsibility as a partner was to assure
a close follow-up of the daily situation. We ourselves tended
to see this follow-up as a "control" in a negative way when in
fact it was really a support. With such support, many unhappy
situations could have perhaps been avoided or detected more
quickly to be able to work on solutions together in a more positive way. Often the people concerned were people with otherwise wonderful qualities. Many of these situations we feel that
we failed through lack of judgment or accompaniment. Again,
time, learning, and experience helped.

LOCAL FEARS ABOUT PERSONS WITH INTELLECTUAL DISABILITIES

Little by little, we gained a better understanding of the situation of people with intellectual disabilities in the Ivory Coast. There were certainly fears. Was the person with a handicap "possessed" by an evil spirit? Was the family being punished? If this was the belief, the person would be kept in their village, but people would be frightened and so avoid contact with them. More traditionally, some of these people could have been eliminated, especially if the handicap was detected at birth. Were these people sick or contagious? Often epileptic seizures or drooling were thought to be contagious. No one would want to touch them or eat out of the same dish, which was the normal way of eating in the neighborhood families and villages. Pregnant women especially would avoid them since there was a danger of contagion. They would be fed but again avoided. I remember once going with N'Goran to watch a local football game. The stadium was full, but I suddenly noticed that despite this, within a few minutes the benches around us had emptied. Often families of Muslim or Christian faith, although they did not understand "why the person was born like this," believed they were still a "gift of Allah," a "gift of God." Then the family looked after them, often with care and sometimes with reverence.

The behavior of the person with the intellectual disability was an important factor in the reaction around them. Families could be pushed beyond their limits in knowing what to do. Sometimes the person would have dangerous behavior, dangerous either to the group or to themselves. There were no support systems for these situations; few had medical treatments or follow-up. We had found Bakari, a small boy who came to live with us, attached by his foot in a chicken coop just outside of his house. We had been shocked by this, but we soon realized after looking for him all around Bouaké every day that his family had become extremely frustrated and were just trying to cope. Bakari found more security in the community, but each time we tried to work things out with his family, Bakari's fear of his father put us back at the starting point. It was essential for us to understand the situation of the person in their own environment and to bring different kinds of support to their family or village to foster understanding, acceptance, and assistance for this more vulnerable member. Gradually, we increased the time spent with families of people with intellectual disabilities.

AMOUIN: A TURNING POINT IN THE COMMUNITY

N'Goran returned to the psychiatric center for an adjustment in his medical treatment. There was a young girl there who was hemiplegic, and her left arm and leg were quite handicapped. She jumped from person to person looking for affection. But since the other people there were themselves not well, they chased her away, sometimes violently. We noticed each day during the meal that N'Goran would put aside the meat or the fish—which obviously was the best part of the meal—and save it for Amouin. More and more often, Amouin would be sitting quietly beside N'Goran, and we saw their relationship growing. When we came to the Ivory Coast, we began a home for adults like L'Arche in Trosly. Though our desire was to discover our way in this new culture, it was still obvious that Trosly was our reference. We had the following questions about taking this little girl: "Wouldn't she be better in her own family?" and "Would we know how to accompany a child with what we had learned and experienced?" We talked with the social worker at the psychiatric center, who told us that everything possible had been done to trace her family but without success. N'Goran was ready to go back to the community, and we realized that we could not leave Amouin but must welcome her in our home. This was in September 1975. Over time, we were to discover the needs of other children abandoned in similar situations.

Obviously, welcoming a child would mean meeting their needs as a child, and then meeting their needs as an adolescent. It was the beginning of quite a pathway! But how wonderful this step was because it opened us to welcoming Bakari shortly after and, later, other children—Gabriel, Binta, Saïcha, Innoncente, Bernard, and Asséto—to make a community that was like a large African family. When one visits the Ivory Coast or other countries in Africa, one is struck by the large families with all ages and the life given by so many interactions in the relationships. Here was already Seydou and N'Goran who brought a certain maturity and wisdom, and all the young adults in the community who were also welcomed: Koffi, Mamadou, Gilbert, Kouadio, N'Dabla, and Poyé.

In France or Canada, one would have difficulty imagining this kind of residential solution with people of all different ages, but in the Ivorian setting and later in the other communities in Africa, it turned out to be extremely rich. Welcoming Amouin opened new possibilities and was the turning point in the history of the community. This was an aspect of our community that was "given" and was in no way part of a preconceived project. It meant that the development of the community would be more diversified, trying to meet the needs of each one.

Amouin did have a very beautiful smile. But she also had an insatiable need for affection and attention. The first years were difficult since she needed both attention and gentle limits. When the assistants became exasperated, N'Goran was the one who she would continually go and just sit beside. N'Goran was calm, attentive, welcoming, and never chased her away. Little by little, Amouin found a deep security in the community, in the relationships, and her beautiful smile became also so peaceful. For Amouin, as for so many others, L'Arche became a real place of security. For Bakari, who needed distance from the violence of his father, the community became a place he didn't need to run from anymore. For each child, it became a place of new life.

SEYDOU'S DEATH

One morning in 1980, we saw that Seydou had not come back home. Having become quite autonomous over the years, he would go out walking after work in the evening. This night there had been a heavy rainstorm. Seydou had been hit by a car during the rainstorm, and we found him in the morgue of the local hospital. Since he had no identification papers, he was marked as "Mr. X." He had become someone so important in the community, finding his place as a wise person. The fact that his life ended alone and in the hospital as "Mr. X" after starting out in the community as "Saturday" and then being revealed as Seydou with a whole history was so difficult.

For Seydou's burial, we did not know where to begin. It was important to respect Seydou's Muslim faith. Our very first and still close neighbors as well as Dr. Baba Coulibaly, a doctor and vice president of our board of directors—all of Muslim faith—came to our aid. We contacted Abdullah and Seydou's friends from the market. They too came to help us. It was important that the body be washed in a certain way and wrapped in a perfect white cloth. Everything was done well. We all gathered around Seydou as he was placed into the grave, and we were told that to respect the Muslim traditions and beliefs, we were not to come back to visit it.

Although Seydou had died as "Mr. X," at this moment he was surrounded by people from all periods of his life: links to his past, his village in Niger, and his family were those who had worked with him as a jewelry merchant; those who had been there to help him over the recent years were Abdullah, the faithful neighbors, Dr. Coulibaly, and all the members of the board of directors; and from these last years were all the community members and the new friends who had enabled him to again find health, stability, and his own profound identity. Death is always hard to live, and a sudden death is especially a shock. Seydou was our founding member and the first member to leave us. But we were at peace knowing all that had been brought together around our wise and quiet Seydou.

CONTACT WITH OTHER L'ARCHE COMMUNITIES AND THE INTERNATIONAL COUNCIL

In May 1975, the International Federation meeting of L'Arche at Shadow Lake in Canada named a new international council. I became a part of this council to represent the community in Africa and other nascent projects, initially including L'Arche in Haiti! I was able to visit the Haitian community twice and to discover this small community that, like ours, welcomed children as well as people of all ages, but in such a different cultural setting. It was extremely rich.

The official inauguration of L'Arche Bouaké took place in 1976, and the whole international council (except Jean who was ill) participated in this event and held its meeting at the Benedictine monastery. Later, just before an international council meeting in Bangalore, India, we were able to spend a few days of meeting and sharing together: Gabrielle from India, Robert from Haiti, and myself with the international coordinator and vice-coordinator. What did we learn about L'Arche in these very different cultures? What were our similarities and differences? What did L'Arche in our various countries have to say to the international federation? The number of L'Arche communities exploded over these years!

Bishop Bernard Agré from Man on the western border had been an inspiration and an important contact since the beginning of the project of L'Arche in the Ivory Coast. He reconfirmed his invitation to come to his diocese to begin a L'Arche community there, promised to give us land to begin, and was enthusiastic and insistent in his invitation. It was a tempting idea. Up until then, things had gone relatively smoothly for the new foundation in Bouaké. A second community relatively nearby could be a real support. We knew we could count on Bishop Agré's support, and we had the desire to accept his warm invitation. Bishop Agré had been invited to the L'Arche International meeting at Shadow Lake in May 1975, and Jean Vanier had been invited to give a retreat in Man in August 1975. I was sent once before the retreat to see the situation in Man, to talk more with Bishop Agré, and to prepare the retreat. A community began in Man with another team but, within a few years, closed for a variety of reasons. There were three handicapped persons at that time. One was reintegrated into his village and two came to the community in Bouaké.

For me, the nine years that I spent on the international council was an enriching experience! The international council gave me contact with other L'Arche communities in many different countries and permitted me to explore deeper questions with the council about how to foster new communities that came with the evolution of L'Arche. Since I often came back and forth through France, I was able to keep my links with L'Arche Trosly, which was supportive and nourishing.

DECIDING TO LEAVE THE IVORY COAST COMMUNITY

For some reason, I started to feel that I was living things in a different way, and Jean encouraged me to be attentive. I felt more aware of not being from the same culture. This seems obvious, but the cultural isolation became a heavy feeling. I also found it more difficult when team members left, friendships ended, and a new team had to be rebuilt. I realized I lacked energy now for things that previously could have been lived as challenges. A time of retreat in Trosly with Fr. Andre Dejaers, a Jesuit priest and friend, brought peaceful confirmation that it was time to move on. This being said, it was obviously hard to leave. To be a part of the foundation of the community and above all to witness the sacred pathway of each one had created deep relationships. I left L'Arche Bouaké in October 1983 and was replaced by Claire de Miribel and then Claude Pariseau, both from communities close to Trosly.

SABBATICAL YEAR AFTER LEAVING

After leaving the Ivory Coast, I was able to take a sabbatical year. My desire for that year was to have a learning experience of accompaniment. I ended up staying for a year with the Community Chemin Neuf, an ecumenical and charismatic community, while they had their own sabbatical year of formation, prayer, and discernment as they considered expanding to the Congo. Since there were many links between L'Arche and Chemin Neuf, since I was coming back from an experience in Africa, and since we shared a focus on accompaniment and discernment, they welcomed me in their community in Paris. How fortunate I was! That year gave me time to rest, to pray, to integrate all that I had lived over the years with L'Arche and especially in Bouaké. At Chemin Neuf, the fraternity, the liturgy, and the quality of the times of training, prayer, and celebration were so nourishing for me! At the end of that year, they accepted the call to the Congo and went on to become present and dynamic in over thirty countries.

RELATIONSHIP WITH PIERRE AND DECIDING TO GET MARRIED

My sabbatical was also a time of personal discernment, and in October 1984, I married Pierre Barraqué. Pierre had spent three years in the community of L'Arche Bouaké, and before that, two years in L'Arche Trosly at the Val Fleuri! For our wedding, there was of course Pierre's family and friends from nearby Versailles, but only my parents were able to come from Canada. There were also longtime friends from L'Arche Trosly, including Jean and Barbara, and many of the members of our first foyer, le Val Fleuri. In addition, friends from L'Arche Bouaké—who were now back in France—came, along with members of Chemin Neuf in Paris and all the members of L'Arche Aigrefoin, where we were headed as a couple! One of the priests who married us was Fr. Bernard Poupard, the longtime abbot of the Benedictine monastery in Bouaké and a close friend.

AFTERWORD

Since 1985, Dawn and Pierre Barraqué have been members of L'Arche Aigrefoin in Versailles, France. There they have discovered L'Arche as "a couple," with their respective places in the community and their place together as a family with four children. Up until her recent retirement, Dawn served as assistant coordinator for the community. She remarks on how it has been "such a grace to witness in the lives of so many assistants how meeting people like our more senior community members can bring deep transformation, even as they have attained for themselves a deep level of human maturity and wisdom. The essence of L'Arche is so alive!"

Chapter 6

"ME AT PEACE?"

L'Arche in Haiti, 1975

ROBERT LAROUCHE

INTRODUCTION:
LOOKING FOR AN ABSOLUTE

Robert Larouche, the founding director of L'Arche in Haiti, grew up in Abitibi in northwest Quebec, Canada. As a teenager, he began to reflect on fundamental questions about the meaning of life: Why am I alive? What is it to be human? Does God exist? In the late 1960s, to explore these questions, Robert chose to leave the familiar world of his family and hometown to study philosophy in Ottawa, Canada's capital city. He realized that he needed distance to find motivation for a radical life choice. He relates, "One of my teachers, a priest who had become a friend and guide for me, said to me, 'I think you are looking for an absolute.'" In the early 1970s, Jean

Vanier gave several lectures in Ottawa on the phi-
losophy of art, speaking of a thirst for an absolute
in the artist's heart and mind. Robert felt it deeply
touched his own thirst. At the end of the lecture,
when Jean invited people to meet him in a student
café, Robert went and heard Jean talk about liv-
ing in L'Arche with people with intellectual dis-
abilities. "I remember asking Jean, 'Are you sure
that they are human?'" He was so caught up in
Aristotle's assertion that rationality is the defining
human criterion that he wondered if people who
were not very rational might not be fully human.
Robert recalls, "Jean's response was very generous
and charitable because he could have told me that
it was I who had a deep personal disability! But he
was nonjudgmental."

Robert's philosophy studies had led him to
question most of his religious beliefs, but when a
friend told him about a retreat Jean Vanier was
leading in Quebec, he decided to attend. "I remem-
ber that Jean spoke about Jesus' encounters with
people: with a rich young man; with a Samaritan
woman; with a tax collector. As he spoke, I too lived
these encounters with Jesus and felt within me a
deep desire to respond. I was also touched by his
words about the wounds of love within each one
of us." Through Jean's talks, Robert opened to a
new vision and awareness "that many people were
rejected and were deeply suffering and striving to
alleviate their pain" while at the same time bearing
"qualities of the heart that they could share." Robert
remarks on how Jean's message drew him: "I was
deeply attracted by this call to a life of compassion.

It was not my normal way of relating to people and looking at the world."

After completing his studies, Robert returned to his hometown in Quebec and, for three years, taught philosophy. He read Jean Vanier's writings and was struck by his emphasis on weakness. He also explored the writings of Jean's spiritual mentor, Père Thomas Philippe. Both spoke of suffering, the essential relational nature of human beings, and how the path to wholeness is through love and friendship rather than reason and autonomy. Robert included Jean's thought in his teaching. Although he liked teaching, Robert began realizing that philosophy was "not the absolute I was looking for" and that instead "I was more attracted to the world of relationship." During these three years, Robert also began to visit people with intellectual disabilities who lived in poor conditions in a large group home. Robert came each week with his guitar and was welcomed. He was struck by their thirst for friendship and felt "a compassion that was new for me." He reflects, "My way of looking at life, my philosophy, was changed by this experience." In 1973, Robert proposed to begin a group home in the spirit of L'Arche. He was invited by the local government agency to prepare a budget. Jean, however, advised him to come first to L'Arche Trosly in France for a year of experience, commenting, "First you must learn the laws of community."

The account now continues in Robert's own voice.

A CRY AND CALL FOR L'ARCHE

First, a founding moment from when I initially went to Haiti with Jean Vanier in 1975: During this trip we visited the psychiatric hospital in Port-au-Prince. As we were walking around the various wards, a little girl ran up to us and clung to us and cried out, "Daddy, Daddy, Daddy!" She tried to jump into our arms but at that moment was thrown to the ground by an epileptic seizure. I took her in my arms and put her on a bed in the ward. A few minutes later, we met with the director of the hospital, Dr. Lamarque Douyon. He was forthright and said to us, "L'Arche is needed here in Haiti. I have people in my hospital who need a home. I am afraid that if they stay here, they will die psychologically and even physically." We asked about whom he was speaking. He said, "Come and see," and took us to the very same little girl we had left on the bed. "She is the one who needs a home." Jean looked at Nadine and me and said, "But we have never welcomed children in L'Arche before." And in the next breath added, "But why not?" Her name was Yveline and she was the seed that called L'Arche to Haiti.

LEARNING THE LAWS OF COMMUNITY

In 1974, I had resigned from my job as a teacher to follow Jean's invitation to come to L'Arche Trosly. In my heart I knew this was a decisive choice, a turning point in my life. I had no intention of returning to teaching. When I arrived in Trosly, Jean asked me how long I was intending to stay. I replied that I had no time limits. In fact, I only stayed nine months in Trosly, but it was a time rich with new learning.

My first home in L'Arche was called La Petite Source, a home for women with intellectual disabilities. True to my training as a teacher, I set about relating to the members of my household as an educator, but soon discovered that I was the one who needed to learn. For example, one of the women in the house was a smoker and I thought it was my job to persuade her, for her well-being, to stop smoking. My teammates soon challenged me, arguing that I was taking charge and being overly controlling, that I was not engaging in a mutual relationship. When another woman in the house fell in love with me, my initial response was to run away, but again my fellow assistants helped me understand what was happening, to be present to her gifts and needs so that she and I too might both mature.

I also got to know Jacques Bregola and René Leroy. Both men taught me a lot about what it means to live with a disability, and what a struggle it is for all of us to accept, never mind love, ourselves as we are. Jacques was a challenging man. He tended to be violent toward the young assistants in the house because, I suspect, we represented all he wanted to be. Nonetheless, he also wanted to be our friend. With the advice and support of our psychiatrist, Erol Franko, I was encouraged to engage firmly with Jacques whenever there was an outburst. As a result, he began to respect and trust me, and to learn to be with me without conflict. When Jacques and René asked me to be their godfather at their baptisms, I knew we had become friends.

During the nine months in Trosly, I also discovered the importance of structures and meetings in building community. It seemed as if our whole week was punctuated by meetings: house meetings, pedagogical meetings, planning meetings, community meetings, and more. On top of that there were community celebrations! Yet each was essential. They nourished us as a community and as individuals. Those first nine months in Trosly showed me that L'Arche was a good place for my own growth.

GOING TO HAITI WITH JEAN

In 1975, Jean Vanier told me that he had been invited to go to Haiti to preach a retreat for young people. The invitation came from two quite different sources: one was from two religious working in Haiti—Sr. Micheline Vinet of the Sisters of St. Anne, who worked in a secretarial school, and Fr. Jacques Beaudry, a cleric of St. Viateur and the director of a retreat house in Port-au-Prince. Both were close to the young people of Haiti and felt that Jean's experience in L'Arche would speak to their questions and needs. The second source was the Haitian ambassador in Canada, Mr. Philippe Cantave, who had heard about Jean and wanted him to found a community in Haiti. Jean saw in these two invitations possibilities for the foundation of a community in Haiti.

Jean decided to go and preach the retreat, and invited me and Nadine Tokar, an assistant in Trosly with an interest in Latin America, to accompany him to Haiti and Brazil. One of the goals of the trip was to discern whether there were enough signs and adequate conditions for the eventual foundation of a community in Haiti and Brazil. I was very naive about Haiti, not even knowing where it was on the map! During our three-week stay, Jean preached two retreats for groups of young adults. Our encounters with them opened our eyes to the reality of Haiti and their disillusionment. They came from the diverse social mix of Port-au-Prince, where well-off neighborhoods were situated next to densely populated and socially explosive slums. The country had been ravaged with political violence and was burdened with a dictatorship. Although strongly rooted in their faith, many young people saw no future for themselves in Haiti and considered leaving. Jean's words and call to commitment with the poor challenged them. Yet realistically what prospects lay before them? It became clear to Jean that if L'Arche was to be born in Haiti, it had to be a poor reality among the poor.

SIGNS FOR STARTING L'ARCHE IN HAITI

Throughout our stay in Haiti, Nadine, Jean, and I had been looking out for any signs that would confirm that it was God's will to found a community. We were looking for people who would support such a foundation—Haitian citizens who were open to the cry of people with disabilities and ready to embrace the experience of Christian community as lived in L'Arche. As the weeks went by, I began to sense that the resources were there. The encounter with Yveline had helped the whole project take flesh. The seed for the community was planted in and through Yveline. But another event also became an important sign.

Toward the end of the visit, Jean was invited to give a public talk aimed at professional and civic leaders in Port-au-Prince. The four hundred seats of the hall at the Collège l'Impasse Lavaud were filled with health professionals, government representatives, grassroots medical workers, and civil servants. On the way to the hall, Jean turned to me and said, "Robert, are you ready to stay?" Jean's talk stirred a real desire to act, so people's questions after it were very practical: "What must we do to start such a community?" "Who will help us start?" "We are ready to be involved but where will the money come from?" Jean invited me to the stage to address the meeting. I said that I was ready to stay in Haiti and with their support wished to establish the foundations for a community of L'Arche. Jean then invited those who wanted to support the beginning of a new community to an informal gathering at a restaurant nearby. People key to the founding of L'Arche in Haiti came to that first meeting: Dr. Douyon, the psychiatrist; Marie Carmel Lafontant, who was then the general secretary of the Ministry of Social Affairs; Lucien Cantave, an agronomist and brother of the Haitian Ambassador to Canada; and five or six other prominent social leaders. Fr. Beaudry was also present. We agreed to create a board and to prepare a constitution for presentation to the appropriate government department for approval.

RETURNING TO HAITI ALONE

We went on to Brazil for three weeks together, then Jean and Nadine returned to France and I returned alone to Haiti. I was quite afraid. Here I was all alone and charged with the task of putting in place solid foundations to begin a new community of L'Arche. My initiation into the Haitian culture and language was facilitated by Fr. Beaudry, who welcomed me into his community, the Foyer de Charité. It was here that I discovered the vibrant spirit of togetherness of the Haitian people and their omnipresent sense of God's providence and leadership. *Si Bondye vle* ("if God wants") were the most frequently used words in any conversation. In the city itself, Exodus 14:14 was inscribed everywhere—on buses, on restaurants, on funeral homes: *"The* LORD *will fight for you, and you have only to keep still."* This too helped me understand something of the self-abandonment that forms a part of Haitian culture.

From the beginning, my desire was that the community would be as deeply Haitian as possible: *If God wants!* I thought that there should not be too many foreigners involved in the start-up as that would delay the inculturation of L'Arche in Haiti and thus water down the gift of Haiti to L'Arche. So I began to study Creole, and since I was immersed in it at the Foyer de Charité, I made rapid progress. Every day I visited Robert, who was blind and who lived in the slum adjacent to the Foyer de Charité. He had no work, so he taught me Creole. I visited Yveline. I also visited another institution called L'Asile de Sigueneau, a government-sponsored shelter on the outskirts of Port-au-Prince. It was an overcrowded warehouse for at least two hundred people...people with intellectual or physical disabilities, former prisoners with incurable diseases, and orphans. At this time the AIDS epidemic was starting to appear in Haiti and those who were infected were sent to Sigueneau to die. All its residents—women, men, and children—stayed in dormitories separated by half walls. It was here that I met Jolibois, Jean Robert, Antoine, Bernadette, Justine, Françoise, Raoul, and Garcia, all of whom we would eventually welcome, one by one, into our community.

SEARCHING FOR A HOUSE

The next step was to find a house, but how were we to find one in this city of a million inhabitants? I hired a real estate agent who, seeing that I was a white foreigner, first showed me luxurious houses in high-class neighborhoods. I kept saying, "No, I want a home in a poor neighborhood, a house just like all the other houses in that area." Finally, I was taken to see a one-story house with a cement roof. A little creek ran alongside it, and there was a small garden with a few mango, avocado, and banana trees. This house was in the neighborhood of Carrefour, a densely populated and fast-growing area. The board gave me an ultimatum, "This is the poorest neighborhood that you are allowed to take a house in." Some members even tried to persuade me that it would be better to go higher up into the hills where it would not be so hot. "After all there are poor people there too." All of this was wise counsel, but I did not want to listen as I was determined that the community had to be a poor reality among the poor. Finally, even though it still appeared too rich to me, I agreed to take the house in Carrefour.

When I moved in, the house was bare. I built a few cupboards and some beds. I made a table big enough to seat ten at a meal. I had no fridge. All the food came from the local market just a ten-minute walk away, with vegetables fresh from the land and the chickens still very much alive! However, I did not know how to light a charcoal stove, so I lived off bread and peanut butter.

JEAN ROBERT PACKS HIS BOX

Now I was ready to welcome the first community member. On the advice of an Anglican sister, I went to the asylum, Sigueneau, to meet a man called Jean Robert. Jean Robert, twenty-nine years old, had been sent to the asylum of Sigueneau because his parents had defaulted on the payment of his fees to a boarding home in Port-au-Prince. When I arrived at the asylum I was greeted by this man, dressed in a pair of khaki shorts and a shirt held together by the one or two remaining buttons. I asked him, "Are you Jean Robert?" Although he had no speech, he nodded, "Yes." I said, "Jean Robert, I want to start a home in a neighborhood about thirty kilometers from here. Would you like to come and stay with me?" Jean Robert disappeared back into his ward and pulled out from under his bed a box that held his few possessions. Tucking the box under his arm, he stood there before me, and I understood that he was ready to come with me. So I went home and prepared a formal letter stating that I was taking responsibility for Jean Robert. With this letter signed by the board, I returned to the asylum a few days later to bring Jean Robert home.

By now the peanut butter meals were becoming tiresome. I asked at the Foyer de Charité whether they knew a cook, so Hélène Bélizaire came. Every day she would set out from her home at 7:30 a.m. and go to the central market of Port-au-Prince, buy the food for the day, and catch the bus out to Carrefour. Arriving at 10:30 a.m., she would light the charcoal fire, prepare the main meal of the day, and serve it at one o'clock. We three sat together at one end of our table made for ten! After lunch she would prepare a lighter supper, wash up all the dishes, and leave for home at about 4:30 p.m. Hélène served us faithfully for twenty-five years!

SUMMER CAMP AND FIRST ASSISTANTS

Jean Robert and I busily created a home together. But how were we going to let others know about people with intellectual disabilities and our life together, and invite them to share it with us? I was aware that it was too big a first step to expect young people to come and live with us, but perhaps they would come on holiday with us for a few weeks. My response was to hold a summer camp on the Catholic bishop's land. It was close to the sea and had a swimming pool. So I invited about twelve children with intellectual disabilities from the neighborhood of the Foyer de Charité and the asylum, and twelve young adults who had attended Jean's retreat. It was hard work but great fun, and for many of the young people, it was their first encounter with a person with intellectual disabilities.

Louise Carignan came to the community through that first summer camp. She was visiting Haiti from Quebec. She joined us at the summer camp. Then she missed her flight home and was obliged to remain two more months in Haiti. Initially she asked to stay just until she got a ticket home, but then changed her mind and stayed a whole year. Louise was tremendous. Besides all her other gifts, she was also a nurse and had lived in L'Arche in Victoria, Canada. Later in the year, we were joined by Maria Azevedo, a Brazilian with experience of working with street children in Brazil and knowledge of L'Arche in France. Together we made a good team.

YVELINE CHALLENGES OUR COMPASSION

Yveline had a very important place in the foundation of our community, but her arrival was not easy! She was very demanding and was constantly testing and provoking us. It seemed to me that she did not want to be with us. After two exhausting months, I took Yveline back to the psychiatric institution and said we could not manage. However, the director of the institution simply patted me on the back and said, "You'll be okay Robert, and she will be okay." So I returned home with Yveline but with no advice and no new resources.

Although Yveline's cry for a home and for love was a sign that L'Arche was called to put down roots in Haiti, I really did not understand her.

Yveline had grown up in a slum area of Port-au-Prince, begging food, stealing, hitting, and being beaten. At times she had stripped herself naked and run into the classroom of a school in the neighborhood creating havoc. Finally, her behavior went beyond the limit and she was locked up in the psychiatric institution. In L'Arche, she appeared devoid of feeling with little to nothing with which we could build a relationship. In fact, she seemed intent on destroying and refusing all our attempts to befriend her. During the early months, we were supported by Nadine, who would visit us occasionally and share with us what she saw happening in the community. We thought we were coping well with Yveline, so we were quite taken aback when Nadine observed, "I'm sorry, but you are all running away from her." It was hard to hear, but it was very helpful. Nadine's insights challenged us to mature in our self-understanding and our commitment to understanding and relating to the other. Being with Yveline demanded honesty and constant recommitment! Personally, she taught me to know myself and to grow in compassion.

At this time I was given a book by Bruno Bettelheim, an American psychoanalyst, called *Love Is Not Enough*. This book gave me some understanding of Yveline. He emphasized that all behavior is intelligible and means something for the person concerned. Therefore, if Yveline tore off her clothes or rolled in the mud, she had a reason. We began to "listen" differently and noticed that Yveline would burn her clothes instead of ironing them, but that as she did it, she would look us straight in the eye. It was as if she was provoking and testing our patience, waiting for us to beat her and reject her. As a team we decided that no one would ever respond to Yveline with aggression. We would not affirm her unconscious wish to be seen as a terrible and unlovable person.

"ME, AT PEACE?"

We believed that there was someone else behind that well-defended fortress, a hidden Yveline waiting to be seen and loved. Over the years, Yveline revealed herself to us. She began to reach out and build up a relationship with us. We believed in her despite her own self-disbelief. We watched her make the journey from a child seething with aggression and violence to the Yveline who could trust and be at peace with herself and others.

Yveline preferred to go barefoot, so every night, Louise would bring a bowl of water to her and ask her if Louise could wash her feet. As you can imagine, Yveline's response was to give the bowl a majestic kick. We would wipe up the spilled water and wash her feet nonetheless, but we would not reproach her or tell her off. Day after day, month after month, Louise persisted and was given the same response. It was very tough for Louise. At the end of her tether one evening, she asked me to be there when she washed Yveline's feet. Sensing Louise's fragility, she smiled sadistically as she kicked over the bowl of water. Louise began to cry. Kneeling on the floor with her head in her hands, Louise wept. Yveline was shocked. She looked at Louise and said, "*Abba wap kriye pou mwen?*" (Are you really crying for me?) This was a real turning point in our relationship with Yveline. From that day on she accepted having her feet washed.

Finally, one day Yveline chose to iron her clothes without burning them. She seemed to be beaming with a certain kind of peace. Maria called to us all to come and witness this. It was so new that we thought we should let Yveline know that we had noticed. So Maria said, "*Yveline ou kè poze!*" (Yveline you are at peace!) She responded, "*Mwen menm kè poze?*" (Me, at peace?) It was as much a surprise and new experience for her as for us. Through such small events we witnessed the emergence of the real Yveline.

FIRST HAITIAN ASSISTANTS

From the outset, I was determined that the community should belong to the people of Haiti, and therefore needed to involve young Haitians. The first man to join us had attended Jean's first retreat in Haiti and was called Jérôme Beldorin. He had social action experience in his home region in northwest Haiti, setting up and overseeing a cooperative. Jérôme came to stay for a year. Because he was a well-known leader in his region, others followed. Staying in the community brought them face-to-face with people who were normally rejected. They were deeply touched by the value and dignity afforded to each person. Jérôme often referred to the words of Genesis 1:27: "So God created humankind in his image," adding, "I am rediscovering my own people and their dignity."

Others came to know the community and to share in its life. Among them was Jacqueline Sanon. I first met Jacqueline at a prayer group called "Les assoiffés de Jésus" (Hearts thirsty for Jesus). I shared about our community life and about Yveline and

Jean Robert. Jacqueline was eighteen years old and in charge of the sewing department in a retail store, but she asked to come stay with us each weekend. She shared the bedroom with Yveline, sleeping in the top bunk, from where she had a bird's-eye view of all that happened! Yveline surprisingly tolerated Jacqueline's presence in her room and even began to imitate her and learn from her. She began to want to wear clean clothes and to enjoy wearing pretty dresses, discovering and rejoicing in herself as a girl.

Within a few years we had enough committed Haitian assistants to be able run three houses and a workshop in Carrefour. Their commitment enabled the community to welcome Justine, Bernadette, Raoul, Rose-Marie, Solange, and Véronique.

FORCED TO GROW

At times, growth, both institutional and personal, was forced upon us. Early on we welcomed a teenager named Raoul into the community. We found him near death in a ditch in our neighborhood. Given good food and medical attention, Raoul revived and soon regained his youthful energy. But as he grew in autonomy, his behavior was often delinquent and I was faced with angry neighbors! However, Raoul would not accept any limits from me, and once when I heard that he had been put in jail by the police for threatening to throw a rock at a fire truck, I sighed with relief saying, "Great, he's in jail. Now I can have a day off!" But soon the police came begging me to take Raoul home as they could no longer tolerate him in the jail.

We knew that Raoul had been deeply hurt in his early life because, with the help of a social worker, we found out that he had suffered terrible physical abuse. Raoul and I shared the same community house. I was the house leader, but I felt quite hurt that I did not have the same bond with him as I did with others welcomed into the community. I could not see a way forward despite the support of the local psychiatrist. When Nadine came to visit, she noticed the tension between Raoul and myself and said, "Robert, I do not know what is going on, but Raoul definitely sees something in you that frightens him and so he is not able to grow in freedom." I took her reflection quite personally, asking myself what I was doing wrong. It was true I was not at peace with Raoul. In the end, we decided to ask Salisien, a young assistant who had a nonthreatening way of exercising authority, and who enjoyed being with Raoul, to set up a new house with Raoul. There Raoul found new life and calmed down. Despite occasional outbursts of the old violence, Raoul began to heal and grow.

CELEBRATION AND UNDERSTANDING

As the community developed, I witnessed the wisdom of the twin pillars of community life: celebration and understanding. Our community was one eager to sing and dance to the sound of the drums. When we gathered to celebrate and pray together, we were a people rich in thanksgiving, rejoicing in the new life being given. The simplicity and spontaneity of such celebrations is a gift of the Haitian soul. At the same time, we also knew that to help people find freedom, we needed to learn to understand behaviors and relationships. When we were confronted with difficult and seemingly incomprehensible behaviors and the tension that accompanied them, we sought the help of a local psychiatrist, Dr. Legrand Bijoux. He would listen to our experiences, frustrations, anxieties, and questions, and help us understand what was happening so that we might approach the difficulty in a unified way. Dr. Bijoux later wrote up his experience with the community, exploring the specific therapy offered through shared living.

TRANSFORMATION: THE TENDER GAZE OF JOLIBOIS

Jolibois was ten years old when he came from the Asile de Sigueneau to live with us. During his time at the asylum, he had thrown himself into one of the toilet pits. He survived because another child alerted the staff who pulled him out. Had he done it on purpose or was it an accident? Jolibois was autistic and seemed enclosed in his own world, not talking, crouching low on the ground playing with little objects. He was very fearful when asked to walk anywhere. During the process of teaching Jolibois how to use the toilet and to keep himself clean, he one day crouched on the hole, put his foot down the hole, and mimicked falling down the hole. I felt he was trying to let me know that he was thinking about throwing himself down the hole again and wanted me to know his despair. What was he trying to tell me about himself? Why would he want to end up down a hole full of human excrement?

Over the years, held and loved by the community, Jolibois evolved into a harmonious young man. He grew in courage and learned to walk confidently. He welcomed others and showed deep affection toward those who cared for him. Jolibois never spoke. He just looked at you, then quietly returned to his solitary games. His gaze at times would penetrate you like an arrow of love and its tenderness felt almost too much.

THE STAGES OF LIFE

When we opened a third house, we decided that the children needed to go to school just like other children. My sister Maryse came to start a school in a one-room hut with a thatched roof adjacent to one of our houses. A small creek flowed around the hut, making it a separate location. Maryse made it into a beautiful place. She set about discovering the needs and gifts of each child by inviting each to school for an individual half-hour session. She chose not to work with them in a group because she was wary that the group dynamic would reproduce their difficult behaviors and so limit their growth. The fruit of this decision amazed all of us. Yveline, who was often very challenging at home, was a different person once she had crossed the bridge and entered the school. Alone with Maryse she was cooperative, learning to draw and write and participating with joy in each activity. Through this experience we became aware of the importance of spaces away from home, so that each child could gain a new self-perspective and have a chance to respond and act differently. As we saw with Yveline, in this other context she could discover her capacity to do beautiful things.

There were other members of the community—adults—for whom school was not appropriate. I asked Jean Robert whether he would like to go to work rather than always be at home all day. His desire obliged us to imagine and set up a workshop. Most of the growth and new developments in the community came about out of necessity, in response to the needs of the community members with intellectual disabilities.

TELLING MY COMMITMENT

Over the years, I became aware of the depth of the bonds that had grown between me and the people we had welcomed into our community. For many of them it was a time of major passages in their life, some literally moving from death to life. As I witnessed these resurrections in people, I felt a call. What was this call? Deep down there was an intimate joy and gratitude for being where I was and for the people with whom I was living. I knew that I did not need to consider other options or projects for my life. As I pondered the words of the Gospels and the

Old Testament, especially the prophets, I was touched by their experience of call, and how Jesus called people both directly and through others: "I was a stranger and you welcomed me...I was sick and you took care of me," says Jesus in Matthew 25:35–36.

I began to speak of this sense of calling. When Jean visited and we walked together along the back lanes of our neighborhood, I shared with him this feeling of profound happiness at being in the community in Haiti, and that I sensed it was where God was calling me to put down roots. Later, during an International Council meeting, Jean shared that he had heard people across the Federation of L'Arche asking themselves whether they were being called by God to make a commitment within L'Arche. I was asked to write down what I was living and what commitment meant for me. Back in Haiti I tried to name what was important in my experience and to put words on my deepest desire. I wrote about my bond with Yveline, Jolibois, and Jean Robert and how I wanted to be faithful to them. I also wrote of my bond with the other assistants who, like me, were choosing to share their lives in a community house with people who had been rejected and abandoned in asylums or on the streets, and how I wanted to be faithful to them. I wrote of the importance of our community being inserted into the locality because I had seen how vital it was for Yveline, Jolibois, and Jean Robert to be accepted, and how painful it was for them when they were called derogatory names. I felt the community had a wider role and witness—that of bringing the gifts of people with intellectual disabilities into the lives of the people of the neighborhood, indeed into Haitian culture and society.

I sent my letter to the international coordinator of L'Arche, Sue Mosteller, who circulated it widely within the federation. Then I began to feel vulnerable. I felt my life would always be engaged with building relationships with the poor, as I knew that was part of how I lived out my relationship with God. Being single was important because it enabled me to commit all my energy to the life of my house and its members, but was that commitment for the rest of my life?

"THIS COMMUNITY IS OF THE SPIRIT"

Over time, the community developed a relationship with the archbishop of Port-au-Prince, François Ligonde. We invited him to speak of the place of compassion and care in the Gospels. He was always ready to listen to us, sharing our daily struggles and graces, and then to affirm us in our way of life and our calling. One day he said, "This community is of the Spirit; it is the liveliest movement in the Haitian Church today." He called the assistants to put down their roots in the community, saying, "This is of God. This is not just a social movement. You live with the poor and you face insecurity. Your community does not have lots of well-built buildings, nor does it offer, as religious communities do, a well-prepared formation program, a provision for old age, or even a cemetery! No, you have none of that, but the Spirit is present." By naming our calling, Msgr. Ligonde affirmed our place and role in the Church.

TRUE LIBERATION: RELATIONSHIP WITH THE POOREST OF THE POOR

At the time of the foundation of L'Arche in Carrefour, the Catholic Church in Haiti was very engaged with the theology of liberation. Young people especially longed to actively change the political landscape of Haiti through democratic elections. They thirsted for a horizon of hope rather than the oppression of a violent dictator. The authorities crushed any sign of active opposition. My heart was with those working for change, especially for the poor. Yet I was challenged by a prominent liberation theologian for having affirmed that the poor are a gift in that they call us to transformation. He asked me, "How can you say that the poor are a gift for you, when they are dying and suffering such injustice?" I knew there was truth in both our experiences and understanding.

Our community embodied this struggle in terms of understanding and vision but also literally because of our location in a neighborhood that was often politically tense. Protests and reprisals were a feature of our shared life with our local neighborhood. During this period, Jean, by now an internationally acclaimed personality, came to give a talk in Carrefour. Before the event, I had been informed that the *Tonton Macoutes*, the personal army of the dictator Duvalier, planned to be at the talk. I warned Jean that this public gathering might be used for political ends and lead to violence. In his talk, Jean emphasized that Jesus invites us to respond to the plight of the poor by befriending them, by building community with them. He invited people to transform their society through giving the poor a place, by responding to their need and right to belong, and by changing their own hearts. This was not what many present wanted to hear. At the end of the talk, activists challenged Jean, asking whether what he said was enough in the face of a repressive regime that denied them a political and economic future. They asked him how he would respond in such a situation. Jean said that he could not tell them what to do. This was greeted with applause as it was interpreted as support for their cause and action. However, Jean went on to stress that while the creation of community was "political" because it changed society, it also demanded inner conversion through relationships. After the talk, people came and told me that they had been very disappointed in what Jean had said because he did not overtly affirm them in their struggle and action. Jean himself wondered afterward whether he had supported the young people enough.

How were we to understand our community amid such fervent unrest and searching? Another liberation theologian who became a friend of the community was aware of the turmoil and questions in the hearts of the young people committed in L'Arche. He said to us, "There are two kinds of poor. Those who are on their feet and marching for their liberation; and those who are too weak even to march for their freedom. I wonder whether true liberation will only happen if the marching poor meet and build relationships with the poor who cannot march for themselves?"

REACHING OUT: FAITH AND LIGHT PARTIES

During the first three years of L'Arche in Haiti, many parents came and asked us to welcome their child into our community. We, however, did not want to undermine a culture that traditionally took care of its children with disabilities. We looked for other ways of supporting them. Madame Anne-Marie Pamphile, the mother of a child with intellectual disabilities, wanted to creatively support other parents. This encouraged us to think seriously about what we could do. The answer we came up with was to have parties! In various neighborhoods we would organize a party for all the families with a child with intellectual disabilities. The parents, the children with disabilities, and some of the young people who had attended Jean's retreats would gather together to celebrate and share. The party developed a specific structure: we'd start by welcoming one another, then accompanied by a drummer, we would sing and dance and end with a time of sharing in two groups—one for the parents and the other for the people with disabilities and the students. These parties were magical and at times ecstatic. The students discovered that the people with disabilities, though blind or lame or without speech or in wheelchairs, were ready to have fun and reach out in friendship. Many lasting friendships blossomed. Inspired by a similar movement that had grown up in Europe, we called these parties "Faith and Light."

A PILGRIMAGE OF WITNESS

The parties multiplied and soon there were several groups meeting regularly. Within a few years there were at least a hundred members in different small groups. We decided to come together and go on pilgrimage to the city of Saut d'Eau, which although a center for voodoo worship also had a Catholic Church. Madame Pamphile thought it was a good idea to choose this city because many people who took part in voodoo ceremonies believed that people with intellectual disabilities were possessed by spirits. We wanted to make known the true reality and gift of people with disabilities. The pilgrimage was a great success. We were 150 people and travelled for about five hours in rented trucks with simple wooden benches. We stayed three days in the city and were welcomed by the parish priest and students from the local school. They welcomed us with singing and dancing on the plaza in front of the church. We in our turn presented a skit. There was much hilarity and many new friendships.

However, maybe the strangest participant in our pilgrimage was Madame Max Adolphe, at the time the leader of the *Tontons Macoutes* paramilitary in Haiti. A very feared woman, she was loyal to the dictator, Duvalier. As we were about to set out for Saut d'Eau with our exotic caravan of trucks and people, we were visited by one of Madame Adolphe's henchmen. He announced that his leader was joining the pilgrimage. Madame Pamphile and I were escorted to her car where Madame Adolphe said, "I have heard about this pilgrimage and I believe in it. It is the kind of event I want to participate in." With some anxiety,

Madame Pamphile and I conferred and decided that we would say yes but on condition that she came as a pilgrim like everyone else, without privilege, and that she did not use the pilgrimage for political ends. There were to be no public speeches and no publicized reports. We also asked her to take some pilgrims in her car.

A SURPRISE

The last day of the pilgrimage took us past Madame Adolphe's house, a place with a dreadful reputation for torture and executions. As we passed in front of the house we were stopped by her soldiers and I was told that Madame Max (as she was called by her followers) wanted to see me. I went into her house, and there in her headquarters were two huge tables filled with food and soft drinks. Under the thatched roof of the main hall tables had been beautifully decorated with table cloths—room for 150 people! There were any number of uniformed servers. She cried out, "Bring in your people for a meal!" We enjoyed a tremendous feast and were treated as if we were kings and queens. I was accompanying a little boy named Harry Bobo, who lived with cerebral palsy. He needed so much attention that I was unable to eat. Seeing this, Madame Adolphe came over and said, "I'll look after your little Harry. Let me care for him so that you can eat." She helped him with great sensitivity and competence.

Our community was nonviolent and witnessed to the power of healing through relationships with the poorest of the poor. But finding right relationships in a politically tense, unstable, and violent situation was not easy. I was once personally threatened by the secret police because of Jolibois. He had wandered into the yard of a leader of the *Macoutes* who lived in our neighborhood and was beaten by one of the guards. I was very angry about this and went to tell the guard never to hit Jolibois again. When he heard of the incident, the *Macoutes* leader cornered me against a wall with his car and told me that he would "get me." The Haitian assistants were terrified that he would really kill me and asked me to speak with Madame Adolphe, who came and sorted the issue out with the local leader.

When Duvalier was toppled a few years later there was enormous violence and many people were killed and burned in the streets. I saw terrible things. It was horrible. I heard that Madame Adolphe had escaped to the United States. I have not heard any other news about her, but I believe that our people with a disability called forth her compassion; that something in the witness of our community touched her.

WISDOM TO LEAVE

Over the first five years the community grew rapidly, and we founded three community houses, a school, and a workshop. Twenty-five people with intellectual disabilities found a place of belonging, and fifteen assistants shared their lives with us in different ways and with different degrees of commitment. I imagined this growth would continue, but over the next ten years we welcomed only one new person into the community houses, although many new people came to our school and workshop. We struggled to understand why we seemed to be stuck. In the end I realized that the nature of our journey had shifted. It was no longer the excitement of new people and new projects, the creativity of birthing a community. We were being asked instead to deepen our journey together and help one another become mature members of the community. At a personal level I sensed I too needed to change.

I had led the community for twelve years. When the community renewed my mandate for a fourth term, I was asked to give special attention to preparing new leadership in the community. At the next discernment for leadership, we named a Haitian assistant as the new community leader. I wondered if I should stay. I was aware that as the founding leader I might become an obstacle for the new leader. Should I leave Haiti? Should I go to another community of L'Arche? I was not alone, as across the Federation of L'Arche, many founding leaders were stepping down and looking at how they might remain faithful while allowing new life. The words of Jesus in John 16:7, "It is to your advantage that I go away," were often recalled at the International Council, when we considered the future of former leaders in the federation. I prayed about the next step and decided to leave. I informed the community about my discernment and decision to leave. Some of the younger assistants were upset and said that I was not keeping my promises, that I was not being faithful. Then Yveline stood up and said, "Robert has to grow! Each one of us must grow! The community has to grow!" and sat down.

LOOKING BACK AND LETTING GO

I had been the community leader for eighteen years, so the changes that came under new and local leadership were a challenge for me. The first Haitian leader was Annette Prévilon, followed by Jacqueline Sanon, who had known us since she was a teenager. They brought in change. As the founding leader, I think I was too strongly influenced by my ideas, especially about the community being for the poor among the poor. I had set up houses that were too basic. For example, the roofs were made of tin, which offers little protection. In general, as soon as people in Haiti have a little money, they put on cement roofs for better protection against the summer heat, hurricanes, and stray bullets. When the assistants said they did not feel safe in the houses, I argued that we could be in solidarity with all the other poor in our neighborhood. The young assistants responded, "But we did not come here to be in solidarity with the poor people in our neighborhood. We want to be able to live in community with people with intellectual disabilities for the long haul." It was a legitimate reaction, but it took me time to yield and eventually to embrace their insights.

Many other things changed. Because Jacqueline was Haitian and belonged to the same culture as the local people, she was able to reach out in ways that were inconceivable for me as a foreigner. As soon as she was made leader, she invited a group of thirteen- to eighteen-year-olds from the neighborhood to create a support group for the community. She called them "Les Amis de Jésus" (The Friends of Jesus). Through this group, the young people were asked to animate community celebrations with song and dance; to clean up the yard and fetch water; to help care for the children in our community houses. There were about twenty members, some of whom later became assistants. It was the best way of being present in and to our neighborhood and of sharing through lived experience the gift of people with intellectual disabilities. Coming from Jacqueline, the invitation was from one sister, one family member to another; and the statement that the people with intellectual disabilities were "ours" could only come from someone who was Haitian. With Jacqueline as leader, our neighbors developed a new relationship with L'Arche Carrefour as "their" community, learning to respect Jacqueline and all those who shared their lives in community with people with disabilities.

AFTERWORD: "FRUIT THAT WILL LAST"

The departure from Haiti was not easy for Robert.
He went to the L'Arche community in Amos, Quebec,

for three initial months. Then he returned to L'Arche Trosly in France and stayed there for two years after leaving Haiti. He went back to where he had started for support but had no inner energy. "I was hurting and in deep grief," he acknowledges. Robert took time for reflection and accompaniment as he asked himself fundamental questions about what kind of life commitment he wanted to live next. Finding some peace and moving on from Trosly, Robert returned to Canada and joined the community of L'Arche in Montreal, where he stayed for eight years and met his future wife, Judith. Married in 2001, Robert and Judith first supported the community of Montreal and then, for four years, Robert was the community leader of L'Arche Amos in Quebec.

In January 2013, Robert and Judith were invited by the Catholic bishop of Amos to go for a few years to Kuujjuaq, an Inuit village in Northern Quebec. Their mandate was to build a community with the Catholics of Kuujjuaq, a community "intercultural and ecumenically inspired" and also "inspired by the cry of those who are the weakest." They helped gather a community "that shares the Word, a community of healing, conscious of the deep wounds inflicted on the Inuit people; a community of solidarity with the Inuit." Robert and Judith realized that their inspiration for animating the faith community in Kuujjuaq came largely from all they had learned in L'Arche, especially the time in Haiti for Robert. In the village of Kuujjuaq, Robert and Judith became friends with seven Inuit people with disabilities whose welcome, trust, and openness were especially encouraging. The gift of these friends for going beyond subtle barriers between outsiders and Inuit in the village sustained not only Robert and Judith but also inspired the Catholic community in its desire for unity, healing, and reconciliation. Robert adds, "In this community and village Judith and I found joy, life, fun, and meaning, with a new depth of faith."

Now having returned to Amos, Robert closes, "As I conclude, the following words of Jesus come up in me and seem like a thread in my journey: 'I chose you. And I appointed you to go and bear fruit, fruit that will last'" (John 15:16).

Chapter 7

"DON'T TURN AWAY FROM THE ONE WHO IS YOUR OWN FLESH"

L'Arche in Honduras, 1977

NADINE TOKAR

INTRODUCTION

Nadine Tokar was born and grew up in Paris. Her family was Jewish, from Ukraine and Poland. Her parents had a deep faith and were well integrated into French society. Nadine's grandparents were also very important for her, teaching her about their Jewish faith and Ashkenazi traditions simply by the way that they lived. Nadine recalls, "I come from a very united family. My parents and grandparents expressed with their lives their love of and trust in God, and their respect of others' lives. My family was very wounded by the wars. My grandparents had to flee Russia at the time of the White Revolution because they were Jewish. They came as a family to Paris and had to start again from nothing. During the Second World War, many of my family were killed in concentration camps. This left my family deeply wounded. My brother and I were born after the war in 1947 and 1949."

Looking back at her childhood, Nadine reflects, *"I had a gentle and protected childhood. I received much tenderness and I was well cared for. My father paved the way in our family as his father had before him; a patriarchal system. Later, I would affectionately call him 'my tender dictator.'"* She recalls the importance of Jewish celebrations for her family: *"The Jewish feasts were always celebrated with the family at my grandparents' houses. I have warm memories of much joy and life, songs and dances, delicious food different from the everyday. I must admit that sometimes the long prayers before the meal could be quite boring for a child. However, we were small enough that we would just play together under the table as the adults prayed above us. I enjoyed listening to them, my grandparents, my father, and my uncles chanting."* For Nadine, her family's Jewish faith touched her deeply and brought her close to God. She explains, *"I can't say that I understood what was happening in these moments, but I sensed that it was something important. I also liked to go to the synagogue and watch them praying; to join in the ritual gestures that my grandmothers would*

*explain to me. In these ways, God quickly became
an important part of my young life in a joyful and
living way. I only have joyful memories of these
times where I learned to speak with God as I spoke
to my dad."*

As a youngster, Nadine participated in Jewish youth groups, always searching for a coherence
between faith and life. Then, in 1968 as a university student, she joined in the student protests and
strikes in Paris. She participated in the streets and
helped to feed and support the strikers. However,
she felt a fundamental lack of balance in these
events and an awareness that the students were
destroying more than they were building up. She
remarks, "After May '68 I was confused. I could
see clearly what we were destroying and rejecting.
However, I sensed there was no vision of what we
wanted to build."

Nadine became fortuitously involved with
handicapped people through the French American
Volunteer Association for Handicapped (FAVA).
She volunteered to go with them every weekend to
recreation activities, including swimming. Here she
discovered a new world of joy and authenticity. The
association was organizing the first Special Olym-
pics. She comments, "Two things really touched
me and changed the way that I looked at the world.
First, there was a running race where the three front-
runners who were about to cross the finish line almost
together suddenly turned back to wait for the other
runners so they could all cross the finish together. I
had been taught that to be someone one ought to
be first. Yet here they showed that arriving together

was more important than winning. Second, at a medal ceremony as the gold medal winner left the podium, he burst into tears, saying 'Do you think that now my father will believe that I am some-one?'" She found it deeply moving to see these young people with their keen sense of relationship, their attentiveness to the other, and their profound personal suffering. Through FAVA Nadine also met Gerry McDonald, who had been to L'Arche in Trosly. Gerry insisted that she should come for a visit to the community. The account now continues in Nadine's own voice.

FIRST VISITS TO L'ARCHE TROSLY

I came to L'Arche Trosly with Claire for a visit in 1971. It was Pentecost, I think. I shared a room with others and a big dog. We had an evening at Les Marronniers with Père Thomas. It was my first contact with the Christian world. At L'Arche, people seemed to me to be dirty and crazy! I promised myself never to return. Yet, a few months later, I spent a week of my vacation with a group from L'Arche. While living with them, I was struck by the authenticity, the groundedness, the simplicity, the suffering, and the joy that shone through the "dirtiness" and "craziness." I was also touched by what the assistants were living—these young Christians who were living their faith more authentically than I was in my own milieu.

I wanted to do something special with my life, but I didn't know what. One night during this week, I woke up and suddenly realized it was clear that this was what I was looking for—that I could live my Jewish faith more truly at L'Arche than anywhere else. I understood what my grandmother wanted to say when she imbued me with respect and love of the poorest at the synagogue, and how that is a path toward God. Life at L'Arche seemed to answer the discomfort that I had felt during the protests of 1968. L'Arche was building something with a clear vision! Later that week, I had been scheduled to go to Peru on holiday. Instead, I returned home to Paris, canceled the tickets, and never went to Peru. I had found my place.

SPIRITUAL LIFE AT L'ARCHE CUISE

I was Jewish, and my Jewish faith was important to me, but for the celebrations of Jewish feasts I had to go back to my family and the synagogue. It was quite painful because it wasn't yet the time of interfaith openness, so I found it quite lonely. In my foyer, we prayed each night and read the gospel, and I was very surprised because when I was listening to Jesus saying things like we must give our life, this was obvious for me. I saw that in my grandparents' lives and in my parents' lives daily. The message was clear to me. I began to read the Gospels in secret, and I found they connected to my own life and faith. I was living in the L'Arche community in Cuisse near Trosly but working at FAVA in Paris. Each morning before going to commute to Paris, I went to the little chapel where there was the Blessed Sacrament. I didn't know what was going on there. I didn't know what the Blessed Sacrament meant. It was very early in the morning, so nobody was there, but I needed this time and silence. I just felt well there.

In June 1972, I asked for a week's holiday, and I arranged to go to a Carmelite monastery in Abbeville. This made everyone laugh because it seemed unexpected to them. In fact, we had visited earlier with my L'Arche home when we had gone to Ambleteuse. I was quite impressed with Sr. Marie-Mad and had the desire to go back. So I went there for a week, a very important week. It was there that I met Jesus for the first time, but when I returned home, I kept it secret. I had glimpsed the light, but it was too destabilizing for me.

MEETING JEAN VANIER AND GETTING BAPTIZED

Three years later, Jesus was still there for me, and very strongly there. I had a very hard time because if I had really seen the light, I couldn't go back. For me that meant that I thought I would lose or hurt my family. I just couldn't face misunderstanding or upsetting my identity, and I didn't know anything about Christianity. For me it was more a living than an intellectual understanding. When I met Jean Vanier the first time, I was in Cuise, and the first thing he asked me was, "Do you speak Spanish?" I said, "No," and he replied, "Learn Spanish." Of course I didn't learn. I don't know why he asked me, but the future was to reveal the wisdom of his intuition.

Sometime later, Jean asked me to go with him and Robert Larouche to Haiti and Brazil. Just a week before the trip there was a struggle within me, and Jean asked, "What's happening?" "Jesus bothers me too much," I replied. So he asked me, "What do you want? Do you want to be baptized?" And I responded, "Yes, that's it." At the same second that I said yes, I found peace again. I have never lost that feeling since. I was baptized at five in the morning in the little chapel in Trosly before leaving for Latin America. My faith would be nourished in the Church in Latin America, and my Christianity would flourish there. I hadn't come to L'Arche to find Jesus. God had always been first in my life. I had been searching for an authenticity between my faith, my life, and my values, but not a change of my religion! Anyway, I have often wondered, could I have founded the community in Honduras if I had not met Jesus?

TRIP WITH JEAN VANIER AND ROBERT LAROUCHE TO HAITI AND BRAZIL IN FEBRUARY AND MARCH 1975

Early in 1975, we went for three weeks to Haiti and Brazil. It was quite an experience because it was the first time that I really faced and was touched by the poverty, misery, and joy of people. When I was a little girl, my grandmother was always leading me toward the poor in the synagogue, and at all our family feasts the places of honor were for the poor of the synagogues. However, I had never seen such extreme poverty before. At the same time, in this poverty there was an incredible joy in life and a deep faith. It all spoke to me of the gospel. It was like everything was being prepared in advance by God. It was clear that everything was given for L'Arche and that everything was ready for Robert to begin building L'Arche in Haiti. Then, after the ten days in Haiti, we went to Brazil, and it was a hard experience there because we were received by one hundred Canadian missionary priests and religious and we spent ten days enclosed in a beautiful property but kept away from the local culture. After this time in Brazil, Robert came back to Haiti to continue preparations there.

FIRST STEPS TOWARD FOUNDING L'ARCHE IN HONDURAS

I went back with Jean to Trosly, and on the plane Jean said, "Do you think we should begin L'Arche in Brazil?" I said, "No, I think if we begin L'Arche in Latin America it should be in Honduras." When I said that, I didn't even know where Honduras was! Jean thought I was just teasing him, but three days later, he called me and told me, "The Holy Spirit listened to you."

He had just received an invitation from Bishop Gerin, bishop of Choluteca, to give retreats in Honduras. That was in March. In June 1975, I was supposed to go to Haiti to support Robert, who was beginning L'Arche there. Jean asked me to go to Honduras first, to make some preparations for a retreat there, and to ensure that we did not relive what we had lived in Brazil previously, disconnected from the local people. I went to Honduras, but I didn't speak any Spanish, so I stayed with Canadian sisters while trying to organize the retreat.

After three days, I was upset to be only with Canadian people, so I went out and walked around just to smell, to see the colors, and to discover the faces of the people. I walked and walked and then, becoming tired, I took the first bus passing by. I quickly fell asleep. I only woke up when we arrived at what must have been the terminus because everyone was getting off. It was just in front of a little church, so I went in and spent some time inside. It was a simple, peaceful time with old ladies praying the rosary and all the kids running, eating, screaming—life. I was touched by the congruence of their faith and their life. Then I walked some more and came upon Nueva Suyapa. It was right after Hurricane Fifi, and thousands of people had lost everything. The temporary solution of the government was to have moved them near to the municipal dump. I was really struck by the little plastic shacks and the naked kids. I wrote down the name of the place so that I could take Jean there later.

A few months later, I returned with Jean for the retreats. I don't know how but I was able to arrange with the Canadian priest for the retreat to be open, open to laypeople and religious, unusual in those days. I was insisting that Jean visit Suyapa and the nearby slum. One day during the retreat he suggested everybody would take the afternoon to go and find a place where they could meet marginalized people. Later they would share with the others what they had lived. So then Jean, Fr. Guido, and I walked to the slum called Nueva Suyapa. Fr.

Guido knew a woman there who was a delegate of the Word of God—a movement of laypeople who had initially started in Honduras, but who now are found all over Latin America. The movement was born to celebrate the word and communion. The woman invited us to the celebration of the word of God that she held every Saturday night at her house, and we went at the end of the retreat. It was such an experience—a little house with a dirt floor, the women with their babies and children, some men outside. There were three women at the front sharing the word, passing it back and forth because they couldn't read well. I didn't understand because I couldn't speak Spanish, but what I could understand was the faith and the love. It was deep, and I kept it in my heart.

RAFAEL CALLS L'ARCHE TO HONDURAS

After the retreat, I said to Jean that if L'Arche was to start in Honduras it must be carried by young people. Jean said, "So go back and organize some more retreats for young people." After some time helping Robert in Haiti, I went back to Honduras to organize the retreats. During this time of preparation, I also began to get to know the reality of handicapped people in Honduras. One of the sisters went with me to look at hospitals where handicapped people were living. We visited the children's hospital and asked the social worker if there were any abandoned handicapped children and she said no, but then she called us back and said there was one in the orthopedic section. I went there, first crossing through another room of children, to a very small isolated room. The nurse said, "He's dangerous," and I found a little boy of six completely nude, in a cage—Rafael.

He had been abandoned the day he was born in this hospital, very handicapped with his legs behind his body; he had already suffered many operations. He had a lovely face but was like a savage child, like a little animal. I stayed quite awhile trying to communicate with him. I tried reaching to him through the cage. At that moment, the phrase of Isaiah 58:7, to not turn away from the one who is your own flesh, came to dwell in my heart. It was clear that he couldn't live his life in this cage. His whole being was calling for L'Arche in Honduras. He needed it desperately. I sensed that Jesus was calling me, and I said yes to Jesus, yes to Rafael. I didn't know where this would lead, but I deeply felt that this was right. I went back to Haiti to support Robert with all of that in my heart, then returned to Trosly. There I told Jean about Rafael in that cage in the hospital. It was clear that this was my call to Honduras, my little annunciation! At that time there were no international structures in L'Arche, nor an international coordinator. So Jean just said, "Go ahead." That is how L'Arche came to exist in Honduras.

FINDING A PLACE TO STAY

Right after Jean said to go ahead, we had the second federation in Shadow Lake, and we named Sue Mosteller as the first international coordinator. I met with Jean and Sue and said let me have time, I can't begin L'Arche right away in Honduras. I don't speak Spanish. I want to live with a family. I need to meet the culture, to meet the people and to understand the way they live. I didn't want to build a French community there. From the beginning, I had said L'Arche must begin with Honduran people. I was French so I wanted to live first the reality of the local people.

In November 1975, I went again with Jean to Honduras for a retreat with young people whom we had organized. When we arrived in Honduras, the priest who welcomed us at the airport said, "Why are you here?" While I was gone, a Canadian priest in charge of youth pastorate decided there would be no youth retreat with Jean Vanier because youth should be evangelized by young people. So we arrived to nothing. I was able to organize a retreat with talks from Jean in the morning. In the afternoon, we arranged to walk to the slum with all the young people who wanted to come, and we had organized something with the local people there at night. We went to see the priest there in Nueva Suyapa, and he was very welcoming and found a place for us to stay, a little house.

Each day while we were walking through the slum, Jean would ask me, "Where will you move to?" I said, "I don't know." Each day he asked, "Where will you live?" I replied, "I don't know." Truly I didn't know, but I was peaceful. I knew that the answer would be given at the right moment. The last day of the retreat, while we were walking, we found ourselves in front of the house of Dona Vilma, where we had celebrated the word originally, and a group of women recognized us, brought us into the house, and gave us coffee and cookies. The daughters of Dona Vilma remembered us from before. We tried to talk a little bit and suddenly it was clear to me that it was there that I wanted to live. So I asked them if it was possible to come and live with them. They were very excited. I said to Jean, "I know now where I want to live" "Where?" "Here!" He said, "Okay."

MOVING TO HONDURAS

Jean and I then left and went to Guatemala, and I decided not to accompany him to Haiti. I knew it would be too hard for me to return to my beloved Haiti. I wouldn't have the courage to go back by myself to Honduras then, but I needed to go now. So we separated, and I went back to Honduras by bus. When I left Jean, I had a strong feeling of loneliness. I was completely alone with something much too big for me without knowing anything, just alone with this call and with Jesus.

I returned to Nueva Suyapa and came upon Dona Maria, Dona Vilma's neighbor, who was washing clothes on the stone. She hadn't believed that I would come back. What I hadn't understood was that between my two visits with Jean, Dona Vilma had died. Dona Maria tried to explain to me that no one was living anymore in Dona Vilma's house but that I could stay with her family. That's where I stayed for a year. I learned life, the life of poor people in Honduras. I learned to speak Spanish with them and with the kids on the street. I would come home eager to show off my new language skills, but unbeknownst to me, the first thing the kids taught me were "bad words!"

BUILDING THE FIRST BOARD

After about ten months living with Dona Maria's family, I was very happy, but I knew I was there to create a home for Rafael and others that I had gotten to know, such as Marcia, Lita, Suyapa, and Denis. So I had to create a board. I didn't know anybody. I had only a list of people from the first retreat, so I took it and tried to remember any names. I only remembered one name: Micky de Pineda. I explained, "I'm Nadine and we met at the first retreat. Now I'm here and need to create a board, but I don't know anybody. Could you help me?" She said, "Okay, come." Obviously, she was gifted in putting people together.

I remember at the first meeting I gave a presentation of the project of L'Arche to all these important people from the city. I was twenty-five and they were laughing because I was speaking the Spanish of the rural people, not their more formal Spanish. I talked about L'Arche, about the project, about Rafael, Marcia. During my year living in Nueva Suyapa I visited lots of institutions and hospitals, so I knew the reality of the people with disabilities. These people who had gathered all said yes to the project that first day.

It was obvious for me, and it's still obvious, that L'Arche is God's project because it wasn't possible that they would say yes simply to me. They were saying yes to something much bigger. I have a deep gratitude to Jorge and Virginia Valle, Oscar and Noly Kafaty, Roberto and Micky Pineda, Humberto and Cécilia Prats, and all the members of the founding board for their trust, support, and love. There was a military government at this time, so it took a long time for our L'Arche project to get official recognition. For the military, all foreigners, all strangers were suspect, especially those with religious connections. Lots of things had to be done to get something like a L'Arche house recognized by the government, but the board did them. I participated, I learned, but I couldn't have done it myself.

FINDING THE FIRST HOUSE

Where to begin? I had been in Nueva Suyapa from the beginning and had the impression that God and Mary had led me to this place. The church of Suyapa is a pilgrimage church, Mary of Suyapa is the national patron, and I had a feeling that Mary wanted L'Arche close to her. However, the board was not very happy with the idea. It was hard for me to accept, but I knew the house could not be in Nueva Suyapa because of physically handicapped people and their needs. I knew we would likely have some people in wheelchairs, so I decided to find a house in Suyapa proper. I went to see the priest there, Bishop Caceres. I asked if he knew of a house. He said, "I have one, come." There was a place that had been a seminary and then a school run by religious sisters—it was a big old wooden house.

Living in my little house in Nueva Suyapa, I felt it was too big, so I said no, it's not what we need.

At one point, I found a house that was not as big. I was so happy. To me it was ideal. I was leaving for Haiti the next day for two weeks, so I arranged with people that we would sign the papers when I returned. While in Haiti I was very concerned about the house, so when Robert Larouche asked if I could stay a little longer, I said no I had to go back to arrange for this house. When I came back, I went straight on to the house and found that they had given it to a family just the day before! I was so disappointed, but at the same time I told myself, okay, now I know we will be just where God wants us. That gave me security and strength.

I continued to search. It was hard work. Each morning, I went down the hill to Mass and asked all the neighbors if they knew of a little house we could use. I became so discouraged. The board said they could help find a house in another place, so I was beginning to think that maybe they were right and that I needed to open my mind and heart. In this moment of thinking maybe they're right, I went to Mass at six in the morning. I asked people if they knew of any house, as I did each day. However, this time, three different people told me to go see Bishop Caceres. At first I said to myself, I know the house, so no thank you. But after the third person, I went to see Bishop Caceres after Mass. I asked, "Could we go to visit the house again?" "Sure," he said. We went, and somehow I didn't visit the house in the same way. Suddenly I could imagine Marcia— who I had been getting to know in an asylum—in the house with her wheelchair, I saw Rafael who didn't walk, I saw the neighbors, and I knew that it was the right place. It was hard for me to change from my little house to this big house, but it was obviously the right place at that point.

THE GUIDING OF GOD

I didn't really have any ideal except to create a home for Rafael once I met him in the children's hospital. I simply had a sense of being guided to Suyapa, the neighborhood where we started. It was obvious that we would try to find a home for Rafael and others in that poor neighborhood. People might say we were idealistic. It's not that I had an ideal of being poor. Poverty's no joke. Poverty wasn't an ideal, it was reality. I came to L'Arche very much with a sense of God's guidance and found that in Honduras also. Why had I arrived in Suyapa? It was Providence for me. I didn't speak Spanish. I didn't know the place. I certainly made lots of mistakes, but I had no preconceived idea or ideal in going there. If you ask about ideals, it was just to discern day by day where the light was guiding us.

The time of the foundation of a community is a very special time because it is really the time when you can touch the grace of God. Really, you touch it—it is incredible—you know you are not alone. You are on the right path. After that time, it's not to touch the grace but to trust it—it's different. The other important thing was that in those early days, we had fun. One of my good friends from back then reminds me that while it was crazy in many ways, what people today may not know is that even though at times it was hard, we really had a lot of fun!

BEGINNING IN THE HOUSE

We began January 7, 1977, in that big house. We had to build some small wooden walls to make bedrooms. What was important for me was to really live like the neighbors so that the neighbors could participate in our lives, and that the people of L'Arche could find themselves belonging in the life of the neighborhood. It was the first indication that handicapped people lived among them. Our life was very simple, living what the neighbors were living. A long time after the foundation, when we started working on inculturation, our simple lifestyle was brought into question. I understand that when you are lacking everything—food, comfort, and security—you want something different, something more. Perhaps I was too idealistic, but for me it was essential to be partners with the local neighbors so that handicapped people would be well integrated.

FIRST ASSISTANTS

Before we began, I received a letter from Regine in Trosly whom I did not know, and who was moved by my letters to the community about working toward the founding of L'Arche in Honduras. Regine said she had been praying about whether to offer herself to help in Honduras. One day while she was in Compiegne pondering it all down by the river, she suddenly saw a boat passing by and the name of the boat was "Nadine," so she said, "Well, I have my answer!" Then she wrote to me and said she wanted to come. I was moved because God was answering me; I would not be beginning alone. That was the start of a long journey of fruitful work, rich complementarity, and deep friendship. Moreover, the board said yes.

Dona Maria had been saying to everybody that she was going to begin L'Arche with us. So when everything was ready to welcome people, we began the first house with her. She came to be with us daily. Soon after we started, Vilma, a young Honduran student who was eighteen, came to live with us, and then another Honduran named Rosita arrived. Then Yves, a young engineer from France, came for two years. It was helpful when Rafael came to have a man on the team. I was perhaps sometimes too strict with foreign assistants and wasn't always attentive as I might have been to their needs. If so, it was because I found it important for the integration of the community to be open to the neighborhood. The first assistants would stay for years. Today, they are married and have careers, but we lived such strong, challenging, and joyful moments together that L'Arche remains an important place for each of them. They remain faithful. I am so grateful for each one.

FIRST CORE MEMBERS—MARCIA, LITA, RAFAEL

In Honduras in the 1970s, there was a military government that didn't like foreign organizations, especially ones with religious connotations. So the board didn't want us to welcome children like Rafael until we got official recognition. We had to wait more than one and a half years for that official recognition before welcoming Rafael. Meanwhile we started the house with Marcia and Lita, who were young adults.

I met Marcia in an asylum where she had been abandoned at age two. I met her at the entrance and she asked, "Where are you living? When are you taking me to your home?" She would ask this again each time I came to visit.

Lita was a neighbor when I was living at Dona Maria's house the year before starting the community. When her father discovered that she had become handicapped as a child, he abandoned her mother with the three children. She was often left alone in the house naked while her mother left for market day, trying to find little jobs to be able to nourish her three kids. Her mother would say in front of Lita, "It's too much, I suffer too much with her!" Lita needed to discover who she was because at home she didn't exist except as a burden. Once she was in L'Arche, we discovered that she had intense desires and a strong sense of what she wanted. At first, when she came at age seventeen, she looked like a seven-year-old, but after six months in L'Arche, she began to grow as a young woman. She was very sensitive and intuitive. She couldn't talk, but she knew how to be attentive to what people around her were living.

Then, after a year and a half, we received official recognition and we welcomed Rafael. Because we had been waiting for so long, the whole neighborhood was looking forward to his arrival, giving us clothes from their children. A neighbor even came with me in his car to pick him up from the hospital.

Rafael was like an animal, very energetic and demanding. He didn't differentiate between a sheet of paper, a piece of wood, or a person. One day, after six months, Rafael came crawling from elsewhere in the house into a room where some of us were gathered. I was struck that he was suddenly noticing people outside himself and wanted to join us. Later, he learned to stand and then went to our little school. He became more and more joyful, but always very demanding. As a teenager, his body grew, but instead of getting stronger, he got weaker and weaker.

WORKSHOP AND SCHOOL

With the arrival of Rafael in the house, we began a workshop for Marcia and Lita as well as a few others, such as Esperanza, from the neighborhood. In the workshop we made *pichingos*, traditional little dolls, and very soon we also began to make mops to clean the floor, which we still do. From the beginning, we wanted to do things that were helpful for people outside so that the work of Marcia, Lita, and others would be recognized and valued.

We loved to go to the market to sell or to have the neighbors come into the house to buy mops. Marcia was very proud. I remember someone in the market one day bargaining down the price. I said it was not possible, but she was discussing it.

238

Marcia straightened up from her wheelchair and said, "What do you think the work is costing us?" The lady said okay, gave us the money, and took a mop.

Handicapped people in Honduras were not treated as they are here. There they were the poorest of the poor, objects of pity. Very often when we went with our people from L'Arche into the streets, we were given money, which upset me. I think L'Arche offered another vision, another way to look at handicapped people. It was going to be a long journey. It was complicated when we began the little school and the workshop. Three people living in the neighborhood with their very poor families came to us daily to attend the workshop. We knew other families with handicapped kids in very difficult situations at home. They were not really living, just sitting in dirt, another kind of abandonment. Even though we offered the school and workshop each day, it was too much for them. To bring the child would have required them to give the child a bath each day, to put on clothes, and to give them food. In a way, at the beginning we were disturbing people. So it was a long, long journey, and a challenge for us to accept them where they were, and to begin to work from where they were rather than from our vision.

CLAUDIA

A week after Rafael first came, we saw it was impossible to have just one child as a little king with too many mothers, so we welcomed another child named Claudia. I went to the institution for handicapped children and asked the director for an easy child because Rafael was already very challenging. She introduced us to Claudia, a tiny blind girl of six years. We didn't know anything about her or her story, but we decided to welcome her. When I left the institution with her, she began screaming. She screamed day and night for the next two years!

We tried all day long to tire Claudia out by taking her running for exercise. Claudia was blind and autistic. We discovered that they had tried to put her in the psychiatric hospital for adults, which was a terrible place. Just imagining Claudia there gave us the strength to continue to go ahead because it was difficult to face her anguish without professional and medical help.

At night we tried to live with Claudia screaming by having a rotation of one assistant each night who was responsible for her. At the suggestion of the psychiatrist, who pointed out that Claudia had never had the experience of being unique for another, one of us was chosen to be the mother figure for Claudia, to be her sole reference, to "rebirth" her. This process, after nine months of a constant mothering presence, allowed her to open a bit to the others and to find peace. What is interesting is that welcoming the kids—Rafael and Claudia, then Johnny, David, and others—helped Marcia and Lita to become adults. It was a very interesting dynamic.

PAULA AND MARCIA

There was a woman named Paula who had developed a progressive neurological disorder. She had been in the same asylum as Marcia and had become a friend of our community. She was in a bed completely paralyzed and had depended on others for thirty years. She really carried the foundation of the community in her heart and her prayers. Each time we welcomed a new person I would bring her a photo and she would pray for them. I deeply believe that because of Paula, we were able to live with Claudia and everybody else. We would visit her and bring her to the community for feasts or Christmas or Easter. With Paula especially, Marcia became a very compassionate person. Marcia was often the one taking care of Paula at the asylum. Even with her own hemiplegia, Marcia would help her eat, offering a spoonful of food for Paula and then taking two for herself! I really saw Marcia with such a heart of compassion, and I think she was able to cope with Raphael and Claudia because of that heart of compassion.

Paula was a precious support for me. She was a living gospel. She never complained, although she certainly had much to complain about. She asked me only one thing—to arrange for her burial. She wanted to be buried at L'Arche because at the asylum, when someone dies, they disappear into a mass grave, and half an hour later there is someone else in their bed. It is a hard reality. Thank God, although I was travelling a lot around the time of Paula's death, on the actual day she died, I was there, and we were able to have a mass and give her a proper burial.

PRAYER AND CHURCH LIFE

We lived beside the church of Suyapa, a pilgrimage place with lots of Masses, so we could go to Mass easily, early in the morning or at night. Right from the beginning, and even as I was living with Dona Maria, we would pray in the home before going to bed. Then when Marcia and Lita came, we prayed with them and went to Mass on Sunday together. People were so rooted in their Catholic faith that for everyone this was normal. In the home, we used a candle for a few years. We also used scripture or the *I Walk with Jesus* books. People would choose a page and say something about why they chose it. It was very simple, just saying thanks for things that happened in the day. Then, after a few years, someone said of the candle, "I don't like it—it's like a funeral." So we stopped using the candle and people placed what they wanted for prayers like flowers or images. Prayer life was so obvious and natural. It was part of local life.

Marcia was baptized in the asylum when she was two years old because they had thought that she was going to die.

She had a godmother who was an employee there, but she had disappeared. One day at the beginning of the community during breakfast, I remember saying to Marcia, "Would you like to make your first communion one day?" "Yes. Yes. I would love to." "So, if you want to, we will need to prepare."

Then we went to Mass. At the moment of communion, I was praying and suddenly opened my eyes to see Marcia in front of the priest who was giving her communion. I said, "God, now, this is your business!"

Lita was baptized when she first arrived. We decided to prepare her for her first communion at our home, but we also felt it was important for her to participate with the other kids in the parish. The kids went for a two-day retreat before their first communion, but Lita wasn't with them because she had not had the same preparation. During that retreat they were supposed to live their first confession, so I wanted also to find a priest who would hear Lita's confession. I had so much difficulty finding a priest—everybody said, "No, she's an angel—no need." In the end, we were able to find a Jesuit, a Guatemalan who was passing through. I prepared two chairs and opened the *I Walk with Jesus* book of Jean at a page about forgiveness. The priest told me to stay near because it would not take time. I left them but it took a long time. The priest came out after they were done. She hadn't spoken, they had shared a time of silence, but she had expressed herself clearly. When he sat down with Lita, she began to bring her hand to her heart in the gesture of contrition, which was amazing because we had never taught her that. He was profoundly moved.

SUYAPA

Suyapa was a little girl who was my neighbor when I had lived with Dona Maria for the year before starting the community.

She suffered from epilepsy. When she was three years old her little brother had died, and she had overheard her aunt say to her mother that it would be better if it had been Suyapa who had died. Then she ran away for the first time, and they found her the next day. She continued to run away all the time after that. I became familiar with the city of Tegucigalpa, especially by night, from looking for her so many times.

We welcomed her—she was eight years old. She had lived on the street—everything you can imagine. When she came, she was full of violence and acted out often, so we had very full, intense days. When we arrived at the prayer at night, she always said, "I thank you Jesus for the good day you gave us" and everybody was surprised as we all were exhausted because of her violence. I realized that Suyapa couldn't go to bed without reconciliation, and that this prayer was her way of being reconciled so that she was able to sleep peacefully. I think she knew she was difficult, but she had the strong feeling that Jesus could save her. The day of her first communion she was radiant, saying to people on the street, "Do you know that I have Jesus in my heart now?"

Each year, we held a retreat where assistants and core members were paired up. When she was sixteen years old I had the privilege of being with her. There was a day of reconciliation where we prepared ourselves together and went to confession separately. I left Suyapa with the priest, and she returned radiant, saying that the priest had embraced her at the end. She said that the priest was so good, so good. Suddenly her face became serious. She took my hand and asked me, "Does that mean that God is as good as this priest?" It was amazing that an adolescent who was so disturbed and violent could reveal to a Jesuit the heart of his vocation, to reveal the tenderness of God. When he heard what she had said, he was really touched and couldn't stop kissing people for the rest of the retreat!

COLONIAL LEGACY

If you read the story of Honduras, you learn a lot. All the countries of Central America have almost the same story, but Honduras has suffered the most from colonization, not just from the Spanish, but also from the Mexicans, Guatemalans, etcetera. It got to a point that to express indigenous culture through dress, songs, art, or cooking meant to be killed. So you had beautiful indigenous people such as Dona Maria feeling they had no value and no self-confidence at all. Most of the assistants came with this legacy, without any confidence in themselves, without any sense of their value.

Some people are a mix of indigenous and Spanish, but they don't accept it, denying the indigenous part. Sadly, I often had the feeling of a country quite depressed and without a sense of pride or of the value of their country and people. People are very beautiful, but they don't know it. The minority of the population is rich, and the majority is poor, although today the middle class has more influence. The poor were not aware of their beauty or of their value. For assistants, most of whom came from this reality, the question was how to help them recognize their own value, even as they helped the core members do the same.

BOARD TENSIONS AND DIFFICULTIES

The reality is that, from the beginning, there was a tension, a very strong tension in the community between the board and the assistants of the community because all the members of the board came from privilege. We were grateful for them, as well as for their contacts and their ability to organize and to raise money. They were very valued people, very dedicated, but they had difficulties understanding the littleness of L'Arche, especially in a country where the needs were so great. There was always a tension, a strong tension. On the one hand, I was thankful for them for all they had done and all they were doing, and I had a strong respect and affection for them. However, it was a struggle for me not to become judgmental.

We were living among the poor and saw the consequences of poverty all around us. We were amid a strong social challenge. Once, during a community day, both worlds came together— the assistants, Dona Maria, Maria Conchita, and all the members of the community, even the board members. Everyone was listening and sharing in groups or giving witness. I remember hearing a few board members listening to Dona Maria, Maria Conchit, or a young assistant and saying, "Wow, what wisdom in these ladies." I thought, that's the miracle of L'Arche. That is the mission of Rafael, Marcia, and Claudia: to bring these two worlds together, to help break down the walls and the fears, because they called each of us to the unity required for their growth. For Marcia, the difference of class didn't exist. She loved people by their names, and she had a relationship with each of us—assistant, board member, or neighbor. In Latin America, we depend on the board for money to live, so the question of money was very sensitive. They would often question our expenditures that they did not understand, and yet they lived lives that to us sometimes seemed more than comfortable. It was yet another challenge in the search for unity.

Remaining nonjudgmental was my greatest challenge. I loved these people, but I had to struggle with myself not to judge them, to remember that first they were good people doing a lot. I had to struggle because I found myself in between these two tensions, helping the board to understand the community, which they needed to run like a business, and helping the assistants to understand the board. Moreover, the local assistants saw that the board treated foreigners like Regine, Chica, or me differently from themselves, and that made them very angry with us. It wasn't very easy to live that, and it remains difficult. That tension is part of the community's life, but tension also helped us to grow.

DEATH OF RAFAEL

The doctors had said that Rafael would not live beyond his teens, but we had ignored it. As a teenager, his body got weaker, and he died when he was twenty-one years old. In his last few days when I sat with him, he often looked at me with great intensity. His look seemed to say that we had fulfilled our mission together. I was entering a time of transition around my leadership, and I felt he was encouraging me to move on.

Rafael died and I will always remember his funeral in the church of Suyapa. It was full of people, such different people— all the neighbors, the little ladies of the market, the board members, the minister of health, all kinds of people. That day I thought, well, that's the fecundity of Rafael's life, his mission to help bring these people together. I trust strongly that the tension of bringing very different kinds of people together is part of our story. It's part of the mission of L'Arche. It's not easy to live, but it is part of the vocation of people with disabilities because of their simplicity and their spontaneity. They do not differentiate between classes or religions. They love, that is all. They call out to be loved, by whomever. It is their strength and their beauty, and it's for this reason that this tension has meaning.

SUFFERING OF BEING A FOREIGNER

I had the feeling that God really gave me these people, gave me Honduras as my people, and I put down roots there and lived my life there. When people asked me, "How long are you going to stay?" it was clear to me that I had no limits. But after ten years or maybe more, I realized the reality was that I was French, a foreigner. That was quite hard because when I was there, I felt at home, but I remained a stranger even if there were very strong friendships. People would say, "You are really one of us," but also people were calling me, even with a lot of tenderness, *gringita* (foreigner). But that is what I was, what I am, and that made me suffer a lot. It took a long time for me to accept that reality, but that was the reality. Not accepting it at first was my big suffering and my big illusion. My reality was that I always remained a foreigner.

REGIONAL AND ZONE COORDINATOR

Somehow the death of Rafael helped me to move on from being the founder of L'Arche in Honduras. His death helped me to let go and to make a passage toward being open to new roles. Twelve years after founding the community, I was asked to be regional coordinator and assumed that role for nine years. After that I became zone coordinator for ten years, until 2002. I had the privilege of living in Honduras for thirty-two years and of being witness to and accompanying all the foundations in Latin America. Even after all these years, I have the feeling that, as an international federation, we must seek to facilitate their own way of living L'Arche, respectful of their culture and reality. The challenge is to allow space for true mutuality to flourish because we have so much to learn and receive from them, as they from us.

Fr. Geodefroy Midy, a Haitian Jesuit priest and a great friend of L'Arche, used to say that missionaries sometimes forget to take off their shoes when they arrive at a new mission, that they fail to recognize that God has arrived before them! At L'Arche we are not missionaries, but we really must learn to take off our shoes.

BACK IN FRANCE

In 2002, Nadine left Honduras for a sabbatical and returned to France. She spent time accompanying her father who was ill and who died at the end of that year. As she was preparing to return, there was not yet clear leadership for the Latin American zone, so she and the international coordinator felt it was not a good time to return. Nadine remarks, "One thing I always found difficult was the fact that simply by being a foreigner, there was always the option of being accorded privilege and power. It was clear to me that I didn't want to go back with power or privilege. I just wanted to go back to live with the people and to become more and more one of them. For that reason, to be able to return to Honduras, I needed someone with responsibility there before me to help me find the right place.

Nadine remained in France and has a role of welcoming and accompanying in L'Arche de Cuise where she now lives. She remarks, "I am still in France and it would seem that it is here that I will grow old. Our journey is not always as we expected." In closing she invokes Thomas Merton, "I will lead you by the way that you cannot possibly understand, because I want it to be the quickest way."

AFTERWORD

JEAN VANIER

I read these chapters with a lot of emotion, deeply touched by what each founder experienced and lived during the beginnings of his or her community: their loneliness, their courage, and their faith. Many of these foundations appeared as completely crazy in some cultures where people with intellectual disabilities were seen as not fully human, maybe even the fruit of sin. How could people in these cultures believe in this vision of L'Arche, where we are called to live with such people in small family homes inserted in a neighborhood?

What energized these founders was their belief that L'Arche was a work of God and that they were called by God to found a new type of community: here was their strength and their hope. Along the journey of the foundation came signs of the presence of God: people they met who understood and encouraged them; some who wanted to be committed to them; others who gave land, time, money, houses, and so on. These signs came as confirmations that what they were trying to accomplish was for and from God and that God would always be with them. So from its earliest days, L'Arche has been founded by many people bringing something to life together.

These founders were also supported by many friends from the community of L'Arche in Trosly or other communities. We were all together in the same boat (the ark). We were all motivated by the same vision, the same hope, the same faith. We had all experienced the beauty of people with intellectual disabilities and how they brought us closer to Jesus and were, in a way, a presence of Jesus. These founders felt called to live poorly with the poor in the way of the Gospels, reading in the events of each day signs of the Holy Spirit leading them through joy and pain, through failures and successes into the kingdom of God. Personally, I had been at the beginnings of these foundations in different ways and felt deeply called to support them with visits and letters. And of course, I sent money from an international fund and I was able, with others and the international council, to encourage other assistants to be part of these new adventures.

These founders who had their gifts but also their weaknesses became signs of hope for many other people. I feel deeply grateful to these founders who were in some ways like Abraham and Sarah, who left their home and land, not knowing where God would lead them. For some founders, it was not a new land but a new way of living.

These new foundations opened L'Arche up to new forms of unity: unity between different Christian churches, unity between different religions, and differences among human beings. I give thanks to these men and women who dared to follow God into a new way of living, discovering the beauty of each person whatever their culture, religion, capacities, or incapacities.

These founders opened up the universal meaning of L'Arche. They were witnesses to the terrible separation that exists in our world between the rich and the poor, those who are admired and respected because of their competence, and those who are humiliated because of their handicaps. They were witnesses also that God has chosen the weak and the foolish to confound those who are closed up in their heads and in power. They revealed that if we enter into a relationship with those who have been humiliated and rejected, we are transformed and healed; together we discover a new road to peace.

STUDY GUIDE

Each chapter in this book contains a different story and can be discussed by a book group in any order or selectively by interest. *Sharing Life* can also be used as a basis for individual retreat.

If you wish to reflect on the book individually, share your thoughts with God in prayer and journaling. Sit quietly and companionably with God, taking time to listen.

GENERAL QUESTIONS

1. In each chapter, what drew you into the founder's story? Where did their story most touch you? How and why?
2. Reflect back on the founders' journeys. What do you see as important stages in their stories? Where do they experience surprises, unexpected changes, crises, challenges, or transformations?
3. How does each founder speak of Jesus and his or her relationship with Jesus? In what ways does their following of Jesus move you, confuse you, surprise you, intrigue you, or inspire you?
4. Where do the founders experience difficulty, struggle, pain? What helps them deal with such experiences? How is their faith affected? Share a

challenging experience in your own journey and how it impacted your life and faith.

5. How does each founder speak of leaving the community that they began? What touched and struck you especially about their departure? Share about a time when you had to move on from something important to you, reflecting on ways in which your departure was both hard but blessed.

QUESTIONS FOR INDIVIDUAL CHAPTERS

Introduction: "There Was a Lightness in Us"

1. Review the ways in which the story of the founding of L'Arche in Trosly has evolved over the years. How has this evolving story been one of faith? What aspects of the evolving story are new or unexpected for you?

2. Think about the six surprises outlined here concerning the founders and their stories. Which surprises catch your attention? Why?

Chapter 1: "These Are Our Friends"

1. Steve, Ann, Bill, and Peter began the first L'Arche community in Canada during a time of social change. What were some of the important innovations, both at Daybreak and in Canadian society, in the community's first decade?

2. How did experiences of pilgrimage and ecumenism shape the Daybreak community? Share a time in your own life when either a pilgrimage or an ecumenical encounter has helped your faith grow.

Chapter 2: "Gathering into One"

1. L'Arche has grown from the beginning through international connections and contacts. As you read Gabrielle's story, what international threads did she bring to the founding of L'Arche in India? Reflecting on your own life, what have been important international influences on your own journey?

2. India, the third country to have a L'Arche foundation, is very different from France or Canada. What unique challenges and gifts did Gabrielle discover as L'Arche took root in India? Where do the particulars of India and its people especially touch you in this story?

Chapter 3: "We Learned to Chew Slowly"

1. How did George and Barbara make mistakes that forced them to adjust their plans and expectations as they began L'Arche in the United States? How did the community nevertheless take root? Ponder your own life and share a time when things might have started badly but worked out well over time. How did you experience grace or God amid the mess?

2. George's story about the founding of L'Arche Erie is full of memorable people. Pick one or two people in the story and share how they touched or intrigued you. Does the story remind you of an important person in your own life?

Chapter 4: "Give the Bread That You Are"

1. Thérèse traces the root of L'Arche in the UK to an uncomfortable and difficult experience with

suffering. How was that experience compelling for her and for her founding of the community? Share an experience of suffering that has moved and motivated you.

2. Thérèse experienced burnout and exhaustion and took several months to recover, walking by the sea and not thinking about L'Arche—and then went on to found L'Arche London. Have you had a time of exhaustion or depression? What made you renew your vision and motivation?

Chapter 5: "What about Africa?"

1. In founding the first L'Arche community in Africa, Dawn and her companions take a great leap into the unknown. How does her faith sustain her? Share about a time in your own journey when you have made a leap of faith with others and how God sustained you.

2. Like L'Arche in India, L'Arche in the Ivory Coast takes root as an interfaith community. How does Dawn's story bear witness to this interfaith reality, even in dealing with death? Share about a time when you have been moved by another faith tradition.

Chapter 6: "Me at Peace?"

1. In Robert's story of founding L'Arche in Haiti, what signs does he follow in his path towards beginning the community? Tell about a time in your own faith life when you felt led to do something for others or for God.

2. Robert tells of Jean Vanier's and his own difficult and cautious engagement with political forces in the

early years of L'Arche in Haiti. What strikes you as important wisdom in their experiences as you hear Robert's story? Share about a time when you had to negotiate difficult political situations whether at work, in your church, neighborhood, or in society. How has your faith helped you in such a situation?

Chapter 7: "Don't Turn Away from the One Who Is Your Own Flesh"

1. In Nadine's story of founding L'Arche in Honduras, responding to poverty is essential to her call. What does she say about the community's establishment among the poor? Tell about a time when you have had a significant experience of poverty or have been struck by poverty in an important way for you. How has your faith been affected?

2. Nadine's faith journey is full of surprises, shifts, and changes. Her path unfolds both by faithful prayer and intuition. Do any of her unexpected experiences and points of transformation intrigue you? Share about a time when God surprised you or drew you in an unexpected way.

Afterword by Jean Vanier

1. In his afterword, Jean Vanier writes, "These founders opened up the universal meaning of L'Arche." Thinking back through all the stories you read, what do you feel is universal and what particularly moves you in the witness of L'Arche?

2. Thinking back through all the stories you read, which founder's story especially inspires your own vision for the world? What do you hope for in our world today?